T.S. Eliot: Mystic, Son and Lover

T.S. Eliot
Mystic, Son and
Lover

DONALD J. CHILDS

THE ATHLONE PRESS
London

First published 1997 by
THE ATHLONE PRESS LTD
1 Park Drive, London NW11 7SG

© Donald J Childs 1997

British Library Cataloguing in Publication Data
*A catalogue record for this book is available
from the British Library*

ISBN 0 485 11493 3

Library of Congress Cataloging-in-Publication Data
Childs, Donald J.
  T.S. Eliot : mystic, son, and lover / Donald J. Childs.
    p.   cm.
  Includes bibliographical references and index.
  ISBN 0-312-16417-3
  1. Eliot, T.S. (Thomas Stearns), 1888–1965–Philosophy.
  2. Eliot, T.S. (Thomas Stearns), 1888–1965–Psychology.
  3. Poets, American–20th century–Psychology.   4. Man-woman
relationships in literature.   5. Mothers and sons in literature.
  6. Mysticism in literature.   7. Love in literature.   I. Title.
PS3509.L43Z64924   1997
821'.912–dc20
                                               96-24155
                                                    CIP

Typeset by
Bibloset

Printed and bound in Great Britain by
Cambridge University Press

For Janet, Kathleen and Emma

Contents

Preface

T.S. Eliot's value in what he once referred to as the stock market of literary reputations began to fall with his death in 1965. Partially responsible for the decline was an *ad hominem* criticism for the most part muted while he was alive. Martin Seymour-Smith's assessment of Eliot's career as poet is an extreme example:

> Eliot is a minor poet: he cannot write about love; he lacks real sympathy, or empathy; he is frigid. . . . Skill, accomplishment, sensibility – even these are not enough to make a major poet. 'Prufrock' is the best as well as the earliest of Eliot's important poems: it is the only one that tries to deal, fully, with his own problem: with his lack of feeling . . . but even as early as 'Prufrock' his procedures tend to function as a substitute for an original poetic impulse. This he never has. . . . As a poem [*The Waste Land*] fails: all traces of the experience that prompted it have been carefully removed. . . . The *Four Quartets* . . . represent an evasion of experience, a failure to examine an incapacity for experience. For all the many ambitious exegeses that have been made of them, it is safe to predict that they will not survive as major poetry.[1]

Not persuasive as an argument that Eliot fails as a poet, this passage is more interesting as evidence that his success as a critic was not complete, insofar as Seymour-Smith attempts by his complaints – about 'lack of feeling', absence of 'original poetic impulse' and 'evasion of experience' – to re-establish the very romantic criteria of literary value that Eliot strove to disestablish. In short, Seymour-Smith reacts against the New Criticism associated with Eliot. Although he writes in the grip of a nostalgia for a time before New Criticism, Seymour-Smith is at least accurate in sensing that with Eliot's death an old orthodoxy passes. The orthodoxy that replaced New Criticism, however, was not Seymour-Smith's older romantic orthodoxy but the orthodoxy of the new new criticism – poststructuralism and its descendents.

Universally acknowledged as a seminal influence in the development of New Criticism, Eliot is not surprisingly caught in the poststructural shadow that eclipses it. The aspect of Eliot that poststructuralism suspects of unorthodoxy concerns his so-called 'mysticism'. The word has never had a precise denotation. In *Mysticism in English Literature* (1913), Caroline Spurgeon notes that 'Mysticism is a term so irresponsibly applied in English that it has become the first duty of those who use it to explain what they mean by it.' The problem is that 'mysticism is often used in a semi-contemptuous way to denote vaguely any kind of occultism or spiritualism, or any specially curious or fantastic views about God and the universe.'[2] The same is true today in the world of literary criticism, the word 'mysticism' being used to denote vaguely any metaphysics of presence in which the signifier is conceived 'as a transparency yielding an unobstructed view of a privileged and autonomous signified (truth, reality, being).'[3] T.S. Eliot's reputation as something of a mystic therefore spells nothing but trouble for his standing in the stock market of literary reputations.

The offending mysticism is a problem in the criticism and the poetry. In an ingenious analysis of the politics of Eliot's canon formation, John Guillory identifies Eliot's mysticism – without identifying it as such – as the element in his criticism that is metaphysically and politically suspect and that Cleanth Brooks elaborates and institutionalizes as New Criticism. Guillory argues that Eliot's infamous valuing of minor poets above major ones is an assertion of 'the marginal relation of the poem to truth'. Minor poets are valuable because, whether they know it or not, they are orthodox. That is, they are informed by *doxa* – true opinion, or right tradition. The point to note, suggests Guillory, is that the content of this *doxa* does not matter to Eliot; what matters is 'the decline of [the] elite [that] delivers orthodoxy to the rulers *and to the poets.*' It is this elite, according to Guillory, that Eliot and Brooks conspire to reconstitute not as a clergy, but as literary critics. Brooks's definition of poetry as the 'language of paradox' – a development of Eliot's implicitly aphasic posture before both *doxa* itself and the particular poems that transmit it – constructs the literary critic as a devotee of the *doxa* 'standing alongside or beyond' (*para*) the poem:

The poem becomes an ostensive act, beyond which lies a conceivably recoverable *doxa*. I believe that 'pointing without saying' is what we mean now by New Critical formalism. The pedagogical device of close reading as well as the prohibition of paraphrase relate to the perceived muteness of the literary work, which is imitated by the gestural aphasia of the teacher. He or she can only point to that truth which must not be spoken.

Eliot is thus responsible for a radically logocentric critical practice 'satisfying . . . the longing for consensus, for a metaphysics of the same – a longing expressed by the posited "unity" of the literary work.'[4] It is this metaphysically naive celebration of the mystical experience of unity against which Guillory and poststructural critics in general react: not only does this logocentric metaphysics invest power in a priesthood guarding the *logos* within the literary canon, but it also reinforces the tyranny of a logocentric culture that represses difference in favour of the same. Such hierarchies must be undone; undoing the mystical Eliot is a step in this direction.

The posture of aphasia before truth or reality that Guillory identifies as the radical hermeneutic posture in Eliot's and New Criticism's ideological endeavour is clearly depicted in Eliot's poetry as a mystical posture – a mystical aphasia before 'the still point of the turning world':

Except for the point, the still point,
There would be no dance, and there is only the dance.
I can only say, *there* we have been: but I cannot say where.
And I cannot say, how long, for that is to place it in time.[5]

Perry Meisel finds in such poetry a mystical impulse as dangerous as the one Guillory finds in the criticism. Eliot's poetics by the time of *Four Quartets* comes to rest 'on an appeal . . . to the authority of a frankly divine agency whose truths the writer simply transcribes as though a prophet newly inspired.' The result is 'less responsibility towards language, more toward belief in unquestioned ground.'[6]

Eliot himself might have preferred that Guillory and Meisel represent his critic or poet as pointing not to the truth that 'must not be spoken', but rather to the truth that *cannot* be spoken. He regards the inability to speak as a function not of a divine injunction but of a human incapacity: 'there can be no permanent reality if there is no permanent truth. I am of course quite ready to admit that human apprehension of truth varies, changes and perhaps develops, but that is a property of human imperfection rather than of truth.'[7] The important point, however, concerns the posture and experience of aphasia – however one explains it – for this mystical aphasia becomes institutionalized as New Criticism on the one hand, and the subject of so much of Eliot's post-conversion poetry on the other. From Eliot's turn-of-the-century study of the phenomenon as a philosophy student to his mid-century experience of it as represented in *Four Quartets*, mystical aphasia is the quintessential figure in his poetry and prose for the apparent acceptance of the metaphysics of presence that is so ideologically suspect from the poststructural point of view.

Readers of all sorts are virtually unanimous in acknowledging Eliot's mystical temperament, but not nearly unanimous in categorizing it. Few would dissent from Kristian Smidt's observation: 'Eliot may not strictly speaking be a mystic, . . . but there is an essential similarity between his glimpses of a higher pattern in his personal history and the ecstatic union with the divine which the great mystics have attempted to describe.'[8] Some, like F.M. Ishak, are less doubtful about Eliot's status as a mystic: 'Eliot has endeavoured to draw attention to the fountain-source of mystical reality, not by way of ratiocination, but through the threads of mystical experiences that are woven together in the very texture of his poetry.'[9] W.H. Auden and Anne Fremantle include Eliot in their collection of Protestant mystics.[10] Still others move beyond the general question of whether or not Eliot was a mystic to the more particular question of what sort of mystic he was. Sister Corona Sharp discovers a Christian mystic drawing inspiration from St John of the Cross, whose works Eliot drew on 'to formulate the mystical journey in his own intellectual way.'[11] F.O. Matthiessen finds in Eliot evidence of the Puritan mind's 'trust in moments of vision'.[12] P.S. Sri discovers that 'Eliot's approach to "the still point" is remarkably similar to the tolerant and pragmatic approach of the "Forest Philosophers" who composed the Upanishads and of Krishna, the divine author and spokesman of the *Gita*.'[13] The threads of Eliot's mystical experiences clearly make a many-coloured coat.

Its many-coloured threads, moreover, are found in poetry as

distinct as *Four Quartets* and the unpublished pieces contemporary
with 'The Love Song of J. Alfred Prufrock'. The former, generally
seen as the most mystical of Eliot's poems, has attracted the most
attention in this regard. Helen Gardner finds in it a clear pattern of
Christian mystical contemplation: contemplative focus shifts from
grace in 'Burnt Norton', to atonement, incarnation and the holy
spirit, respectively, in each of the following quartets.[14] Staffan
Bergsten finds that the Eliot of 'Burnt Norton', 'as a Christian,
strives . . . to apprehend the timeless pattern in time, to find an
eternal purpose in temporal life.'[15] Similarly, R.L. Brett concludes
that the quartets 'are meditations upon the Christian understanding
of Time and Eternity and lead to a mystical apprehension of a unity
beyond the contradictions of human history and experience.'[16]
More recently, however, Lyndall Gordon has concluded from her
study of Eliot's unpublished poems that he:

> began to measure his life by the divine goal as far back as his
> student days, in 1910 and 1911, and that the turning-point
> came not when he was baptized in 1927 but in 1914 when
> he first interested himself in the motives, the ordeals, and the
> achievements of saints.[17]

Largely sympathetic to Eliot's religious quest, these scholars and
critics do not represent the only point of view on Eliot's mysticism.
Harold Bloom shares Seymour-Smith's disdainful and revisionary
attitude toward Eliot and his anti-romanticism – decanonizing
the poet and critic in terms uniquely his own. In favour of
a 'stronger' poet like Wallace Stevens who is more capable
of the transumption of romanticism necessary in the modern
world, Bloom seems to identify Eliot's mystical impulse as the
source of his 'malign influence'.[18] Eliot's definition of literary
tradition envisions 'a simultaneous order defying temporality'
and so 'releases literary time from the burden of anxiety that is
always a constituent of every other version of temporality.'[19] The
aspiration towards a mystical apprehension of a unity beyond the
contradictions of human time is the problem. According to the
Bloomian Perry Meisel, this aspiration makes Eliot 'unwholesome',
'noxiously . . . protofascist', 'merely pedantic', and 'escapist'.[20]
C.K. Stead reaches similar conclusions. By the time of 'Burnt
Norton', 'Eliot threw his poetry totally into the service of his
religious-political commitment. . . . [But] the language does not

give one to believe in Eliot's mystical perceptions, nor even in his philosophical competence.'[21] Terry Eagleton is equally suspicious of the posture of 'self-abnegatingly humble' authoritarianism that he finds in 'Tradition and the Individual Talent' – a posture that he characterizes as mystical:

> [According to Eliot,] a literary work can be valid only by existing in the Tradition, as a Christian can be saved only by living in God. . . . This, like divine grace, is an inscrutable affair: the Tradition, like the Almighty or some whimsical absolute monarch, sometimes withholds its favour from 'major' literary reputations and bestows it instead on some humble little text buried in the historical backwoods. Membership of the club is by invitation only: some writers, such as T.S. Eliot, just do discover that the Tradition . . . is spontaneously welling up within them, but as with the recipients of divine grace this is not a question of personal merit, and there is nothing you can do about it one way or the other.[22]

In each case, the mystical impulse is marked as something that is at best aesthetically irresponsible or at worst politically reprehensible.

Such a poststructural critic as Luce Irigaray, however, suggests that the mystical impulse need not be politically or metaphysically incorrect. She locates in mystical experience a field in which woman escapes marginalization as object of the masculine gaze – the 'only place in the history of the West in which woman speaks and acts so publicly.'[23] As Toril Moi explains, Irigaray finds that 'the mystic's ignorance, her utter abjection before the divine, was part and parcel of the feminine condition she was brought up in.' By accepting this patriarchal subjection, she 'paradoxically opens up a space where her own pleasure can unfold. Though still circumscribed by male discourse, this is a space that nevertheless is vast enough for her to feel no longer exiled.'[24] As far as women are concerned, then, there is no equation between mysticism and an unhealthy metaphysics and politics. Does the same hold true for men? Irigaray notes that in the history of Western mysticism, 'the poorest in science and the most ignorant were the most eloquent, the richest in revelations. Historically, that is, woman. Or at least the "feminine".'[25] Her qualification here allows that a poststructurally 'healthy' version of mysticism may also be accessible to men who have somehow come to appreciate within phallocentric discourse some part of the marginalization that defines the 'feminine'.[26] From this point of view, to have discovered a mystical impulse in Eliot is not thereby to have discovered a vicious politics, a moribund metaphysics or an uninteresting aesthetics.

It is interesting to note, therefore, that whether scholars and critics admire Eliot's mystical impulse or condemn it, they tend to agree that it represents a version of the logocentric impulse so suspect in a poststructural world. Critics like Gardner, Sharp, Gordon and Paul Murray – sympathetic to Eliot's religious quest – explain his mysticism as fundamentally cognate with the quest for communion with God that informs the mysticism in the Christian tradition. This tradition more often than not represents what Irigaray would call mysticism theologized – mysticism made 'teleological by providing it with a (masculine) object'.[27] Those unsympathetic to what appears to be a quest for the One signifier of Truth, Reality or Being tend to regard Eliot's mysticism as synonymous with logocentrism – the general type of the faith in an absolute ground that ostensibly ruins his later poetry. To judge by what scholars and critics have had to say so far, then, Eliot's mysticism is apparently uncompromised by either New Critical irony or deconstructive *différance*. It would seem that his notorious declaration in *For Lancelot Andrewes* – 'The point of view may be expressed as classicist in literature, royalist in politics, and anglo-catholic in religion' – has made it difficult to conceive of Eliot as anything but uninterestingly and unredeemably logocentric.[28] And yet that the mystical moments in Eliot's poetry or that the definitions of mysticism provided in his prose necessarily entail the mystifyingly logocentric metaphysics so regularly located in this writing is by no means clear.

That we ought to revise interpretations of Eliot's work so as to acknowledge the latently poststructural dimension of his sensibility from the time of his early work in philosophy is suggested by the recent work of critics and scholars like Cleo McNelly Kearns, Sanford Schwartz, Walter Benn Michaels, Harriet Davidson, Richard Shusterman, Michael Beehler and James Longenbach. Kearns, for instance, studying the Indic dimension of Eliot's poetry and thought, has suggested that it is possible to interpret the religious dimension of Eliot's poetry as in part a continuation of the epistemological enquiry begun in the dissertation of 1916, *Knowledge and Experience in the Philosophy of F.H. Bradley*.[29] She sees the dissertation as 'in part a refutation of mystical philosophy'. It emphasizes the fact that all we can know as human beings is a succession of points of view – the fact that Kearns finds Eliot emphasizing by means of his juxtaposition of Indic and Christian religious traditions: 'Indic tradition, among many other points of view, is essential . . . , for only through its counterpoint can Eliot enact the destabilization of an old perspective and the movement to a new one, which is all we know, at least in this life, of transcendence.'[30]

Other readings of Eliot's dissertation and related philosophical essays demonstrate the extent to which Eliot was drawn towards the anti-metaphysical position represented by much turn-of-the-century philosophy. In such philosophy in general, and to a large extent in Eliot's particular engagement with it, Schwartz locates what he calls 'the matrix of modernism' – 'the shared assumption' of modern psychology, philosophy, anthropology, and art 'that consciousness is not fully transparent to itself'.[31] Michaels observes that 'It is customary . . . to regard Eliot as a fairly straightforward idealist and to identify the primacy of experience and of some version of the subjective self as his central philosophical concerns.' But this is a mistake. Michaels argues that Eliot for the most part aligns himself in his dissertation with pragmatism's 'critique of the notion of ground':

> Eliot's pragmatism does not consist in any simple repudiation of the ultimate although it generally begins with the denial that certain seemingly fundamental distinctions (between the given and the constructed, for example, or the real and the ideal) have any ultimate justification. And at least one form of the relativism (or scepticism) with which pragmatism is sometimes identified is clearly a possible consequence of this initial denial. But Eliot's argument does not stop here; he insists that the fact that we can adduce no ultimate justification for such distinctions does not mean that they are in any sense 'invalid'. They have their 'practical' significance; they are only local and unstable but they are real.[32]

Michaels finds in the dissertation, as Shusterman finds in the subsequent literary and socio-political prose, both pragmatism's resistance to the metaphysics of presence and its groping towards an understanding of what a universe without an ultimate ground might amount to.[33]

Davidson presents a similarly anti-metaphysical interpretation of Eliot's philosophical point of view: 'Eliot is drawn to the lack of essences in Bradley's metaphysics, but is not at all interested in a logical absolute as foundational for truth.'[34] She grounds in Eliot's dissertation, therefore, the Heideggerian reading of *The Waste Land* initiated by William V. Spanos. Attempting 'to retrieve the poem . . . for a post-Modern audience', the latter argues that:

> *The Waste Land*, far from achieving a privileged status as autonomous object outside of temporal existence, as has been claimed both by its admirers and detractors alike, is in fact basically *open-ended*, a *historical* poem that demystifies the reader's traditional, i.e. logocentric, expectations and engages him in history in the mode of dis-covery or dis-closure.[35]

Yet Davidson finds in the reading by Spanos 'the limits of phenomenological interpretation which does not put the subject in question'; she argues that 'Eliot maintains Bradley's skepticism about the self but joins it with a very modern existentialism and non-subjective pragmatism, all of which sets in motion a spinning hermeneutic.' She finds in the early criticism and poetry:

> a hermeneutic ontology, similar to that being developed contemporaneously by Heidegger. . . . Always, Eliot is holding extremes together in a profound phenomenological recognition that neither extreme is sufficient but neither is expendable, and [that] there is no absolute ground on which to stand in judgement.[36]

Focusing less upon the dissertation, but surveying a wider range of Eliot's prose – both his essays on literature and his later books on orthodoxy, Christianity and culture – Shusterman reaches similar conclusions about Eliot's hermeneutic philosophy. For him, Eliot's hermeneutic impulse is best explained in terms of the work of Hans-Georg Gadamer.[37]

Beehler also returns to the dissertation, recovering the poststructural aspect of this work as a constituent in Eliot's philosophical and poetic voice, not so much through Davidson's recourse to the general '*Zeitgeist* of modernism' as through a study of the particular influence of the semiotic of Charles Sanders Peirce.[38] According to Beehler,

> When Eliot refers in the dissertation to signs or symbols, he has in mind Peirce's sense of symbols and icons, but not his sense of index. This exclusion is provocative because it points towards Eliot's emphasis upon the differential aspect of Peirce's semiotics and opens the dissertation to a reading that insists upon difference without appeal to a unique cognitive identity or a unified immediate experience.

Beehler argues that 'Eliot's marginal meditations on signs and symbols interrupt in and radically disturb [the dissertation's] central philosophy.' This marginal aspect of the dissertation – what Beehler calls 'Eliot's semiology' – 'affects any logically coherent theory, for it is the logic of philosophy, the unified *logos* of philosophical knowledge, with which it interferes.' It similarly interrupts and disturbs Eliot's theology, the unified *logos* of his Chrisitan knowledge. Concerned to overcome the critical consensus as to the logocentric nature of Eliot's philosophical, critical and poetic sensibility, Beehler therefore distinguishes between 'Eliot the theologian', the persona heeded so far by most scholars and critics, and 'Eliot the philosopher', the disruptive persona only just beginning to be heard.[39]

James Longenbach, however, is the only one so far to have begun to appreciate the role of Eliot's interest in mysticism in the poststructurally prescient philosophical point of view that he had developed by the 1920s. He warns that 'Eliot's invocation of theories of mysticism and vision should not be taken lightly'. Bringing together such apparently disparate texts as Eliot's dissertation, his reviews of turn-of-the-century neo-scholastic theology and many of his various observations about mysticism, Longenbach finds in *The Waste Land* a quest for a mystical vision of reality. He defines the mysticism to which Eliot aspires in this poem as a kind of 'visionary power' that allows one to 'transcend the "normal equipoise" and perceive the "systematic" interconnectedness of all things, earthly and ethereal, past and present.'[40] Interested primarily in modern poetry's engagement with history as hermeneutic, and only secondarily in Eliot's mysticism as an example of such a hermenuetic, Longenbach nonetheless points the way to an appreciation of the complexity and sophistication of Eliot's understanding of mysticism – especially in his interpretation of the relationship between Eliot and Dante.[41]

These readings of Eliot's early work in philosophy and its continuing influence upon his writing provide a useful general framework for the reconsideration of Eliot's mysticism that I undertake in the following pages. This mysticism cannot be understood without an appreciation of the perspective that Eliot achieved through his work in philosophy at Harvard and Oxford. His research at this time acquainted him not only with turn-of-the-century philosophy, but also with turn-of-the-century studies of mysticism and theology. One can trace through the poetry, criticism and philosophy subsequent to Eliot's early work in these areas mystical moments of one sort or another in which the strains between 'Eliot the theologian' and 'Eliot the philosopher' become evident. Apparently offering intimations of the absolute that resolves all contradictions, Eliot's mystical moments inevitably recall in their very effort to express such intimations the dissertation's insights with regard to the inescapability of difference. As Eliot notes in his dissertation: 'Metaphysical systems are condemned to go up like a rocket and come down like a stick' (KE, 168). So are Eliot's mystical moments.

Yet just as important as the philosophical aspect of my study is its psycho-biographical aspect. In any attempt to understand Eliot's mysticism, an appreciation of the poststructural perspective that Eliot achieved through his study of philosophy at Harvard and Oxford takes us only so far. A fuller understanding requires, on the one hand, an appreciation of the self-diagnosed mother-complex that he found himself sharing with D.H. Lawrence and, on the other, an appreciation of the visionary experiences that attended the almost pathological misogyny that developed during his troubled first marriage. As much as the turn-of-the-century anti-metaphysical academic mood, Eliot's lived experiences led him to appreciate the void that was both the medium and the message of his mystical vision.

As Lyndall Gordon demonstrates in *Eliot's Early Years*, Eliot's interest in mysticism was always more than academic and intellectual. He had his own mystical experiences.[42] What needs to be emphasized is the extent to which these mystical experiences were functions of his relationships with human beings. In *Eliot's*

New Life, Gordon has revealed how important a role Eliot's unconsummated love for his own Beatrice, Emily Hale, played in his spiritual life.[43] Yet just as important in any effort to define Eliot's mystical experiences is an appreciation of the role in his spiritual life of his ambivalently consummated love for his first wife, Vivien. Together, they created a relationship that made possible for Eliot the visions of human emptiness and depravity that he immediately understood as mystical experiences. Eliot constructed from the dark night of his marriage a mystical misogyny with as significant a spiritual import for him as the more traditional mystical experiences documented in the many turn-of-the-century studies of mysticism with which he was familiar.

Such studies, however, also made Eliot aware that certain mystical experiences could be explained in terms of psychopathology. Always possessing a lively sense of the liability of others to misinterpret their own intense emotional experience as an experience of the divine, Eliot came to suspect that he had fallen victim to the same temptation, despite extreme vigilance. He worried that he was a repressed version of D.H. Lawrence. Careful attention to the pattern of his alternating identification with and distancing of himself from Lawrence in writing about him that spans twenty years reveals Eliot's fear that he too suffered from what he called Lawrence's 'mother-complex' (a term Eliot preferred to Freud's term 'oedipus complex'). Explaining Lawrence's mysticism in terms of such a psychopathology, Eliot can be seen to be projecting onto Lawrence his anxiety about the part played in his own mysticism by his tortured experience of his roles as obsessed son and misogynistic lover.

Acknowledgements

Quotations from unpublished material by T.S. Eliot are © Valerie Eliot, 1996, and are reprinted by permission of Mrs Eliot. Excerpts from T.S. Eliot's *The Collected Poems and Plays of T.S. Eliot, The Waste Land: A Facsimile and Transcript of the Original Drafts Including the Annotations of Ezra Pound*, edited by Valerie Eliot, *The Letters of T.S. Eliot, Volume I 1898-1922*, edited by Valerie Eliot, and *The Varieties of Metaphysical Poetry*, edited and introduced by Ronald Schuchard, are reprinted by permission of Faber and Faber Ltd. Permission to quote published material controlled by Harcourt Brace & Company is acknowledged on the copyright page.

Several paragraphs in Chapters 4 and 8 first appeared in 'Metamorphoses, Metaphysics, and Mysticism from "The Death of Saint Narcissus" to *Burnt Norton*', *Classical and Modern Literature: A Quarterly*, **13** (1992), 15–29, and part of Chapter 8 also appeared in 'Risking enchantment: the middle way between mysticism and pragmatism in *Four Quartets*', in *Words in Time: New Essays on Eliot's 'Four Quartets'*, ed. by Edward Lobb (London: Athlone Press, 1993), pp. 107–30. Permission to quote this material is gratefully acknowledged.

I wish to thank Mrs Eliot for permission to consult collections of unpublished material by T.S. Eliot, and I wish to thank the following librarians and their staff for assistance in exploring special Eliot collections: Michael A. Halls, King's College Library, Cambridge University; Rodney G. Dennis, Houghton Library, Harvard University; Lola L. Szladits, New York Public Library. For the use of his collection of Eliot's uncollected prose, I am grateful to Edward Lobb. For financial support of early research activities, I am grateful to the Social Sciences and Humanities Research Council of Canada, the Webster Research Fellowship programme of Queen's University at Kingston, Canada, and the Calgary Institute for the Humanities at the University of Calgary. I wish also to thank the Faculty of Arts at the University of Ottawa for a sabbatical half-leave in 1993 during which most of this book was written and for financial assistance in the payment of permission fees.

Finally, I wish to express my appreciation to relatives, friends and colleagues who have encouraged and supported my work on Eliot, especially Donald and Vera Childs, Laurie Maguire, Bernhard Radloff, A.C. Hamilton, R.L. Brett and Carson Elliott. Most of all, however, I wish to thank Janet Childs for her tireless help in this project and all the other projects that we share.

Introduction

In Eliot's neglected short story 'Eeldrop and Appleplex' (1917), Eeldrop – a thinly disguised version of Eliot himself – is described 'as a sceptic, with a taste for mysticism'.[1] There is neither a briefer nor a more accurate way of describing Eliot's own religious and philosophical point of view – whether in 1917 or in the 1940s, when he completed his most 'mystical' poem (*Four Quartets*). In 1917, however, for Eliot to come even this close to acknowledging publicly a mystical sensibility was to run the risk of incurring the disdain of such an admired mentor as Bertrand Russell, who in 1914 – the very year that he instructed Eliot for a term at Harvard and the very year in which Eliot's personal study of mysticism was at its height – attacked the modern taste for mysticism.

In his essay 'Mysticism and Logic', Russell prescribes for the age as a whole the very regime of tempering the mystical sensibility with a dose of scepticism that Eliot would himself adopt. Russell acknowledges the contemporary taste for mysticism reflected in the popularity of Henri Bergson's 'mystical' philosophy and tries to bring the mystically-minded back into the fold of science and logic:

> Metaphysics, or the attempt to conceive the world as a whole by means of thought, has been developed, from the first, by the union and conflict of two very different human impulses, the one urging men towards mysticism, the other urging them towards science. . . . But the greatest men have felt the need both of science and of mysticism.

When push comes to shove, however, Russell is less charitable: 'Mysticism is, in essence, little more than a certain intensity and depth of feeling in regard to what is believed about the universe'; it is 'to be commended as an attitude towards life, not as a creed about the world.' People who take seriously such a 'mysticism' as Bergson's philosophy of intuition 'ought to return to running wild in the woods, dyeing themselves with woad and living on hips and hawes.'[2]

The tension between the mystical and the scientific temperament that Russell highlights was an important element in the
European *Zeitgeist* at the beginning of the twentieth century. This
tension can be understood as an aspect of what Schwartz calls the
'matrix of modernism':

> In seemingly independent developments, the disciplines devoted
> to the study of the psyche, the sign, and society were reorganizing
> around the opposition between the world of ordinary awareness
> and the hidden structures that condition it.
>
> In philosophy, the same tendency appears as an opposition
> between conceptual abstraction and immediate experience, or,
> more generally, between the instrumental conventions that
> shape ordinary life and the original flux of concrete sensations.[3]

In response to the scientific, materialist rationalism of the nineteenth century, the variety of phenomena gathered into the term
'mysticism' at the beginning of the twentieth century offered
an alternative epistemology – opposing the material with the
spiritual, the intellectual with the intuitive, the external with the
internal.

The taste for mysticism was shared by many more than
Eeldrop/Eliot. As an alternative epistemology, 'mysticism' appealed
to philosophers like Henri Bergson and William James, certain
Roman Catholic and Anglican theologians and a wide variety
of people interested in the occult (spiritualists, theosophists and
psychical researchers). It also appealed to poets. Pound and Yeats
were extremely knowledgeable about the occult.[4] Other poets as
distinct as the Georgian Rupert Brooke and the Imagists Richard
Aldington and John Gould Fletcher advertised their mysticism. 'Do
not leap or turn pale at the word Mysticism, I do not mean any
religious thing . . . ' writes Brooke, 'It consists just in looking at
people and things as themselves – neither as useful nor moral nor
ugly nor anything else; but just as being.'[5] Aldington's account
of the poetic process as an experience of reverence and mystery
is similar:

> By 'reverence', I understand . . . an intimate and spontaneous
> conviction that what is not me, what is outside me, is far greater
> and more interesting than I am. . . . By the sense of mystery
> I understand the experience of certain places and times when

one's whole nature seems to be in touch with a presence, a *genius loci*, a potency.[6]

Fletcher adopts Ernest Fenellosa's account of Zen Buddhism's doctrine of the interdependence of human beings and inanimate nature to illustrate the nature of the poetic process by an account of the hypothetical project of writing a poem about a book:

> I should link up my personality and the personality of the book, and make each a part of the other. In this way I should strive to evoke a soul out of this piece of inanimate matter, a something characteristic and structural inherent in this inorganic form which is friendly to me and responds to my mood.[7]

Mystical experience seems as important to these ostensibly modern poets as it was to such romantic precursors as Wordsworth and Shelley.

From this point of view, it might seem as though Russell were vainly attempting to hold back a tide of mysticism that was coming in after the ebbing of Arnold's Sea of Faith. But he was not without support. Just as much evidence of the turn-of-the-century *Zeitgeist*, but less comfortable with its mystical aspect, was T.E. Hulme – representative of a poetic constituency determined to eliminate the mystical element in modern literature. A Bergsonian in one of his guises, Hulme can claim – like Brooke, Aldington and Fletcher – that 'the function of the artist is to pierce through here and there, accidentally as it were, the veil placed between us and reality.'[8] Such an aesthetic is as mystical as it is romantic. Yet however willing (as he on occasion was) to champion Bergson against Russell, Hulme can, virtually in the same breath, also argue that it is wrong to speak of poetry 'as the means by which the soul soar[s] into higher regions, and as a means by which it bec[omes] merged into a higher kind of reality.'[9] Romantics, he complains, are always 'bringing in some of the emotions that are grouped round the word infinite'.[10] In particular, 'W.B. Yeats attempts to enoble his craft by strenuously believing in [a] supernatural world, race-memory, magic. . . . This is an attempt to bring in an infinity again.'[11]

For everyone who saw some form of mysticism as a viable modern response to the scientific, materialist, rationalist aspects of the nineteenth century, inhospitable to the human spirit, there was another who saw in any form of mysticism a recourse to the no longer viable coping strategies of the romantics. How could one be more anti-modern than such a mystic? For evidence of the impact of this conflicted *Zeitgeist* upon Eliot, one can turn to the early essays with which he launches his career as literary critic. Without anticipating too much of the arguments to be made in succeeding chapters, I offer here brief portraits of the two Eliots that emerge from this background of competing mystical and scientific temperaments.

The effect of encountering the ideas of Hulme in London by 1916 was to confirm for Eliot the importance of the anti-mystical influence of his Harvard teachers Irving Babbitt and George Santayana. Before Eliot left America, the latter had encouraged him to equate mysticism with romanticism. According to Babbitt, romanticism is a 'revulsion from the rational' that masquerades as a quest for a 'heavenly idealism'.[12] According to Santayana, the romantic imagination is mystical insofar as it discredits intellect:

> We long for higher faculties, neglecting those we have, we yearn for intuition, closing our eyes upon experience. We become mystical. . . . Mysticism will be satisfied only with the absolute, and as the absolute, by its very definition, is not representable by any specific faculty, it must be approached through the abandonment of all. The lights of life must be extinguished that the light of the absolute may shine, and the possession of everything must be saved by the surrender of everything in particular.[13]

For Santayana, Babbitt, Russell and Hulme, to label someone a mystic is to label that person a romantic – a friend of the nineteenth century, an enemy of the twentieth.

The impact of these mentors upon Eliot is evident in the latter's most famous essay, 'Tradition and the Individual Talent' (1919). Eliot's respect for the scientific temperament celebrated by Babbitt, Santayana and Russell is evident in his notorious metaphor for explaining the relationship between depersonalization and tradition in terms of a chemical catalyst: 'I . . . invite you to consider, as a suggestive analogy, the action which takes place when a bit of finely filated platinum is introduced into a chamber containing oxygen and sulphur dioxide.'[14] A suspicion of mysticism is suggested by his proposal to halt the essay at 'the frontier of metaphysics or mysticism' and so to confine the essay to the 'practical conclusions' that can be 'applied by the responsible person interested in poetry' (SE, 21–2). He echoes Hulme – 'the most fertile brain of my generation' – who argues that poetry is not a means of soaring 'into higher regions' or becoming 'merged into a higher kind of reality': 'It is nothing of the sort, [but rather] . . . a means of expression just as prose is, and if you can't justify it from that point of view it's not worth preserving.'[15]

According to Hulme, our first postulate should be 'the impossibility . . . of expressing the absolute values of religion and ethics in terms of the essentially relative categories of life'.[16] Eliot's 'first postulate' in 'Tradition and the Individual Talent' (1919) is very similar. His goal is to 'divert interest from the poet to the poetry' and so, like Hulme, to circumscribe the poetic enterprise within the essentially relative categories of words (SE, 22). Eliot's point of contact with Hulme is revealed in his reference to Aristotle's *De Anima*: 'the intellect is doubtless a thing more divine' than the body.[17] Eliot implies that the poet's personality is to the poem as, according to Aristotle, intellect is to the body: that is, personality and intellect are of a different order of reality from poem and body. Personality, like the divine absolute, is apart from and other than the poem; the poem provides no access to the poet's personality. To encourage the pursuit of the poet's personality in his poetry (as romantic poets had done) is therefore to exceed the capacity of language: it is to excite a mysticism bound to be frustrated – it is to excite the pursuit of a presence nowhere to be found, for 'the poet has, not a "personality" to express, but a particular medium, which is only a medium and not a personality' (SE, 19–21). Words, in short, are no more adequate to the other reality of the poet's personality than to the higher reality of the absolute.

This conclusion does not mean that Eliot disapproves of mysticism, for his subject is poetry and his conclusion is simply that poetry is not mysticism. Furthermore, this conclusion is not even a reliable indication that he disapproves of attempts to conjoin mysticism and poetry. In essays contemporary with 'Tradition and the Individual Talent', Eliot reveals a nostalgia for the mystical sensibility that once appeared in literature. In 'Dante' (1920), we find that Dante is an example of the true mystic, and that 'the true mystic is not satisfied merely by feeling, he must pretend at least that he *sees*.'[18] Far from urging us to stop at the border of mysticism, Eliot implies that not being able to cross the border into mystical vision is a sign of our modern degeneration:

> When most of our modern poets confine themselves to what they had perceived, they produce for us, usually, only odds and ends of still life and stage properties; but that does not imply so much that the method of Dante is obsolete, as that our vision is perhaps comparatively restricted. (SW, 171)

Similarly, in 'Philip Massinger' (1920) and 'The Metaphysical Poets' (1921), Eliot outlines a sensibility more 'unified' than the 'ratiocinative' sensibility of the eighteenth century and the 'unbalanced' sensibility of the nineteenth century (SE, 288). Another term for the unified sensibility nostalgically recalled in this analysis would be 'mystical sensibility': the mystical end implied in the development of a sensibility that is 'always forming new wholes' and in which 'Sensation [becomes] word and word [is] sensation' is an experience of the unified Word (SE, 287, 210).

The scepticism and the taste for mysticism endure side by side. Caught between the argument of Russell, Santayana and Babbitt that mysticism and the modern mind are incompatible and the argument of certain philosophers, theologians and occultists that the modern mind must recover its mystical potential, Eliot might seem – like Hulme – to respond by speaking out of both sides of his mouth at once. In the one essay he seems anti-mystical in the way Hulme, Russell, Babbitt and Santayana are anti-mystical; in the others he seems as sympathetic to mysticism as he was when a convert to Bergsonism ten years before. What we must bear in mind, I suggest, is that Eliot's mystical project is not so much to denounce or endorse mysticism as to define it. The attitudes toward mysticism in these essays are only apparently contradictory. They are evidence of a developing knowledge and experience on Eliot's part that lead him, on the one hand, to allow fewer and fewer experiences to be properly labelled mystical and, on the other, to accord to experiences that might properly be so labelled more and more importance.

1

The Meretricious Promise of Fantastic Views

Among the first mysticisms that Eliot entertained as potentially legitimate mysticisms – and as such the main focus of this chapter – were occultism and Bergsonism. The one confined to the salon or circus sideshow, the other to the academy, these extremes bracketed Eliot's understanding of mysticism. His eventual rejection of occultism and Bergsonism is well known. Yet more interesting than his rejection of these mysticisms is the hesitation that he shows on the way to it.

Purging the mystical of the occult, for instance, was the first move for any apologist on behalf of mysticism. In *Mysticism* (1911), Evelyn Underhill complains of the elision between mysticism proper and eccentric phenomena such as the occult:

> One of the most abused words in the English language, it ['Mysticism'] has been used in different and often mutually exclusive senses by religion, poetry, and philosophy: has been claimed as an excuse for every kind of occultism, for dilute transcendentalism, vapid symbolism, religious or aesthetic sentimentality, and bad metaphysics. On the other hand, it has been freely employed as a term of contempt by those who have criticized these things.[1]

As noted above, Spurgeon's complaint is the same: 'mysticism is often used in a semi-contemptuous way to denote vaguely any kind of occultism or spiritualism, or any specially curious or fantastic views about God and the universe.' It has therefore 'become the first duty of those who use [the term] to explain what they mean by it.'[2]

This elision of the mystical and the occult is evident in many of the passages quoted above. Russell's contempt for mysticism leads him to suggest that twentieth-century mystics have degenerated intellectually to the level of the early Britons – superstitious druids who dyed themselves blue. Druidism and mysticism are one. Hulme's anti-mystical assertions make no distinction between

Yeats's belief in the supernatural world and magic, on the one hand, and other less eccentric, more philosophically and theologically respectable ways of searching for a 'higher reality', on the other. For each, the occult is unproblematically a part of the mystical.

The inclination of those with the scientific temperament to place the scientific above the mystical, and the inclination of the more orthodox of those with the mystical temperament to place the properly mystical above the occult, helps to account for Eliot's regular denigration of the occult. If to be a mystic is to be intellectually suspect, to be an occultist is to be beyond the pale indeed. Occultists appear occasionally in Eliot's poetry, but none seems to be taken seriously. Madame Sosostris of *The Waste Land*, 'famous clairvoyante / . . . the wisest woman in Europe, / With a wicked pack of cards', is Eliot's most celebrated occultist (CPP, 62). But there is also Madame Blavatsky, with her 'Seven Sacred Trances', in 'A Cooking Egg', and there are the anonymous occultists in *Four Quartets* who 'Describe the horoscope, haruspicate or scry, / Observe disease in signatures, evoke / Biography from the wrinkles of the palm' (CPP, 189). The good press received by an Augustine or Buddha is not shared by these occultists. When Augustine and the Buddha appear together in *The Waste Land*, Eliot implies that something important has happened: 'The collocation of these two representatives of eastern and western asceticism, as the culmination of this part of the poem, is not an accident' (CPP, 79). In *Four Quartets*, occultisms are merely the 'usual / pastimes and drugs, and features of the press' (CPP, 189).

This denigration of the occult, however, needs to be reconciled with a rather different attitude revealed in a 1935 *Criterion* 'Commentary'. Supplementing *The New English Weekly*'s obituary number on A.R. Orage, an occultist whom Eliot had known personally since July of 1922, Eliot acknowledged both his own and other contributors' disdain for 'Orage's preoccupation with certain forms of mysticism': 'I deprecate Orage's mysticism as much as anyone does.'[3] Eliot uses the word 'mysticism' to denote 'occultism'. In deprecating mysticism, then, he is deprecating occultism – an activity that he condemned elsewhere at this time as an interest in 'the wrong supernatural world'.[4] To this point, the attitude toward the occult in the *Criterion* 'Commentary' is in agreement with that in the poetry. Yet Eliot continues by suggesting that 'while it [Orage's mysticism] was something that I think should be opposed if he were still alive, it was something that I think we should, in a fashion, accept now that he is dead.'[5] Eliot urges his readers to 'accept' Orage's occultism – urges a tolerant attitude toward the peculiar combination of spiritualism and theosophy that P.D. Ouspensky and George Gurdjieff conveyed to Orage in the 1920s. This is not an attitude toward occultism on Eliot's part with which we are familiar.

More remarkable still is the autobiographical hint that Eliot provides as a preface to his qualification of his deprecation of occultism: 'Perhaps my own attitude is suggestive of the reformed drunkard's abhorrence of intemperance.'[6] Having suggested a plausible interpretation of his attitude in response to no prompting but his own, and then refusing to deny the interpretation that he has thus put into circulation, Eliot implies that he was once an occultist – or at least sympathetic to occultism. The period of occult inebriation to which he alludes in 1935 probably refers to his experiences of 1920 and 1921. Eliot attended seances at this time sponsored by the difficult patron of the *Criterion* in its early years, Lady Rothermere. The seances in London were presided over by Ouspensky, with whom Lady Rothermere vainly attempted to make Eliot converse in Sanskrit, a language he had studied at Harvard.[7] Although Vivien Eliot scornfully described Lady Rothermere a year later as 'in that asylum for the insane called La Prieuré where she does religious dances naked' (this was Gurdjieff's Institute for the Harmonious Development of Man; the dancing was designed to elevate consciousness), Eliot's 1935 confession suggests that he maintained a more open mind about the occult than did Vivien.[8]

There were three main kinds of occultists in Eliot's Boston and London, and Eliot had met them all: spiritualists, psychical researchers and theosophists. According to Janet Oppenheim, spiritualists 'were likely to attend seances in an accepting frame of mind'. Since they believed 'in human survival after death and in the possible activity of disembodied human spirits, they did not hesitate to assert the reality of communication with the dead and to accept as genuine most of the phenomena that they witnessed at seances.' The psychical researchers, however, trod with greater circumspection and even, in some cases, skepticism. Eager to investigate the allegedly spiritualistic phenomena as exhaustively as possible, they did not consider a critical mind inappropriate in the seance room. They were attracted to the subject, not only because it apparently offered a chance to prove immortality, but also because it presented the opportunity to explore the mysteries of the human mind. In all their investigations, psychical researchers claimed to be gathering information objectively, collecting the facts needed for strict scientific evaluation.[9]

Theosophists were as much interested in the spirit world and immortality as spiritualists and psychical researchers, but their approach to these matters was distinct. Inspired by Madame Blavatsky, the nineteenth-century promoter of a term that conjures up 'a rich variety of associations with the cabalist, neo–Platonic, and Hermetic strands in western philosophic and religious thought', theosophists disapproved of seances.[10] First, seances forced the return of souls otherwise progressing to higher spiritual realms. Second, given that the best souls were moving away from the astral plane intertwined with the earthly plane, the souls likely to be contacted in seances were those of the most reprobate, and perhaps even those of the non–human. And so, although Blavatsky's claim to have been initiated into secret wisdom by Mahatmas or Spirit Masters in Tibet initially prompted many spiritualists to join her Theosophical Society, there was inevitably a falling out. Similarly, theosophists and psychical researchers parted company in 1885 when the Society for Psychical Research exposed spiritually fraudulent practices by Blavatsky and her associates.[11]

Eliot was exposed to occultism and occultists in a wide variety of ways. Before he met Orage, and before he met Ouspensky, he had met the ubiquitous occultist – spiritualist, psychical researcher and theosophist in one – W.B. Yeats. In fact, soon after his arrival in London in 1914, Eliot engaged in occasional conversations with Yeats about psychical research – according to Eliot, 'the only thing he ever talk[ed] about, except Dublin gossip'.[12] In the evening classes that he was teaching in 1917, two of his students were occultists:

Mrs. Howells and Mrs. Sloggett. Both are mad. Mrs. Howells is a spiritualist, and wanted to give me treatment for a cold in the head. She writes articles on the New Mysticism etc., for a paper called the *Superman*, and presents them to me. Mrs. Slogget writes me letters beginning Dear Teacher, Philosopher and Friend, and her special interests are astrology and politics.[13]

Furthermore, according to Peter Ackroyd, Eliot liked to hear and to tell ghost stories.[14] It is not unlikely, therefore, that in addition to crime reports (especially reports of murders), Eliot also liked to read in Boston and London newspapers the regular reports of extraordinary events in the world of the occult – one of the 'usual . . . features of the press' to which he refers in *Four Quartets* (CPP, 189). With regard to Eliot's knowledge of occultism and occultists, then, 'it is implausible', as Leon Surette argues, 'to suppose that he could have been ignorant of those occultists who were the constant subject of gossip in the newspapers of the day.'[15]

Equally important, however, is the fact that, while a graduate student in philosophy at Harvard from 1910 to 1914, Eliot conducted research that introduced him to a variety of information about the occult. For instance, long before encountering news of the occult world through Yeats, Eliot had demonstrated his own interest in spiritualism. He made several pages of notes on Pierre Janet's *Neuroses et idées fixes*, summarizing two cases of particular interest to him from the many that Janet documents. The first concerns Janet's Observation 51:

A man interests himself passionately in spiritualism. Acquires delusion of malignant spirit, after having been himself a medium *dessinateur* [drawer]. Had felt ideas come to him wh. were not his. Sometimes the words, he felt, were pronounced in his stomach. Cerebral dissociation. When he is in England the Demon speaks English; in Switzerland it talks German.[16]

This passage resurfaces in at least two ways in Eliot's writing ten years later. First, in 'The Metaphysical Poets' (1921), both Eliot's clinical language in diagnosing English literature's split personality and his hope for a 'unification of sensibility' echo his notes on this case of occult neurosis. The suggestion of 'dissociation' between the 'stomach' and the 'cerebral' areas recorded by Eliot in his notes on Janet's book returns as Eliot's own language when he prescribes a cure for the 'dissociation' between sensation and the 'ratiocinative': 'Racine or Donne looked into a good deal more than the heart. One must look into the cerebral cortex, the nervous system, and the digestive tracts' (SE, 288, 290). Second, these notes in a more general way echo in *The Waste Land* (1922): as in Eliot's notes, there are the visit to the spiritualist (Madame Sosostris), the discovery of malignant spirits (the poisonous Belladonna and the crooked merchant), and both the foreign voices in general and the Demons of the *Brihadaranayaka-Upanishad*.

The notes about the second case are also strangely proleptic with regard to *The Waste Land*:

> Woman who showed hereditary traces of hysteria consults Spirits consequent upon a loss in fortune. She found that spirits would write to her by means of her own hand & became *complêtement entêtée* [completely infatuated]. She would do nothing but write. Became sick. Spirits began to do nothing but predict her death over & over. (Notes)

Certainly the poem is 'over & over' a whispering about death – from the Sybil's desire for death in the epigraph to the preparation for death ('Shall I at least set my lands in order?') contemplated in the concluding lines (CPP, 74). More interesting is the fact that *The Waste Land* was for Eliot just such an experience of voices in the midst of sickness: 'it is just a piece of rhythmical grumbling'; 'I wasn't even bothering whether I understood what I was saying'.[17] Indeed, Eliot implies during an apparently autobiographical digression in 'The *Pensées* of Pascal' (1931) that his experiences during the composition of *The Waste Land* might be interpretable as an instance of automatic writing:

> it is a commonplace that some forms of illness are extremely favourable, not only to religious illumination, but to artistic and literary composition. A piece of writing meditated, apparently without progress, for months or years, may suddenly take shape and word. I have no good word to say for the cultivation of automatic writing as the model of literary composition; I doubt whether these moments *can* be cultivated by the writer; but he to whom this happens assuredly has the sensation of being a vehicle rather than a maker. (SE, 405)

Eliot certainly had occasion to recall these notes in 1921 and 1922. He was suffering a breakdown during the composition of

The Waste Land. His own mental illness may well have prompted recollection of the similar experiences of spiritualists that he had once read about. Furthermore, in figuring his experiences within *The Waste Land,* Eliot's recourse – consciously or unconsciously – to the experiences figured in his notes about spiritualism functions not just autobiographically but also thematically. First, the recollection of Janet's cases of neuroses and obsessions helps to balance any impulse in the poem to interpret very similar experiences as *necessarily* having a religious significance. That is, balancing the impulse to present certain experiences in the poem as a mystical intimation of 'the heart of light, the silence', and as the Lord's mystically plucking the speaker out of this world, is Janet's point that people in the grip of such visions are often ill (CPP, 62). In the concluding lines of the poem, for instance, it is not clear whether we are in the midst of vision or madness: the voice of the Thunder seems divine, yet the speaker seems to be in 'ruins', 'mad againe' (CPP, 75). Second, should Eliot or his speaker succumb to the temptation to regard the experiences of voices and visions as religious experiences, the echo of Janet's cases serves as a reminder that malignant spirits speak as many tongues as benevolent spirits. That is, Janet reminds Eliot that just because a vision has a religious dimension does not mean that it is good. Such visions may be no more than 'aethereal rumours', deceptive things appearing 'Only at nightfall' and effective only 'for a moment' (CPP, 74). Eliot remains Eeldrop, a sceptic with a taste for mysticism.

As we shall see in Chapter 2, Underhill makes points like these in *Mysticism,* and Eliot himself records them in the notes that he made during his reading of her book. It begins to be possible to see why Eliot should have taken the time to summarize for himself the details of the cases of misfortunes in the world of the occult that Janet documents, for the experiences of these unknown people resonated with Eliot's own not just in 1921 and 1922, but also in the period from 1911 to 1914, when he made his notes. Lyndall Gordon believes that Eliot experienced a mystical vision in 1910 (recorded in his unpublished poem 'Silence') that affected him profoundly.[18] If Gordon is correct, then Eliot's extensive reading about mysticism in the years that followed can be understood as an attempt to understand his experience of 1910. Certainly his notes on Underhill's *Mysticism* (made some time over the next three or four years) reveal an interest in determining the legitimacy of visions. A substantial portion of the notes involves a transcription of Underhill's observations about voices and visions, concluding with Eliot's summary: '3 main types of visions & voices 1. intellectual, 2. distinct, but recognized as interior, 3. hallucination. 1 is always accurate, 2 & 3 are not always' (Notes).

Reinforcement of any openness of mind that he was prepared to have on this matter was ready to hand at Harvard. Eliot encountered something very close to spiritualism, for instance, in the work of William James, whose book *The Varieties of Religious Experience* was another of Eliot's resources in his study of mysticism (Eliot's notes are limited to the chapter on mysticism). According to Bruce Campbell, 'To qualify as a spiritualist one had only to believe in the individual's survival after death and the ability of the dead to communicate with the living.'[19] In these terms, James very nearly qualified. Before Eliot arrived at Harvard, James had been president of the Society for Psychical Research, a society (flourishing in the second half of the nineteenth and early part of the twentieth century) interested to investigate questions of thought transference, communication with the dead and the occult in general. The society hoped 'to reach conclusions about humanity equally as demonstrable as the conclusions of geologists, biologists, and physicists about the natural world.'[20] James advertised his interest in psychical research openly, quoting from the *Proceedings for the Society for Psychical Research* in *The Varieties of Religious Experience*. He referred approvingly to the attempts by Frederic W.H. Myers (president of the SPR) and Richard Hodgson (president of the American SPR) to prove not just the existence of a spiritual world, but the existence of immortality: 'Facts, I think, are lacking yet to prove "spirit-return", though I have the highest respect for the patient labours of Messrs. Myers, Hodgson, . . . and am somewhat impressed by their favourable conclusions. I consequently leave the matter open.'[21]

Furthermore, at Oxford in the spring of 1915, Eliot was taking 'a short course' in psychology from a one-time office-holder in the SPR, William McDougall.[22] As a member of the SPR, McDougall championed James's psychology as reinforcement for the SPR's claim, as Oppenheim puts it, 'that mechanistic doctrines could not fathom all the secrets of the universe'.[23] One of Eliot's unpublished essays on Kant suggests that Eliot was prepared to accept this part of McDougall's, James's and the SPR's message. His analysis of the relationship between ethics and Kant's critique of practical reason led him to the following conclusion (which he developed more fully in the first chapter of his dissertation):

> To define the mechanical in terms of the moral is to define the moral in terms of the mechanical, and vice versa; the point at which x is resolved into y and at which y is resolved into x [is] the same, and this is the point of meaninglessness. In order to remain in the world of meaning we must preserve the dualism.[24]

It was the preservation of this dualism that McDougall celebrated when remembering James, in an obituary published in the *Proceedings of the Society for Psychical Research*, as one who refused 'to reduce all consciousness to the level of an epiphenomenon or silent spectator; he insisted always on the real efficacy of our consciousness, our feelings, our efforts, our thoughts as teleological co-determinants of our bodily movements.'[25]

In the end, James provided for Eliot what he provided for McDougall: a certain intellectual respectability for a *critical* (as opposed to a wide-eyed) interest in the occult – an interest that, in its more popular forms (as seances, fortune-telling, and so on), was far less critical and far less respectable. In 'William James on Immortality' (1917), Eliot celebrates in James 'the union of sceptical and destructive habits of mind with positive enthusiasm for freedom in philosophy and thought.' Eliot locates in James something similar to the combination of scepticism and a taste for mysticism that he locates in his own persona Eeldrop. Eliot aligns himself further with James by representing James's religious and philosophical experience in the terms by which he represented his own: 'the oppression of dogmatic theology was remote from him, who lived in the atmosphere of Unitarian Harvard; but the oppression of idealistic philosophy and the oppression of scientific materialism were very real to him.'[26] This aspect of James was celebrated by Eliot and McDougall alike – McDougall cherishing it as an articulation of the rationale of the psychical researcher: the desire to provide a middle ground between the mechanical and the spiritual, ideally using the former to demonstrate the latter. Eliot's appreciation of Orage in 1935 suggests that Eliot shared this desire of James, McDougall and the SPR to link the mechanical and the

spiritual: one of the reasons for tolerating Orage's occultism is that
'Orage did a good deal to hold the two together'.[27]

That Eliot was interested in far more than psychologists who
happened also to be psychical researchers is suggested by 'A
Cooking Egg' (1919). His reference to Madame Blavatsky and
her ability to instruct 'In the Seven Sacred Trances' establishes both
the intermediate role between the spiritual and mechanical that
Eliot considered for occultism and his familiarity with theosophical
aspects of the occult:

> I shall not want Pipit in Heaven:
> Madame Blavatsky will instruct me
> In the Seven Sacred Trances;
> Piccarda de Donati will conduct me. (CPP, 44).

In Grover Smith's reading of the poem, the stanza in which
Madame Blavatsky appears functions like the other three central
stanzas of the poem. The first line presents a simple ideal from
the speaker's past – in this case, a young female friend, implicitly
representing a simple, naive religious attitude not adequate to true
'Heaven'. The lines that follow complicate and qualify what was
so simple in the past. There is the saint-like Piccarda de Donati
from Dante's *Paradiso*, representing a much grander version of
Pipit's faith. More insidiously, there is Madame Blavatsky – the
representative figure for an important strand of the popular religious impulse of the poem's present.[28] Her position between the
extremes of a past religious experience judged inadequate and the
perfect religious experience imagined in the *Paradiso* is noteworthy,
for it is the intermediate position between the mundane and the
divine that Eliot contemplates for occultism as a whole.

Eliot probably gathered his information about trance first-hand
from Blavatsky's most notorious book, *The Secret Doctrine*.[29]
The allusion to Blavatsky's book is relatively precise: 'Madame
Blavatsky will instruct me / In the Seven Sacred Trances'. Smith
notes that '*The Secret Doctrine* is full of sevens.'[30] Among them are
the seven cosmic elements, the seven races of humankind, the
seven eternities, the seven powers of nature, and so on. Eliot's
allusion, however, is even more specific than Smith allows. The
line about 'the Seven Sacred Trances' seems to refer to Blavatsky's
explanation of science's characteristic error: science is mistaken

'in believing that, because it has detected in vibratory waves the *proximate* cause of [light, heat, sound, *etc.*], it has, therefore, revealed ALL that lies beyond the threshold of sense.' On the contrary, if the truth be known, 'Occultism has long since penetrated' beyond this proximate cause; 'we must seek for the ultimate causes of light, heat, etc, etc. in . . . *super-sensuous* states – states, however, as fully objective to the spiritual eye of man, as a horse or tree is to the ordinary mortal.' And so the passage to which 'A Cooking Egg' alludes: 'Such states can be perceived by the SEER or the Adept during the hours of trance, under the *Sushumna ray* – the first of the Seven *Mystic* rays of the Sun.' Blavatsky explains that 'The names of the Seven Rays . . . are all mystical, and each has its distinct application in a distinct state of consciousness, for occult purposes.'[31] These are 'the Seven Sacred Trances' of Eliot's poem, the states in which – according to Blavatsky – the gap between matter and spirit (the mechanical and the moral, in Eliot's terms) is bridged.

The allusion in 'A Cooking Egg' to Blavatsky's 'Seven Sacred Trances' represents an important piece in the puzzle of Eliot's attitude toward the occult. The context in *The Secret Doctrine* from which Eliot plucks the idea – an explanation of the reconciliation of science and theosophy – confirms his interest in occultism's claim to mediate between the spiritual and the material. Even the subtitle of the book emphasizes this aspect of theosophy: 'The Synthesis of Science, Religion, and Philosophy'. It is not surprising, therefore, to find that in the 'Commentary' about Orage Eliot explains in very similar terms his conception of the intellectual, spiritual and political function of the occultism of this 'irresponsible religious adventurer'. It was as a mediator between religious and economic 'revolutionists' that Orage's occultism 'had its effect'. On the one hand were the materialists who needed his 'streak of other-worldliness . . . and desire for the absolute'; on the other were the other-wordly 'who needed to be attracted and instructed in social doctrines as far as their prejudices would permit' (Orage was interested in the Social Credit programme of Major Douglas). According to Eliot,

He saw that any real change for the better meant a spiritual revolution; and he saw that no spiritual revolution was of any use unless you had a practical economic scheme. What we need to remember is Orage's mediating position, and we need to work as if he were still here to mediate.

We are really, you see, up against the very difficult problem of the *spiritual* and the *temporal*.[32]

Theosophy and spiritualism are to be tolerated for their practical mediating potential.

By the biographical inference that Eliot encourages, one can conclude that it served Eliot as he sees it serving moderns in general through the particular instance of Orage – as a synthesis of matter and spirit, science and religion, intellect and intuition. As Campbell explains, theosophical teachings:

> respond to two significant challenges to religion in the modern world: how to reconcile the claims of various religions of the world, and how to integrate religion with the findings of modern science. . . . In response, Theosophy set forth a set of beliefs purporting to be a modern presentation of an ageless, universal wisdom–religion. Also, Theosophical teachings were presented as consistent with recent scientific discoveries in geology, astronomy, and biology.[33]

In the end, occultism (with which Eliot acknowledges that he has in the past aligned himself, and whose effect through Orage upon some of his contemporaries he is rather pragmatically still willing to condone in 1935) remains for Eliot an ambivalent modern phenomenon – in his considered judgement, a preoccupation with 'the wrong supernatural world', but nonetheless at least an interest in a supernatural world, and as such (whether in the hands of an 'irresponsible religious adventurer' like Orage, or a more responsible religious adventurer like Eliot) potentially more than the 'pastime' and 'drug' that he came to call it in *Four Quartets*. What needs to be emphasized is that Eliot was for a surprisingly long time at least willing to keep open this occult option in the face of 'the very difficult problem of the *spritual* and the *temporal*' – however much of a teetotaller he may have become with regard to such 'fantastic views' by the time of *Four Quartets*.

Eliot's experience of Bergsonian mysticism was similar to his experience of occult mysticism: here was another attempt to bridge the spiritual and the material. In retrospect, Bergsonism even prompts the same 'reformed . . . abhorrence'. Although Eliot confessed in 1948 that his only 'real conversion, by the deliberate influence of any individual, was a temporary conversion to Bergsonism' (this conversion had occurred years before in 1910–11 when Eliot was attending Bergson's lectures at the Collège de France), he seldom spoke well of Bergsonism.[34] The essays collected in *The Sacred Wood* (1920) make his opinions clear: 'the follies and stupidities of the French, no matter how base, express themselves in the form of ideas – Bergsonism itself is an intellectual construction' (SW, 45). It was a folly and stupidity because it mixed genres:

> Every work of imagination must have a philosophy; and every philosophy must be a work of art – how often have we heard that M. Bergson is an artist! It is a boast of his disciples. . . . Certain works of philosophy can be called works of art . . . [are] clear and beautifully formed thought. But this is not what the admirers of Bergson . . . mean. They mean precisely what is not clear, but what is an emotional stimulus. (SW, 66–7)

Four years later, he echoed these remarks: 'Bergson makes use of science – biology and psychology – and this use sometimes conceals the incoherence of a multiplicity of points of view, not all philosophic.'[35] As a number of critics have shown, however, what Eliot gained from Bergson is indeed substantial in philosophical, theological and poetic terms.[36] According to Philip Le Brun, 'there appears to be an actual failure on Eliot's part to recognize what he gained from Bergson, and perhaps some process of repression is involved.'[37] If there is repression involved in these comments about Bergson and Bergsonism, the thing repressed is Eliot's awareness of the attraction he had once felt toward the emotional stimulus offered by Bergson's 'mixture of thought and vision'. Telling in this regard is the rhetorical question with which he concludes his 1924 discussion of Bergson: 'Has not his promise of immortality a somewhat meretricious captivation?'[38] Eliot implicitly acknowledges his experience of this 'captivation' and his disappointment at its meretriciousness. It turns out that his complaints about Bergsonism here and elsewhere are not so much complaints about a muddled philosophy as complaints about a broken promise. As 'A Paper on Bergson' reveals, Eliot regarded this promise as a broken *mystical* promise – a promise that he had by the 1920s come to regard as founded upon the emotional stimulus of an inadequate and perhaps counterfeit form of mysticism.

What turned him away from the philosophy he had once accepted so enthusiastically was his increasing understanding of the disparity between the Bergsonian objective and the Bergsonian achievement. Bergson's objective, as Eliot understood it, was to determine the intermediate point between space and non-space, between the extended and unextended, between quantity and quality, between real and ideal, and so on – the point, that is, that Eliot later celebrated as a 'moment in and out of time', a moment 'bisecting the world of time, a moment in time but not like a moment of time'. Bergson fails to achieve this objective, but Eliot's careful analysis of the reasons for the failure puts him on the way to his later suggestion that 'to apprehend / The point of intersection of the timeless / With time, is an occupation for the saint' (CPP, 190, 160, 189–90). In retrospect, Eliot tacitly acknowledges that Bergson could not possibly have succeeded.

Eliot's main claim in 'A Paper on Bergson' is that Bergson fails to prove that 'there is no point of contact between the unextended and the extended, between quality and quantity', and so fails to define reality consistently.[39] Eliot allows the premise fundamental to Bergson's first work, *Time and Free Will*, that 'sensation is not measurable'. But he has reservations, asking 'is sensation ever pure from extension?' Has not Bergson, 'so far as he has explained intensity, explained it in numerical terms?'[40] Eliot catches Bergson speaking of 'the *number* of elementary psychic phenomena which we dimly discern in . . . emotion' (TFW, 18, emphasis added). Applying Bergson to Bergson, he argues that to number is to measure and that measurement – and therefore number – applies properly not to quality, but to quantity (not to intensity, but to extension). Bergson explains his apparent inconsistency by suggesting that:

> there are two kinds of multiplicity: that of material objects, to which the conception of number is immediately applicable; and the multiplicity of states of consciousness, which cannot be regarded as numerical without the help of some symbolical representation, in which a necessary element is *space*. (TFW, 87)

Eliot rejects this explanation, wondering whether there are really 'two species – *très différentes* [very different] – of multiplicity; or only one, the space type' (Paper, 4–5).

According to Eliot, Bergson's extended multiplicity is the same as his unextended multiplicity. The only difference is that applying the concept of number to external objects is easier than applying it to internal states: 'it will not *work* as well for mental states as for physical objects' (Paper, 6–7). The problem with mental states, from the point of view of trying to construct relations between them, is, first, that they are always fluctuating and, second, that they are 'always more or less internal' and so relatively inaccessible to objective inspection (Paper, 6). But if the only difference between Bergson's two types of multiplicity consists in the *degree* of difficulty experienced in applying the concept of number to physical objects and mental states, then Eliot cannot see 'any essential difference between the nature of the physical world, for science, and the world of introspection' (Paper, 7). The distinction between the unextended and the extended collapses.

For Eliot, Bergsonism depends conceptually upon the very extension it wishes to marginalize. So much for the pre-eminence of the unextended: 'How can this, then, be that which is most real? It has none of the marks of a final reality' (Paper, 10). Eliot makes the same point in his analysis of *Matter and Memory*, where the absolute is not so much an unextended *durée* of pure time as a pure motion. Pure motion, Eliot complains, has none of the marks of an absolute. This pure motion – like pure time – requires to be extended to be perceived. And so Eliot asks: 'How . . . can this pure motion be extended, if it is *pure* motion; and if it is partly extended, are we not obliged to think of something besides pure motion?' (Paper, 12). In short, Bergson's pure motion is literally inconceivable. The extended thus proves to be a Derridean supplement, both adding to and replacing the unextended.[41]

The metaphysical and epistemological incoherence of Bergsonism is revealed in *Creative Evolution* in which Eliot finds that Bergson has given up trying to claim that pure time and pure motion are 'most real'. Instead, he writes as though life and matter are equal and opposite realities, inversions of the same movement:

In reality, life is a movement, materiality is the inverse movement, and each of these two movements is simple, the matter which forms a world being an undivided flux, and undivided also the life which runs through it, cutting out in it living beings all along its track.[42]

Eliot asks the same question that he has been asking all along: 'Which is the reality, the movement as we perceive it cut up into objects, or in its homogeneous flux?' (Paper, 13). Eliot finds that 'the important point is the almost Manichaean struggle between life & matter' (Paper, 14). In Heraclitean phrases he would recall years later in the epigraph to 'Burnt Norton', he complains: 'Reality, though I should judge *one* at bottom [,] divides itself into a Cartesian dichotomy – the way up, consciousness, and the way down, matter' (Paper, 13–14). In the end, 'reality remains as obscure as ever' (Paper, 16a).

Eliot's criticism of *Time and Free Will*, *Matter and Memory* and *Creative Evolution* establishes the groundwork for the dissertation to follow. In exposing the metaphysical and epistemological conundra that bedevil Bergsonism, Eliot begins to articulate the conclusion about the relation between subject and object that he reaches in *Knowledge and Experience*: 'Everything, from one point of view, is subjective; and everything, from another point of view, is objective; and there is no *absolute* point of view from which a decision may be pronounced' (KE, 21–2). That his criticism of Bergsonism's attempt to mediate between the subjective and the objective has led to this conclusion is evident from his allusion to Bergson's *élan vital* (life force). Eliot explains that immediate experience or feeling (the unextended *durée* intuited by Bergson) is inaccessible to human beings: 'An *élan vital* or "flux" is equally [as much as subjects and objects] abstracted from experience, for it is only in departing from immediate experience that we are aware of such a process.' In fact, it seems to be Bergson's depiction in *Creative Evolution* of the history of the world as the history of mind that Eliot is criticizing a few pages later:

> In time, there are the two sides, subject and object, neither of which is really stable, independent, the measure of the other. In order to consider how the one came to be as it is, we are forced to attribute an artificial absoluteness to the other. We observe, first, the development of mind in an environment which *ex hyposthesi* is not dependent upon mind; and second, in order to conceive the development of the world, in the science of

geology, let us say, we have to present it as it would have looked
had we, with *our* bodies and our nervous systems, been there to
see it. (KE, 22)

Implied here, and made explicit in 1924, is Eliot's claim that the
difference between him and Bergson is that he recognizes what the
latter does not – 'the incoherence of a multiplicity of points of
view'.[43] Eliot knows what Bergson unintentionally demonstrates:
'we can only discuss experience from one side and then from the
other, correcting these partial views' (KE, 19).

What most intrigues Eliot about Bergson's philosophy is the claim
for the possibility of genuine contact with the absolute: 'How is
it that we seize in perception at one & the same time a *state* of
consciousness & a *reality* independent of us?' (Paper, 17–18). Eliot
understands that, according to Bergson, 'We perceive in the quality
itself something which *transcends* (dépasse) sensation' (Paper, 18).
His response to this claim is sceptical: 'But do we?' (Paper, 18).
Paul Douglass's examination of this part of the paper identifies its
main thrust: 'The essay . . . suggests that Bergsonian intuition (pure
perception) cannot itself escape the dictum of *Matter and Memory*:
'*perçevoir signifie immobiliser*' (to perceive means to immobilize)'.[44]
Eliot's complaint is that this dictum opens a gap between subject
and object that cannot be bridged: '*Perçevoir signifie immobiliser!* –
then how can our perception be identical with the object, which,
in itself, is pure motion?' (Paper, 18–19). In perception, do we
actually *experience* the transcendence of which Bergson speaks – the
transcendence from the finite to the infinite, from the contingent
to the absolute? Given that matter, insofar as it is real, is perpetual
flux, and given that to perceive matter is to immobilize it, 'Where
. . . is the reality – in the consciousness, or in that which is
perceived? Where is the one reality to subsume both of these, &
can we or can we not know it?' (Paper, 18–19).

With regard to the paper's references to mysticism, Douglass
notes Eliot's willingness to call Bergsonism a mysticism (albeit
'a weakling mysticism') – explaining the use of the term as
Eliot's acknowledgement of 'the implicit monism of Bergson's
philosophy' (Paper, 22).[45] But he ignores the fact that Eliot
identifies two distinct mystical moments in Bergson's work: 'To
come down to the actual [mystical] statements, we find them to

divide chiefly into two sorts. One tends toward an absolute which *sees* eternity in a single moment' (Paper, 22). The other seems to involve not so much a moment as an evolution towards an absolute. In *Creative Evolution*, Eliot notes, consciousness tends to be presented as 'progressive' (Paper, 23). Consciousness *becomes* the unextended *durée* by means of evolution.

The first sort depends upon intuition. Demonstrating this aspect of Bergson's mysticism, Eliot quotes two passages from *Creative Evolution* on the relationship between individual consciousness and absolute consciousness. In the first passage, Bergson defines reality and our relationship to it:

> For want of a better word we have called it [reality] con-sciousness. But we do not mean the narrowed consciousness that functions in each of us. Our own consciousness is the consciousness of a certain living being, placed in a certain point of space; and though it does indeed move in the same direction as its principle, it is continually drawn the opposite way, obliged, though it goes forward, to look behind. This retrospective vision is . . . the natural function of the intellect [by means of memory], and consequently of distinct consciousness. In order that our consciousness shall coincide with something of its principle, it must detach itself from the *already-made* and attach itself to the *being-made*. It needs that, turning back on itself and twisting on itself, the faculty of *seeing* should be made to be one with the act of *willing* – a painful effort which we can make suddenly, doing violence to our nature, but cannot sustain more than a few moments. (CE, 237)

Here is the mystical tendency 'toward an absolute which *sees* eternity in a single moment'. The other 'utterance in regard to the Absolute' is similar (Paper, 20):

> We must strive to see in order to see, and no longer to see in order to act. Then the Absolute is revealed very near to us and, in a certain measure, in us. . . . It lives with us. Like us, but in certain aspects infinitely more concentrated and more gathered up in itself, it *endures*. (CE, 298–9)

The Absolute 'revealed' in each of these passages 'is a *self-sufficient* reality' (Paper, 20). The Absolute is 'a completed infinite' – there to be experienced mystically at any moment (Paper, 26).

From Eliot's point of view, the problem with an intuitive mysticism like this – one that ostensibly reveals reality in a single moment – is that it cannot possibly achieve a vision of the Absolute: 'Is it [the Absolute] the infinitely quickened rhythm of consciousness, which would, Bergson tells us, be able to seize the whole of this story [the *durée*] in a single perception? This is possible, but it is hardly likely' (Paper, 22–3). Eliot accepts F.H. Bradley's argument that relational knowledge cannot provide knowledge of the Absolute: reality must be one, for plurality necessitates relations that imply a superior unity to which the relations themselves are merely adjectives. Eliot thus quotes Bradley approvingly: 'the absolute, as Bradley says, bears buds & flowers & fruit at once' (Paper, 26). According to Eliot, the Absolute towards which Bergson's philosophy aspires in its mystical moments is an incomplete Absolute (it 'is simply not final'); and so the mysticism that Eliot discovers here is 'a rather weakling mysticism' (Paper, 19, 22).

The second kind of mysticism involves the evolution of continuous memory – the speaker's apparent goal in 'Rhapsody on a Windy Night', a poem that many critics have regarded as one of Eliot's most Bergsonian poems.[46] In 'A Paper on Bergson', however, Eliot argues that the mysticism of continuous memory is as flawed as the mysticism of intuitive vision, for it is 'a futile attempt to emulate a completed infinite by a sequential infinite' (Paper, 26). At this point, Eliot is perhaps recalling his own attempt in 'Rhapsody' to arrive at mystical vision of a completed infinite by assembling in a sequence of hours a sequence of memories that might be made continuous. In retrospect, his conclusion about the mysticism of continuous memory is just as much a conclusion about 'Rhapsody': 'the acquisition of [Bergson's] second kind of *memory*, the continuous type, is only another triumph in spatialisation' (Paper, 24–5).

In 'A Paper on Bergson', the mystical inadequacy that Eliot first locates in the speaker of 'Rhapsody' is now located instead in Bergsonism itself. In 'Rhapsody', the mystical inadequacy comes of the speaker's being compromised by the practical intellect; the last twist of the Bergsonian knife is his acceptance of practical routine: he cannot even transcend his practical relationship to his toothbrush. In 'A Paper on Bergson', the same contamination of pure memory by the spatializing practical intellect is found. The mystical problem is therefore shifted from the mystic to the method: 'it is no more possible that truth should be gained by these means than that a man should ever catch sight of himself with his eyes closed' (Paper, 26). Eliot thus concludes his formal philosophical consideration of Bergsonism by exposing it as not the reconciliation of science and mysticism that so many thought it to be, but rather as a captivating confusion of science and mysticism whose promise of immortality through a communion with the *élan vital* proves entirely meretricious.

Eliot's conclusion from his epistemological criticism of Bergson's mysticism would seem to be that mysticism – as experience of the Absolute – is impossible. In *Knowledge and Experience*, Eliot recognizes that it is a problem facing human being itself – not just Bergsonism – that we can aspire to the completed infinite of the Absolute only within the sequential infinite of human experience: 'no actual experience could be merely immediate, for if it were, we should certainly know nothing about it' (KE, 18). There would be no subject–object relation in which the knowledge could occur. His conclusion in 'A Paper on Bergson' with regard to Bergson's desire to find a position intermediate between subject and object is the same: 'In the abs[solute] A is already so completely B, & B is so completely A, that there is nothing to say about either . . . . This is my interpretation of Bergson' (Paper, 26).

What Eliot had begun to articulate in 'A Paper on Bergson' is the 'Humpty-Dumpty' insight he recorded in *Knowledge and Experience*: 'if we attempt to put the world together again, after having divided it into consciousness and objects, we are condemned to failure. We cannot create experience out of entities which are independent of experience' (KE, 30). The most that we can hope to achieve is a practical, as opposed to an absolute, knowledge – the kind of practical knowledge that in 'Rhapsody on a Windy Night' and 'A Paper on Bergson' Eliot located at the epistemological limits of Bergson's mystical moments.

Although he found the philosophy inadequate, Eliot nonetheless remained fascinated by Bergson's mystical ambitions. The mysticism that he discovered was indeed deficient – 'a weakling mysticism'. Yet because the word *mysticism* has acquired a pejorative connotation, one ought not to succumb to the temptation to read Eliot's description of Bergsonism as 'a weakling mysticism' as a double criticism: 'the philosophy is not only weak, but it is also mystical.' In fact, Eliot is not complaining at all that the philosophy is mystical: in Bergson, 'there are . . . suggestions, more than suggestions, of leading towards an absolute; suggestions which have often led Bergson's critics to call him mystic. With this appellation I am not disposed to quarrel' (Paper, 22). He is complaining that the mysticism is not strong enough; it will not stand up to rigorous philosophical analysis.

The continuing seductiveness for Eliot of Bergson's mystical ambitions is evident in 'Eeldrop and Appleplex'. Written in 1917 – when Eliot's rejection of Bergson might have seemed full-blown – this story is very similar to the poems of the early period that Eliot himself identified as Bergsonian.

It develops the same squalid urban setting one finds in 'The Love Song of J. Alfred Prufrock', 'Preludes' and 'Rhapsody on a Windy Night': 'The suburban evening was grey and yellow on Sunday; the gardens of the small houses to left and right were rank with ivy and tall grass and lilac bushes; the tropical South London verdure was dusty above and mouldy below; the tepid air swarmed with flies' (E&A II, 16). The two characters Eliot introduces, Eeldrop and Appleplex, have 'rented two small rooms in a disreputable part of town'. Furthermore, 'They had chosen the rooms and neighborhood with great care' (E&A I, 7). Of course not only Eeldrop and Appleplex have been careful in choosing their neighbourhood; so has Eliot. Just as he chose in 'Rhapsody on a Windy Night' to look for the double significance of the everyday world in the streets of Paris, so in 'Eeldrop and Appleplex' he looks for it amongst the 'evil neighborhoods' of London. The shady street with the riotous neighbourhoods nearby is perfect: 'over it hung the cloud of a respectability which has something to conceal' (E&A I, 7). Like Eliot, Eeldrop and Appleplex are interested to see through the cloud, to draw back the veil, which the everyday world places between consciousness and reality.

As I suggested above, Eeldrop seems to be Eliot. In March of 1917, the latter began work for the Colonial and Foreign Department of Lloyd's Bank. In the first instalment of the story in May, Eeldrop says to Appleplex, 'I am, I confess to you, in private life, a bank-clerk' (E&A I, 11).

There is also Appleplex, who provides the angle of vision complementary to Eeldrop's:

Each pursued his own line of enquiry. Appleplex, who had the gift of an extraordinary address with the lower classes of both sexes, questioned the onlookers [as people arrested were brought to the local police station], and usually extracted full and inconsistent histories: Eeldrop preserved a more passive demeanour, listened to the conversation of the people among themselves, registered in his mind their oaths, their redundance of phrase, their various manners of spitting, and the cries of the victim from the hall of justice within. (E&A I, 7–8)

Appleplex is perhaps Ezra Pound, or Eliot's alter ego. Yet one can see Eeldrop and Appleplex as one mind – the same mind speaking from two different perspectives: 'It may be added that Eeldrop was a sceptic, with a taste for mysticism, and Appleplex a materialist with a leaning toward scepticism' (E&A I, 8). They are the voice of Eliot, a person split into the turn-of-the-century's mystical and materialist moods – moods that manage to converge towards scepticism.

'Eeldrop and Appleplex' is a final consideration of the Bergsonian goal and a final criticism of the Bergsonian method. Acting upon their Bergsonian insight that the everyday, practical world is the dead world of the intellect, Eeldrop and Appleplex withdraw to their rooms:

Both were endeavoring to escape not the commonplace, respect-able or even the domestic, but the too well pigeon-holed, too taken-for-granted, too highly systematized areas, and, – in the language of those whom they sought to avoid – they wished 'to apprehend the human soul in its concrete individuality'. (E&A I, 8)

The goal is the Bergsonian goal; but the desire is to avoid the fate of Bergsonians themselves. When Appleplex mentions that a certain Mrs Howexden has recommended that he read Bergson, Eeldrop replies: 'Our philosophy is quite irrelevant. The essential is, that our philosophy should spring from our point of view and not return upon itself to explain our point of view' (E&A I, 10). His point is that we must beware the tendency to substitute an *explanation* of our point of view for the point of view itself. 'A philosophy about intuition', Eeldrop argues, 'is somewhat less likely to be intuitive than any other' (E&A I, 10). After all, to articulate such a philosophy is to intellectualize it. 'Bergson', he points out, 'is an intellectualist' (E&A I, 11). Appleplex seems about to claim that at least he and Eeldrop are individualists. 'Individualists. No! ! nor anti-intellectualists', Eeldrop exclaims. 'These also are labels' – just as Bergsonism is a label. 'We cannot escape the label, but let it be one which carries no distinction, and arouses no self-consciousness. Sufficient that we should find simple labels, and not further exploit them' (E&A I, 10–11). In true Bergsonian fashion, Eeldrop tries to avoid reducing experience to a word that will replace the experience in question. Philosophy must not be what Roland Barthes calls 'readerly', must not be an exercise in which philosophers merely discover their own closed point of view. It must be 'writerly', a creative, productive exercise that refuses to 'exploit' experience by totalizing it, an exercise that is open to the play in a point of view and so open to a point of view's difference from itself.[47]

Eliot's metaphor for Bergson is the figure of Edith, who is introduced in the second 'Eeldrop and Appleplex' instalment:

> 'On such a night as this', said Eeldrop, 'I often think of Scheherazade, and wonder what has become of her.'
>
> Appleplex rose without speaking and turned to the files which contained the documents for his 'Survey of Contemporary Society'. . . . 'The lady you mention', he rejoined at last, 'whom I have listed not under S. but as Edith, alias Scheherazade, has left but few evidences in my possession.' (E&A II, 16–17)

She is associated from the beginning, by both Eeldrop and Appleplex, with Scheherazade – the narrator of *The Arabian Nights* who postponed her tale's climax each night so as to prevent her husband from killing her (as he needs to, has to, wants to). Like Bergson, Scheherazade/Edith is the archetypal deferrer: she interrupts her narrative and prevents the closure that would for her mean death just as Bergson replaces the fixed and static with the living duration of flux by interrupting the practical intellect's relentless progress towards its practical goals. Appleplex is suspicious of Scheherazade/Edith: 'I want to know why she misses. I cannot altogether analyse her "into a combination of known elements" but I fail to touch anything definitely unanalysable' (E&A II, 18). In other words, Bergsonism is not merely a matter of intellect; it is not just a 'combination of known elements' –

not just the intellectual analysis that Bergson himself dismisses (in
words that Appleplex borrows) as an 'operation which reduces the
object to elements already known'.[48] But neither is it intuitive
– 'unanalysable'. Appleplex, in the end, is unimpressed by the
mysterious Scheherazade/Edith/Bergson:

> I find in her a quantity of shrewd observation, an excellent
> fund of criticism, but I cannot connect them into any peculiar
> vision. . . . Everyone says of her, 'How perfectly impenetrable!'
> I suspect that within there is only the confusion of a dusty garret.
> (E&A II, 18)

Eliot repeats here, through the voice of Appleplex, the substance of his observations in 'A Paper on Bergson'. Bergson,
like Scheherazade/Edith, is unable to escape the confusion of his
own rhetoric. Bergson fails as a philosopher, it turns out, just as
Scheherazade/Edith fails as an artist: he cannot escape the intellect.
According to Eeldrop:

> The artist is part of him a drifter, at the mercy of impressions,
> and another part of him allows this to happen for the sake of
> making use of the unhappy creature. But in Edith the division
> is merely the rational, the cold and detached part of the artist,
> itself divided. Her material, her experience, that is, is already
> a mental product, already digested by reason. Hence Edith (I
> only at this moment arrive at understanding) is really the most
> orderly person in existence, and the most rational. Nothing
> ever happens to her; everything that happens is her own doing.
> (E&A II, 19)

Edith is 'readerly'; she finds in herself what she expects to find.
'Edith', Appleplex concludes, 'is the least detached of all persons,
since to be detached is to be detached from one's self, to stand
by and criticise coldly one's own passions and vicissitudes. But
in Edith *the critic is coaching the combatant*' (E&A II, 19, emphasis
added). This is Eliot's conclusion about Bergson: the latter has
not really distinguished between intellect and intuition; he has
merely distinguished between varieties of intellect (as in his only
apparent distinction between numerical and non-numerical kinds
of multiplicity). Bergson, therefore, 'is really the most orderly
person in existence, and the most rational' – certainly not the artist
that many a Bergsonian took him to be.

In 'Eeldrop and Appleplex', then, Eliot explains that it is not important to *be* a Bergsonian (indeed, to be one – in the sense of being no more than a label – may be detrimental to one's spiritual health); rather, it is important to *experience* what Bergson defines as the end of his philosophy: a pseudo-mystical vision of a heterogeneous world. Eeldrop celebrates the importance of such vision in the first 'Eeldrop and Appleplex' instalment, explaining the momentary significance of a fellow diner:

> why was he for a moment an object of interest to us? . . . We were able to detach him from his classification and regard him for a moment as an unique being, a soul, however insignificant, with a history of its own, once for all. It is these moments which we prize, and which alone are revealing. For any vital truth is incapable of being applied to another case: the essential is unique. Perhaps that is why it is so neglected: because it is useless. (E&A I, 8–9)

Like a good Bergsonian, Appleplex also raises the useless (the heterogeneous) above the practical (the homogeneous). The former is more real, and so he not only celebrates, but also seeks, the experience that is most real: 'We aim at experience in the particular centres in which alone it is evil. We avoid classification. We do not deny it. But when a man is classified something is lost' (E&A I, 10). Yes, Eeldrop agrees, human beings are so classified and catalogued that 'Many are not quite real at any moment' (E&A I, 10). 'The majority of mankind', Appleplex asserts, 'live on paper currency: they use terms which are merely good for so much reality, they never see actual coinage' (E&A I, 10). Reality, Bergson himself explains, is 'the gold coin for which we never seem able to finish giving small change.'[49]

Even after 'A Paper on Bergson', then, Eliot seems to agree with Bergson that some sort of mystical vision of reality might reasonably remain the goal of our philosophies. His devastating criticism in 'A Paper on Bergson' was no more fatal to his interest in Bergson than his disdain for occultism was fatal to his interest in an occultist like Orage. Bergsonism was for Eliot what he would later call a point of departure: 'what the poet looks for in his reading is not a philosophy – not a body of doctrine or even a consistent point of view which he endeavours to *understand* – but a point of departure.'[50] Bergsonism was important not for its body of intellectual doctrine, nor for its definition of intuition as something that could be *understood*, but for its quest for an in-between point of view that could be *lived* – a point of view between the intellectual and the intuitive, the material and the moral, the temporal and the spiritual. This was Eliot's point of departure – both in his temporary conversion to Bergsonism and in his less temporary tolerance of the occult.

2

Philosophy Perceived

Between the extremes of the fantastic views of occultists and
Bergsonians, Eliot found another kind of mysticism. By 1913–14,
he had begun extensive research on the subject of more traditional
religious mysticisms, particularly Christian mysticism. Surviving
notes in the form of index cards indicate close attention to a
number of books: *Studies in Mystical Religion*, by R.F. Jones; *Etudes
d'Histoire et du Psychologie du Mysticisme* (Studies in the History and
Psychology of Mysticism), by H. Delacroix; *Christian Mysticism* and
Studies of English Mystics, by W.R. Inge; *Essai sur les fondements
de la Connaissance Mystiques* (An Essay on the Basis of Mystical
Knowledge), by E. Récéjac; *Mysticism*, by Evelyn Underhill.
He planned to read a number of other studies (although no
notes survive to indicate that he did so): *The Mystical Element
of Religion*, by F. von Hügel; *Personal Idealism and Mysticism*, by
W.R. Inge, *Essai sur le mysticisme spéculatif en Allemagne au XIVe
siècle* (An Essay on Speculative Mysticism in Germany During the
Fourteenth Century), by H. Delacroix.[1] Gordon points to these
notes as part of her evidence for her conclusion that 'The turning
point in Eliot's life came not at the time of his baptism in 1927,
but in 1914 when he was circling, in moments of agitation, on
the edge of conversion.'[2] Eloise Knapp Hay rejects Gordon's
conclusion that at this time 'Eliot's imagination toyed with the
saint's ambitious task', pointing out that his notes 'were equally
explicit on the pathologies of mysticism, and [that] it was these
pathological aspects that Eliot first treated in poetry' (particularly
in 'The Death of Saint Narcissus' and 'The Love Song of Saint
Sebastian'). She suggests that the reading in question 'was done
chiefly for Josiah Royce's seminar on comparative methodology in
the fall and winter of 1913–14.'[3]

For many of the books and essays that Eliot read at this time,
one can easily guess the academic motive behind his reading. He
probably read a book like F.B. Jevons' *An Introduction to the History
of Religion* with Royce's course in mind, as Hay suggests. The eight
pages of notes that he made were no doubt used to prepare the

two seminars that he conducted in the course – seminars focusing upon the description, explanation and interpretation of primitive religions.[4] But he presumably read books like J. Burnet's *Early Greek Philosophy* and G.T.W. Patrick's *Heraclitus of Ephesus* for other philosophy courses that he was taking or in which he was acting as a teaching assistant. In other words, not all of the books were read with the requirements of Royce's course in mind. More importantly, not all the books were read with a clear academic purpose in mind. Eliot pursues the subject of mysticism far beyond any application such reading might have had in Royce's course. In fact, these readings seem unrelated to any other course that he was taking or teaching. Yet they represent the largest part of his actual reading, and the subject of Christian mysticism represents the largest part of the list of books and articles that he intended to consult. That mysticism in particular – as opposed to religious experience in general – held a peculiar fascination for Eliot is confirmed by his notes on William James' *The Varieties of Religious Experience*, for he made notes only on the chapter concerning mysticism. Similarly, his notes on books like E. Murisier's *Les Maladies des sentiments religieux* (The Diseases of the Religious Passions) and P. Janet's *Neuroses et idées fixes* (Neuroses and Obsessions) indicate that it was the analysis of mystical experience that he found of interest in these works. If Gordon overemphasizes the spiritual significance of this reading for Eliot, Hay underemphasizes it by suggesting that it represents for the most part an academic exercise. Eliot's research into Christian mysticism is undoubtedly another important part of the life-long investigation of mysticism that begins in these early years.

Of the many works that Eliot read, the most important was Evelyn Underhill's *Mysticism: A Study in the Nature and Development of Man's Spiritual Consciousness*. Eliot's notes on her work are among the most extensive of the notes that he made. Furthermore, they are of a different nature: whereas from the other books he took observations about this or that aspect of mystical experience, he noted in Underhill's work (as though the information were definitive) the precise stages and substages of the mystical experiences that she detailed. Moreover, Eliot seems to have used her bibliography as the basis of his own list of books to read – accepting Underhill's judgement as to the most valuable of the many texts available to students of mysticism. For instance, he seems to quote Underhill's 'Indispensable' beside his note concerning F. von Hügel's *The Mystical Element of Religion* (Notes). Similarly, Underhill is a likely source for Eliot's association of Bergson and Heraclitus in 'A Paper on Bergson': 'Reality, though I should judge *one* at bottom [,] divides itself into a Cartesian dichotomy – the way up, consciousness, and the way down, matter' (Paper, 13–14). Underhill argues that Vitalism – her name for Bergson's Life Force philosophy – is ironically a '"new" way of seeing the Real [that] goes back to Heracleitus' (*Mysticism*, 33).

More than ten years later, her work's continuing impact on Eliot is evident. In her Appendix, 'A Historical Sketch of European Mysticism', there is a passage on Richard of St Victor that Eliot seems to have noted carefully:

> by the beginning of the twelfth century . . . [there was] another mystic almost as great, though now less famous [than St Bernard]: the Scotch or Irish Richard of St Victor (*ob. c.* 1173), whom Dante held to be 'in contemplation more than man'. Richard's master and contemporary, the scholastic philosopher Hugh (1097–1141) of the same Abbey of St Victor at Paris, is also generally reckoned amongst the mystics of this period, but with less reason. (*Mysticism*, 546)

In his Clark Lectures (1925–6), Eliot's introduction of Richard is strikingly similar:

> The most interesting example of a twelfth-century mystic that I know, and an example which should throw considerable light upon Dante, is Richard of St Victor. Richard was, like the great philosopher Hugh of St Victor, a Scotchman who became prior of the Victorine monastery, the Ricardo of [the] *Paradiso*, Canto [X]:
>   '*Che a considerar fu più che viro*'.
>   'Who in contemplation was more than man'.
>
>   (*Varieties*, 101)

The similarities – the claim that Richard is one of the most interesting mystics of the twelfth century, the reference to his Scottishness, the reference to his monastery, the reference to the same three figures (Richard, Hugh and Dante), and the quotation of Dante's words – suggest that Eliot has borrowed heavily here from Underhill. It is not out of the question that Eliot retained this information from his first reading, but it is more likely that he used Underhill's book in the course of brushing up his knowledge of mysticism in preparation for his Clark Lectures. Either scenario testifies to Underhill's continuing influence.

One of Eliot's first observations in his notes on Underhill's *Mysticism* is that the beginning of the book is 'given over to consideration of mysticism in relation to phil[osophy], psch[ology], etc. & is not informing.' Perhaps this comment is a matter-of-fact dismissal of a philosophical and psychological competence less able and less informed than his own. (Underhill was an amateur – in the best and worst senses of the word.) It may be a backhanded acknowledgement that Underhill's philosophical and psychological conclusion – that Bergsonism is a weakling mysticism – is already evident to Eliot.[5] Interestingly, however, Underhill's argument in the first part of her book overlaps a good deal of Eliot's in 'A Paper on Bergson'. Gordon dates the latter from 1913 or 1914; the notes on Underhill's book were made no earlier than 1912, for Eliot used a 1912 edition of her book.[6] Much of the reading included with the note cards on Underhill's *Mysticism* was for philosophy courses that Eliot was taking or teaching in 1913 and 1914, so one might provisionally date this period of reading as beginning in 1913 (Eliot was from 1913 a teaching assistant in the Department of Philosophy at Harvard, teaching undergraduates).[7] Furthermore, Underhill's book was one of the first that Eliot read (serving as a bibliographical source for other reading on mysticism that he did and planned to do). It is likely, then, that Eliot studied Underhill before writing his paper on Bergson. If so, there is reason to suggest that the closeness of the arguments that these two critics of Bergson make is not coincidental.

Eliot does not allow Bergson's Heraclitean claim to have discovered and defined the true *logos*, and neither does Underhill: 'the utter immanance of the Vitalists' will not do; Vitalism would be 'declared by the mystics to be incomplete' (*Mysticism*, 49). In fact, Underhill makes the same two-pronged argument that Eliot was to use in 'A Paper on Bergson':

On the one hand is his [man's] ineradicable intuition of a remote, unchanging Somewhat calling him: on the other there is his longing for and as clear intuition of an intimate, adorable Somewhat, companioning him. Man's true Real, his only adequate God, must be great enough to embrace this sublime paradox, to take up these apparent negations into a higher synthesis. (*Mysticism*, 49)

As we have seen, Eliot agrees that Bergson's 'Real' cannot do this. He finds Bergson suspended between these mystical objects – the transcendental self-sufficient reality and the still-to-be-evolved real immanent within us. His conclusion can be stated in Underhill's words: 'Neither the utter transcendence of extreme Absolutism, nor the utter immanence of the Vitalists will do' (*Mysticism*, 49). In Eliot's terms, these mysticisms are 'simply not final': 'Where . . . is the reality – in the consciousness, or in that which is perceived? Where is the one reality to subsume both of these, & can we or can we not know it?' (Paper, 18–19).

In Eliot's notes on *Mysticism* – and in many of the comments that he would go on to make about mysticism and its analogues – the point to note is the importance that Eliot accords the distinction between transcendental and immanental mysticisms that Underhill makes in situating Bergson within the mystical universe. After noting these two 'theologico-mystico doctrines', Eliot writes that 'The mystic must divide the aspects under which he knows the Godhead, if he is to deal with them in a fruitful or comprehensible way. Two aspects [1] Personal [2] Absolute' (Notes). The practical consequences of Eliot's close attention to Underhill's insistence on this epistemologically necessary distinction between the immanently personal and transcendentally absolute points of view are manifold. In the dissertation to follow, the inevitability of these two points of view forms the backbone of the whole argument: 'Everything, from one point of view, is subjective; and everything, from another point of view, is objective; and there is no *absolute* point of view from which a decision may be pronounced' (KE, 21–2). In 'Tradition and the Individual Talent', the same tension that Underhill and Eliot define as constitutive of our knowledge and experience of the Real turns out to be constitutive of our knowledge and experience of the literary Real as well – the tension between the individual's experience and point of view on the one hand, and something much more comprehensive on the other.

In fact, Underhill's interest in the 'Personal' as a factor in knowledge and experience of the Godhead informs 'Tradition and the Individual Talent' in significant ways. She points out that mysticism is an intensely personal experience that has found its best means of communication, its surest metaphors, in the language of the Christian faith, for Christianity begins by restating 'the truths of metaphysics in terms of personality' – the personality of Christ himself (*Mysticism*, 125). As Eliot records in his notes, 'The incarnation is for the mystic a perpetual cosmic and personal process. The mystics see in the historic life of Christ an epitome – an exhibition – of the essentials of all spiritual life.' From this point of view, 'the essence of the mystic life consists in the remaking of personality: its entrance into a conscious relation with the absolute' (*Mysticism*, 448). This remaking of the personality consists largely in giving it up: the self

> has got to learn to cease to be its 'own centre and circumfer-
> ence': to make that final surrender which is the price of final
> peace. . . . So long as the subject still feels himself to be
> *somewhat* he has not yet annihilated selfhood and come to the
> ground where his being can be united with the Being of God.
> (*Mysticism*, 475–8)

The self must become nothing and the will must become quiet, for to will one's spiritual reward is to assert personality: only when the mystic 'learns to cease thinking of himself at all, in however depreciatory a sense; when he abolishes even such selfhood as lies in a desire for the sensible presence of God, will . . . harmony be obtained' (*Mysticism*, 478). Paradoxically, then, the mystic 'obtains satisfaction because he does not seek it; completes his personality because he gives it up' (*Mysticism*, 110).

The language by which Underhill describes the mystic's struggle to overcome human personality in favour of the divine personality shows up in Eliot's explanation in 'Tradition and the Individual Talent' of the poet's need to overcome idiosyncratic personality in favour of a more universal poetic personality. In language that Eagleton recognizes as simultaneously mystical and right-wing, Eliot suggests that the poet makes 'a continual surrender of himself as he is at the moment to something which is more valuable'; the 'progress of an artist is a continual self-sacrifice, a continual extinction of personality'; poetry 'is not the expression of personality, but an escape from personality'; the 'poet cannot reach this impersonality without surrendering himself wholly to the work to be done' (SE, 17, 21, 22).[8] This process of aesthetic self-abnegation is the first step in an argument that asserts the priority of external authority. In 'The Function of Criticism' (1923), Eliot develops further the language of self-surrender and self-sacrifice: 'There is . . . something outside of the artist to which he owes allegiance, a devotion to which he must surrender and sacrifice himself in order to earn and to obtain his unique position' (SE, 24). The language of 'devotion' makes more explicit the mystical connotation of the language of self-sacrifice. Eliot also suggests that those who interrogate the self in order to find God are, as mystics, no better than 'palpitating Narcissi' – again confirming the origin of much of his rhetoric here in his study of mysticism (SE, 27). He had learned from Underhill that 'Immanence [is] apt to degenerate into pantheism' (Notes); he had observed in 'A Paper on Bergson' that Bergson's immanental mysticism 'is simply not final' (Paper, 19); he notes in 'The Function of Criticism' that an immanental epistemology often 'breathes the eternal message of vanity, fear, and lust' (SE, 27). In so humble a beginning as Underhill's warning about the dangers of grounding a mysticism upon the self (in which the divine is located as immanent), Eliot discovered a suspicion of the vain, impermanent, degenerating self that he could work into his ubiquitous argument that the self – whether in mysticism, post-Cartesian epistemology or literary writing – needs to be sacrificed to something greater.

Furthermore, Underhill contributes not just to the destabilization of self as 'centre and circumference' of reality (the destabilization as much a part of Eliot's dissertation as a part of his literary criticism); she also contributes to Eliot's articulation of the hermeneutic process that emerges from his contemplation of the relation between past and present in literary activity. In the preface to her work, Underhill states that 'mysticism avowedly deals with the individual not as he stands in relation to the civilization of his time, but as he stands in relation to truths that are timeless' (Mysticism, ix). Substitute 'literature' for 'mysticism' and the words serve equally well as a preface to 'Tradition and the Individual Talent', where Eliot develops a similar understanding of the relationship between the present and the past, the contemporary and the timeless, the individual and the tradition. Underhill's account of mystical writing as a tradition is similar to Eliot's account of literary writing as a tradition:

> Each mystic, original though he be, yet owes much to the inherited acquirement of his spiritual ancestors. These ancestors form his tradition, are the classic examples on which his education is based; and from them he takes the language which they have sought out and constructed as a means of telling their adventures to the world. It is by their help too, very often, that he elucidates for himself the meaning of the dim perceptions of his amazed soul. From his own experiences he adds to this store; and hands on an enriched tradition of the transcendental life to the next spiritual genius evolved by the race. (*Mysticism*, 542)

Virtually any sentence about tradition and the historical sense from 'Tradition and the Individual Talent' could be inserted into this passage.

Although Underhill speaks of an 'inherited acquirement', her reference to a process of 'education' in which a certain 'language' is 'sought' and 'constructed' suggests a conclusion similar to Eliot's: tradition 'cannot be inherited, and if you want it you must obtain it by great labour' (SE, 14). The labour itself is the same. According to Underhill, 'as in all other and lesser arts which have been developed by the race, [the mystic's] education consists largely in a humble willingness to submit to the discipline, and profit by the lessons, of the past' (*Mysticism*, 359). Eliot writes of the need for a similarly humble submission to the past: 'What is to be insisted upon is that the poet must develop or procure the consciousness of the past and that he should continue to develop this consciousness throughout his career. What happens is a continual surrender of himself as he is to something which is more valuable' (SE, 17). In each case, the result of this educational labour is the historical sense – 'a perception, not only of the pastness of the past, but of its presence . . . a sense of the timeless as well as of the temporal and of the timeless and of the temporal together' (SE, 14). By means of this historical sense, Underhill and Eliot agree, mystics and writers become immortal. According to Underhill, 'Strange and far away though they [mystics] seem, they are not cut off from us by some impassable abyss. They belong to us. They are our brethren; the giants, the heroes of our race' (*Mysticism*, 534). Eliot's argument is similar: 'not only the best, but the most individual parts of his [the poet's] work may be those in which the dead poets, his ancestors, assert their immortality most vigorously' (SE, 14).

Underhill's analysis of tradition leads to the same hermeneutic circling of knowledge and experience that we find in 'Tradition and the Individual Talent'. Whereas Underhill concludes that 'Tradition runs side by side with experience; the past collaborates with the present', Eliot concludes that 'Whoever has approved this idea of order, of the form of European, of English literature will not find it preposterous that the past should be altered by the present as much as the present is directed by the past' (*Mysticism*, 359, SE, 15). As Davidson explains,

> The present and the past cannot ever be known apart from each other, for they hermeneutically define each other. Knowledge of the past is mostly knowledge of the point of view from which we see the past, while knowledge of one's point of view is mostly knowledge of the past which determines this point of view.[9]

The implication of the idea of tradition that Underhill and Eliot share is that ultimately the Real is not something to be known and experienced, but knowledge and experience themselves.

The only passage that Eliot quotes verbatim from *Mysticism* suggests that it is indeed the hermeneutic aspect of Underhill's explanation of mysticism that strikes him as interesting:

> If we would cease, once for all, to regard visions & voices as objective, and be content to see in them forms of symbolic expression, ways in which the subconscious activity of the spiritual self reaches the surface mind, many of the disharmonies noticeable would fade away. Visionary experience . . . is a picture which the mind constructs . . . from raw materials already at its disposal. (Notes, *Mysticism*, 325)

This hint that human consciousness – whether as an everyday consciousness or as a visionary consciousness – is never simple or pure but always already constructed in some way is reflected both in Eliot's dissertation and in 'Tradition and the Individual Talent'. In the former, 'the line between the experienced, or the given, and the constructed can nowhere be clearly drawn' (KE, 18). In the latter, the poet's mind is this line between the given and the constructed – imagined not as a line, however, but as an invisible container: 'The poet's mind is in fact a receptacle for seizing and storing up numberless feelings, phrases, images, which remain there until all the particles which can unite to form a new compound are present together' (SE, 19). The line between the old and the new and between the tradition and the individual talent can nowhere be clearly drawn.

In this broadly hermeneutic context, Eliot's proposal to halt 'Tradition and the Individual Talent' at 'the frontier of metaphysics or mysticism' deserves careful scrutiny. It implies that there is a line that one ought not to cross if one wishes to remain in the world of the 'practical' and the 'responsible' (SE, 21–2). Eliot seems to suggest – like Hulme – that literature ought not to aspire to express the infinite; its practical and responsible task is to communicate. He thus apparently rules out metaphysics or mysticism in literature. Yet he contradicts himself. Focusing his argument just a few pages before against 'the metaphysical theory of the substantial unity of the soul', he implies that his complaint about the romantic celebration of personality derives not so much from the introduction of metaphysics itself into literature as from the introduction of a particular metaphysical mistake – the overestimation of the importance of the self or soul. The romantics were caught up in the wrong metaphysics; with the right metaphysics, they might have been unobjectionable.

Eliot's shift from a quarrel with the romantics' particular metaphysical or mystical mistake to his much broader proposal 'to halt at the frontier of metaphysics or mysticism' can be explained by his dissertation. In the latter, it is not just the metaphysics associated with the self or soul that is problematic, but metaphysics in general. The problem with metaphysics is that it is a fiction: 'For a metaphysics to be accepted, good-will is essential' (KE, 168). In an essay for *The Monist* on Leibniz and Bradley in 1916, he develops this line further:

> Bradley's universe . . . is only by an act of faith unified. . . . The Absolute responds only to an imaginary demand of thought, and satisfies only an imaginary demand of feeling. Pretending to be something which makes finite centres cohere, it turns out to be merely the assertion that they do. And this assertion is only true so far as we here and now find it to be so.[10]

Metaphysics is a cooperative construction. Underhill alerts Eliot to the fact that so is a certain kind of mysticism. The passage on visionary experience that Eliot quotes from her emphasizes the constructedness of the visionary mystical experience. Her warning – recorded by Eliot – is that visions are not necessarily reliable (Notes). Eliot draws the same conclusion about metaphysical visions: they may be authoritative for those who have them, but not for others.

From this point of view, the line in question in 'Tradition and the Individual Talent' suggests not only that Eliot is refusing to cross the frontier *from* the practical and responsible world *into* the mistaken mysticism and metaphysics of romanticism, but also that he is refusing to cross from a certain metaphysics or mysticism (within the confines of which a responsible person can draw practical conclusions) into something different. That is, by reading the line against the background of Eliot's close study of Underhill and against the background of his related work in philosophy (and perhaps against the line's apparent grain), one finds that Eliot imagines the poet as having proceeded *within* the familiar territory of a certain mysticism or metaphysics to the limit of the horizon of understanding that such a mysticism or metaphysics makes possible. The line deconstructs its anti-metaphysical and anti-mystical surface: the point of its subtext is not to suggest that what remains to be said in poetry by breaching the boundary in question is mistakenly metaphysical or mystical, but rather to acknowledge that outside the metaphysics or mysticism that we inhabit there can be nothing practical and responsible to be said to those who remain within.

That the subtext in question is a significant one is indicated by Eliot's Preface to the 1928 edition of *The Sacred Wood* where he raises again the question of borders and the poet's response to them. As though with 'Tradition and the Individual Talent' in mind, he takes back his suggestion that there is a border at which criticism must stop:

> poetry . . . certainly has something to do with morals, and with religion, and even with politics perhaps, though we cannot say what. If I ask myself . . . why I prefer the poetry of Dante to that of Shakespeare, I should have to say, because it seems to me to illustrate a saner attitude toward the mystery of life. And in these

questions, and others which we cannot avoid, we appear already to be leaving the domain of criticism of 'poetry'. So we cannot stop at any point. The best that we can hope to do is to agree upon a point from which to start. (SW, x)

The phrase 'practical conclusions . . . [that] can be applied by the responsible person interested in poetry' in 'Tradition and the Individual Talent' becomes here 'the domain of criticism of "poetry"'. Similarly, the 'mysticism' and 'metaphysics' of the earlier essay become here 'the mystery of life' – now Eliot's main concern.

Mysticism and metaphysics move thereby from the margin of literary study in the 1919 essay to the centre of literary study in the 1928 Preface – but only briefly. For Eliot's point is that there is no centre and no margin: there is only 'an attitude toward the mystery of life' – whether that attitude be the poet's or the critic's. Life is a mystery, and our attitude toward it comprises a metaphysics or a mysticism with its own centres and margins – such as Eliot's own metaphysical or mystical attitude here, which places Dante near the centre of truth and Shakespeare nearer the margin. What is true of a metaphysics in the dissertation – 'For a metaphysics to be accepted, good-will is essential. Two men must *intend* the same object, and *both* men must admit that the object intended is the same' (KE, 168) – is true of criticism here: 'The best that we can hope to do is to agree upon a point from which to start.'

As in the dissertation, so in both of Eliot's essays: to raise the question of metaphysics is to raise the question of belief. As Michaels explains,

> what Eliot means when he calls reality conventional is that the real is what we *believe*, and that we cannot anchor our beliefs in something more real than they are. . . . If they are really our beliefs, we must believe them. Other beliefs are not less firmly grounded in the real than ours; they are just wrong, they don't agree with ours.[11]

The dissertation makes explicit what Eliot implies in the 1928 Preface to *The Sacred Wood* when he declares that Dante's attitude toward the mystery of life is saner than Shakespeare's: Eliot's beliefs agree more fully with Dante's than with Shakespeare's.

*   *   *

Eliot's essay on Dante a year later (1929) goes to great lengths to cover this question – both in the sense of addressing it and in the sense of hiding it from view. The first line of the essay implies that the appreciation of poetry ideally begins in the moment of immediate experience: 'In my own experience of the appreciation of poetry I have always found that the less I knew about the poet and his work, before I began to read it, the better' (SE, 237). To know nothing about the poet and his work would presumably be best of all. Eliot thus enters again upon the argument in 'Tradition and the Individual Talent' that a poem can be perceived as an object independent of the subject that created it and the subject that perceives it.

The question of the relationship between belief (whether Dante's or the reader's) and the experience of the poetic object is an extension of Eliot's earlier investigation of the relationship between point of view and experience in general. Asserting that 'the line between the experienced, or the given, and the constructed can nowhere be clearly drawn', and that 'the difference in no instance holds good outside of a relative and fluctuating point of view', Eliot concludes that 'no experience is only immediate' (KE, 18). In the 1929 essay on Dante and the 1928 Preface to *The Sacred Wood*, Eliot finally addresses the contradiction that arises by arguing, on the one hand, that no experience is only immediate and, on the other, that poetic experience can be. The issue erupts in what Eliot calls 'a diversion . . . concerning the nature of Belief':

> you cannot afford to *ignore* Dante's philosophical and theological beliefs, or to skip the passages which express them most clearly; but . . . . You are not called upon to believe what Dante believed, for your belief will not give you a groat's worth more of understanding and appreciation; but you are called upon more and more to understand it. . . . It is a matter of knowledge and ignorance, not of belief or scepticism. (SE, 257–8)

This claim is not inconsistent with claims in the earlier essays that the poet's emotions are not the 'significant' emotions in poetry (SE, 22). Yet that this anti-romantic assertion is no more the last word than the right word on the subject of the poem's ontological independence as object is revealed by a lengthy note that supplements the diversion.[12]

Apparently as a result of I.A. Richards's 'incomprehensible' observation about *The Waste Land* – in it, the poet effected 'a complete severance between his poetry and *all* beliefs' – Eliot is moved to define his argument and its terms more clearly: '*If* there is "literature", *if* there is "poetry", then it must be possible to have full literary or poetic appreciation without sharing the beliefs of the poet. This is as far as my thesis goes in the present essay' (SE, 269).[13] Eliot's thesis is an adaptation of Richards's observations in *Practical Criticism*. Unless you admit that 'full appreciation of poetry is possible without belief in what the poet believed', in the end 'you will be forced to admit that there is very little poetry that you can appreciate, and that your appreciation of it will be a function of your philosophy or theology or something else' (SE, 269–70).[14] Where he parts from Richards is in his disagreement that poet or reader can be separated from *all* belief. On the one hand, 'we are forced to believe that there is a particular relation' between 'Dante's beliefs as a man and his beliefs as a poet' and 'that the poet means what he says' (SE, 269). Eliot accepts a logocentric conception of literature as sign system: it represents the poet's beliefs. On the other hand, 'I cannot, in practice, wholly separate my poetic appreciation from my personal beliefs' (SE, 271). Appreciation of poetry is to some extent 'a function of your philosophy or theology or something else' – the thing that Richards and Eliot deny.

On the one hand, he recognizes that his assertion in this essay and in 'Tradition and the Individual Talent' that poetry can be appreciated practically and responsibly outside a particular metaphysics or mysticism is itself a metaphysics, asserting the ontological autonomy of the poem. Eliot finds himself supporting a metaphysical theory of the substantial unity of poetry and the substantial unity of criticism: 'If you deny the theory that full poetic appreciation is possible without belief in what the poet believed, you deny the existence of "poetry" as well as "criticism"' (SE, 269). Like the Derridean supplement, Eliot's note both adds to and replaces his main text, for it turns out that the appreciation of poetry is not just a matter of 'knowledge and ignorance', but also a matter of 'belief or scepticism'. On the other hand, he finds his metaphysics inadequate, for his reading practice contradicts his thesis about the ontological status of poetry and criticism: 'It would appear that "literary appreciation" is an abstraction, and pure poetry a phantom' (SE, 271).

As much in his essay 'Dante' (1929) as in his dissertation, it is the practice that reveals the metaphysics and justifies the theory:

> All of our terms turn out to be unreal abstractions; but we can defend them, and give them a kind of reality and validity (the only validity which they can possess or can need) by showing that they express the theory of knowledge which is implicit in all our practical activity. (KE, 18)

Practical activity in the matter of belief and understanding is contradictory:

> I am quite aware of the ambiguity of the word 'understand'. In one sense, it means to understand without believing, for unless you understand a view of life (let us say) without believing in it, the word 'understand' loses all meaning, and the act of choice between one view and another is reduced to caprice. But if you yourself are convinced of a certain view of life, then you irresistibly and inevitably believe that if anyone else comes to 'understand' it fully, his understanding *must* terminate in belief. It is possible, and sometimes necessary, to argue that full understanding must identify itself with full belief. (SE, 270)

Eliot's '*general* theory' of 'poetic belief and understanding' will remain 'embryonic' until it can express the theory of knowledge implicit in such a contradiction (SE, 269).

The subtext at the beginning of the third part of 'Tradition and the Individual Talent' has finally reached the surface: Eliot recognizes that criticism cannot be the exercise of dispassionate objectivity that his rhetoric calls for; rather, it must be an attempt to identify the limit of the horizon of understanding made possible by the metaphysics or mysticism that one always already inhabits. Such a metaphysics or mysticism is revealed in the practical activity of responsible persons confined within it. The insight latent in Eliot's essays is again the hermeneutic insight that the world is always already meaningful. As Davidson explains, 'Eliot asserts that we know everything and nothing, because the distinction between appearance and reality cannot be maintained. Finite existence is all there is – completely unknown to us in its essence and completely known to us in our practical lives, our world.'[15] Implied in Eliot's essays is the double awareness that we know everything and that we know nothing – the double awareness of the mysticism that

Underhill locates in the constructedness of visionary experience, and the double awareness that Eliot locates in his own definition of metaphysics. We are at once in complete communion with the Real, and yet the Real is merely conventional. 'Tradition and the Individual Talent' seems to suggest that knowledge outside that which has 'practical consequences' for the reading of poetry is metaphysical or mystical; at the same time, there is no knowledge that is not a function of a conventional absolute – and therefore metaphysical or mystical.[16]

In the end, Eliot's interest in the mystic's claim to an experience of 'non-subjectivity' (evident in essays like 'Dante' (1929) and 'Tradition and the Individual Talent') locates two contradictory impulses: first, the traditional mystical impulse to know and to experience the essence of the Real as universal truth; second, the dissertation impulse to reconceive the Real as always a function of local practice and convention. As we shall see in Chapter 8, however, it is only in *Four Quartets* that Eliot can finally express the theory of knowledge latent in this contradiction.

According to Eliot, what it is to inhabit the local practice and convention that he calls a metaphysics or mysticism is shown by Dante, and once again it is Underhill who nudges him in this direction. His identification of Dante as a poet with one of the 'saner' attitudes towards the mystery of life was encouraged by her. She concedes that Dante is a poet before he is a mystic: 'not for [mystical vision] were my proper wings [fitted], save that my mind was smitten by a flash wherein its will came to it.'[17] Yet his mysticism is as perfect as his poetry; the *Divine Comedy* is 'a faithful and detailed description of the Mystic Way' (*Mysticism*, 154). In a line from the *Paradiso* quoted often by Eliot and quoted by Arnold as a touchstone of great poetry, Underhill finds the state of utter self-surrender that represents the touchstone of true mysticism: '*la sua volontate è nostra pace*' (His will is our peace).[18] Not surprisingly, then, in her attempt to rehabilitate mysticism, Underhill cites Dante more than she cites almost any other mystic.

Dante's greatest virtue as mystic is to demonstrate that the 'full spiritual consciousness of the true mystic is developed not in one, but in two apparently opposite but really complementary directions' (*Mysticism*, 42). These are the directions of immanence and transcendence so important in Underhill's explanation of mysticism – so important that Eliot began his own notes at this point. In the *Paradiso*, Dante sees 'both the two courts of heaven manifested'.[19] According to Underhill, 'he sees Reality first as the streaming River of Light, the flux of things; and then, when his sight has been purged, as achieved perfection, the Sempiternal Rose' (*Mysticism*, 47). Like the immanental mystic, Dante finds that the absolute is within creation, a part of becoming; like the transcendental mystic, he finds that the absolute is radically separate from creation, a discrete being. The *Divine Comedy* is for Underhill a classic statement of the twofold nature of mystical vision:

> Certain rare mystics seem able to describe to us a Beatific Vision experienced here and now: a knowledge by contact of the Flaming Heart of Reality which includes in one great whole the planes of Being and Becoming. . . . Its finest literary expression is found in the passage of the 'Paradiso' where Dante tells us how he pierced, for an instant, the secret of the Empyrean. Already he had enjoyed a symbolic vision of two-fold Reality, as the moving River of Light and the still white rose. Now these two aspects vanished, and he saw the One. (*Mysticism*, 406)

Dante forces 'human language to express one of the most sublime visions of the absolute which has ever been crystallized into speech':

> He inherits and fuses into one that loving and artistic reading of reality which was the heart of Franciscan mysticism, and that other ordered vision of the transcendental which the Dominicans through Aquinas poured into the stream of European thought. For the one the spiritual world was all love: for the other all law. For Dante it was both. In the 'Paradiso' his stupendous genius apprehends and shows to us a Beatific Vision in which the symbolic systems of all great mystics . . . are included and explained. (*Mysticism*, 551)

Dante solves the puzzle – 'the puzzle which all explorers of the supersensible have sooner or later to face: *come si convenne l'imago al cerchio* [how the image agrees with the circle], the reconciliation of Infinite and intimate, both known and felt, but neither understood' (*Mysticism*, 125).[20]

Eliot presents Dante's achievement in similar terms. Like Underhill, he explains Dante's pre-eminence both as poet and

mystic by reference to his special visionary power: the vision
of poets and mystics is not 'a device to enable the uninspired
to write verses, but really a mental habit, which when raised
to the point of genius can make a great poet as well as a great
mystic or saint' (SE, 243). Again like Underhill, he locates the
specialness of Dante's visionary power in the fact that *The Divine
Comedy* combines knowing and feeling: 'The mystical experience
is supposed to be valuable because it is a pleasant state of unique
intensity. But the true mystic is not satisfied merely by feeling, he
must pretend at least that he *sees*' (SW, 170). *The Divine Comedy*
provides more than the 'loving and artistic reading of reality'; it also
offers the 'ordered vision of the transcendental': 'seeing visions – a
practice now relegated to the aberrant and uneducated – was once a
significant, interesting, and disciplined kind of dreaming' (SE, 243).
Following Underhill, Eliot finds Dante's simultaneously intense and
disciplined vision to represent the inclusive vision of love and law
characteristic of the 'true mystic'.

The important point to mark is that Dante's philosophy is not
something to be studied: 'Dante, more than any other poet, has
succeeded in dealing with his philosophy, not as a theory . . . or as
his own comment or reflection, but in terms of something *perceived*'
(SW, 170–1). Dante succeeds where Bergson and the speaker in
'Rhapsody' fail. The philosophy is part of Dante's 'vision of life',
and so must appear in a poem in which 'the vision is so nearly
complete': 'we *see* it, as part of the ordered world' (SW, 170).
Eliot's concern is to distinguish between Dante's experience and
the modern experience: 'Dante helps us to provide a criticism of
M. Valéry's "modern poet" who attempts "to produce in us a
state". A state, in itself, is nothing whatever' (SW, 170).

The language of the dissertation erupts once more. Eliot's
distinction here between a perception and an inner state is
the focus of the dissertation's third chapter, 'The Psychologist's
Treatment of Knowledge'. Eliot argues that it is a mistake to regard
the perception of an object – that is, the idea or mental presentation
of an object – as itself an object: 'It is incorrect . . . to say that we
can have sensations of redness; redness is a concept; or to say that
we have sensations of red. The sensation is of a red *something*, a
red spot or area' (KE, 62). Explaining that in turn-of-the-century
psychology 'the idea is conceived to have an existence apart from
its object', Eliot argues instead that 'This existence . . . is simply the

fact of its reference' (KE, 63). As Michaels explains, 'What Eliot
seems to mean here is that . . . sensation cannot be conceived as a
thing. . . . The essence of a perception is its reference to an object'
(179–80). The virtue of *The Divine Comedy* is to present Dante's
philosophy 'in terms of something *perceived*'. It is presented not as
Catholicism (a concept, like red), but as a Catholic something. The
philosophy is not mistaken for a state; it is part of Dante's vision, his
reference to the world – an instance of 'the articulate formulation
of life which human minds make' (SW, 170).

Eliot implies that this aspect of Dante's sensibility is analogous to
mystical experience:

> Dante helps us to provide a criticism of M. Valéry's 'modern
> poet' who attempts 'to produce in us a *state*'. A state, in itself,
> is nothing whatever.
>   M. Valéry's account is quite in harmony with pragmatic
> doctrine, and with the tendencies of such a work as William
> James's *Varieties of Religious Experience*. The mystical experience
> is supposed to be valuable because it is a pleasant state of unique
> intensity. But the true mystic is not satisfied merely by feeling,
> he must pretend at least that he *sees*. (SW, 170)

Both Dante and 'the true mystic' *see*. There is no state intermediate
between subject and object. And so the experience of one's
philosophy or theology as reference – instead of as a concept –
is common to mystics and certain poets.

This experience of a point of view as reference is defined by
Eliot elsewhere as an experience characteristic of the unified
sensibility. The difference in 'Dante' (1920) between the poet
who deals with philosophy 'in terms of something *perceived*' and
the poet who deals with it 'as a theory . . . or as his own
comment or reflection' is developed in 'The Metaphysical Poets'
as 'the difference between the intellectual poet and the reflective
poet' (SW, 170–1; SE, 287). The metaphysical poets are the last
English poets demonstrating a unified sensibility: 'Tennyson and
Browning are poets, and they think; but they do not feel their
thought as immediately as the odour of a rose. A thought to Donne
was an experience; it modified his sensibility' (SE, 287). Dante is
Eliot's prime example of the not yet dissociated sensibility. Dante is
one for whom his philosophy 'has reached the point of immediate

acceptance, . . . it has become almost a physical modification' (SW, 162–3). Eliot agrees with Underhill: Dante feels and knows at once.

Underhill's understanding of Dante's special virtue as a mystic is instrumental in allowing Eliot to locate Dante as the focus of his epistemological nostalgia for a unified sensibility. By means of Dante's example, Underhill argues that mysticism – unlike modern philosophy – suffers no dissociation of being and becoming, infinite and intimate, thought and feeling. Dante's sensibility is therefore for Underhill the archetypally mystical sensibility, a point Eliot follows her in making in 'Dante' (1920). By way of contrast, Eliot suggests that the modern poet exhibits the archetypally dissociated sensibility:

> When most of our modern poets confine themselves to what they had perceived, they produce for us, usually, only odds and ends of still life and stage properties; but that does not imply so much that the method of Dante is obsolete, as that our vision is perhaps comparatively restricted. (SW, 171)

As one of these 'modern poets', Eliot's complaint is that a defective sensibility is his inheritance by means of the restricted epistemological practice of the modern world – an epistemological practice that makes unlikely the experience of a true mysticism.

3

Modernism and Pragmatism

Before analysing *The Waste Land* and The Clark Lectures by the light of Eliot's interest in mysticism, it is necessary to foreground another area in which this interest is explored. Eliot points to it when concluding the passage above in his 1920 essay on Dante with criticism of Paul Valéry's "'modern poet" who attempts "to produce in us a *state*'":

> M. Valéry's account is quite in harmony with pragmatic doctrine, and with the tendencies of such a work as William James's *Varieties of Religious Experience*. The mystical experience is supposed to be valuable because it is a pleasant state of unique intensity. (SW, 170).

By way of contrast, he compares Dante favourably to 'the true mystic' (SW, 170). Eliot implies that pragmatism is connected with a false mysticism.

That Eliot should see a connection between pragmatism and mysticism is not surprising given that his notes upon *The Varieties of Religious Experience* – one of the most famous books of William James, the most famous pragmatist – refer only to the chapter on mysticism. But the immediate stimulus for his reference to pragmatism and mysticism is a sequence of book reviews on modern theology completed a few years before his first Dante essay – reviews in which precisely the alliance between pragmatism and mysticism is under scrutiny.

In reviews for *The International Journal of Ethics* between 1915 and 1918, Eliot read various books related to Anglican and Roman Catholic modernism. The course of reading prompted by the reviews that he wrote allowed him to apply to religion in general and Christian theology in particular the reservations about Absolutes and the interpretation of religious experience that he had developed in his dissertation and related philsophical essays. That a reviewer like Eliot should reflect his own preoccupations in his reviews is not surprising. Nor is it surprising that the books offered him for review should have proven to be closely related to his interests. First, Eliot had ample opportunity over dinner with a member of the journal's editorial board in October of 1915 to explain his interests and expertise. As a result of the dinner, he procured for himself the task of reviewing two books, one on theism and the other on Nietzsche.[1] Second, Philip Jourdain, British editor of *The Monist* (in which Eliot was shortly to publish essays on Leibniz and Bradley) and the *International Journal of Ethics*, allowed Eliot to select the books that he would review: 'Jourdain . . . is the most satisfactory employer I could wish. I have only to suggest an article and he clamours for it, and any book I see advertised and want to review he will send for, for me.'[2]

Pleased with what was for a graduate student in philosophy something of a coup, Eliot took advantage of Jourdain's flexibility to make his reviewing as practical as possible. A prestigious enough endeavour in its own right (Eliot anticipated that his reviewing would 'impress the people at Harvard much more than the same amount of work . . . put in upon the thesis'), reviewing would also serve academic ends: '[I] am reading some of Nietzsche's works which I had not read before, and which I ought to read anyhow before my examinations.'[3] It was equally practical for the student who had spent 'Two years . . . in the study of Sanskrit . . . and a year in the mazes of Patañjali's metaphysics' to review *Brahmadarsanam, or Intuition of the Absolute, Being an Introduction to the Study of Hindu Philosophy*.[4] Similarly, the student who had read Emile Durkheim and Lucien Lévy-Bruhl and written a paper on 'The Interpretation of Primitive Ritual' reviewed *Group Theories of Religion and the Religion of the Individual* and *Elements of Folk Psychology, Outlines of a Psychological History of the Development of Mankind*. Moreover, the student who had at the outbreak of war been at summer school in Marburg for further study of German philosophy reviewed *Philosophy and War*, a topical book on the subject of German philosophy and war.[5]

The demonstrable connection between his own interests and expertise and the books that he reviewed leads one to ask why he should have reviewed books on modern theology – books like *Conscience and Christ: Six Lectures on Christian Ethhics*, by Hastings Rashdall, and *Mens Creatrix*, by William Temple. Rashdall and Temple were leading figures in the Anglican Modernist movement. Did Jourdain suggest that Eliot review them? If so, did he do so because of some expression on Eliot's part of a general interest in religion? Or did Eliot request for review precisely these books, perhaps because of an interest in modern Anglican theology? Modernism relied heavily on pragmatism as the philosophical underpinning of its reformist agenda. If modernism's pragmatism were known to Eliot before he reviewed these and similar works, then one could explain his reviews once again as a function of his practical habits: the student who had read William James reviewed pragmatic modernists. As Eliot himself noted years later, 'Those who know the religious views and religious feelings of William James will know the strength and the weakness of Anglican modernism.'[6]

Whatever the explanation, the result is the spectacle of Eliot's engagement with modernism – an engagement that he comes to recognize by 1920 as a contest with the pragmatic mysticism of modernism.

Modernism was an attempt to accommodate theology to the modern world. Although Eliot accurately observed that 'French "Modernism" and English "Modernism" are quite different', modernism involved in both its Roman Catholic and Anglican versions the reinterpretation of time-worn dogmas within the terms of modern science and modern (that is, post-Kantian) philosophy. As the Catholic modernist George Tyrrel put it, 'By a Modernist, I mean a churchman, of any sort, who believes in the possibility of a synthesis between the essential truth of his religion and the essential truth of modernity.'[7] Accepting Kant's assertion that the mind is active in the construction of its experience, modernists looked for an alternative to the traditional understanding of dogma as representing an absolute and timeless revealed truth. In orthodox Catholic theology – and especially in the scholastic theology renewed in the Catholic Church at the end of the nineteenth century – faith was defined as intellectual assent to such dogma. Modernists, however, argued that truth cannot be embodied in dogma, for dogma is expressed in language, and language changes through time. Truth embodied in language, they argued, is as mutable as language. It will inevitably assume the human shape of the human language that seeks to describe it. Modernists therefore sought a source of spiritual authority beyond dogma, beyond language. This search led them to consider mysticism as a model for modern religious experience.

French modernists were greatly influenced by the so-called mystical philosophy of Henri Bergson – the philosopher whose 'standing-room-only' lectures were the reason that Eliot was in Paris in 1910 and 1911. Perhaps the largest figure on the philosophical landscape of Europe before the war – although since sunk into oblivion – Bergson captured the imagination of his age with his 'time philosophy': reality is a continuous flux, a pure duration, a timeless present; only process is real; the static is merely appearance. Actual experience of the process that is reality is beyond the reach of the intellect. Certain French modernists, intent on arguing that faith must not be understood as an intellectual matter, welcomed Bergson's philosophy. Asserting that intellect is an insufficient witness to divine truth, they found in Bergsonism an anti-intellectualism that complemented their own attempt to locate a new spiritual authority beyond the intellect in the realm of intuition.

Bergson paved the way for the modernist acceptance of the pragmatic interpretation of truth. According to William James, 'The truth of an idea is not a stagnant property inherent in it. Truth *happens* to an idea. It *becomes* true, is *made* true by events.'[8] For Bergson and his modernist followers, if truth is an accurate description of reality, and reality is in process, then truth too is in process. The static Truth that we mark with a capital T is actually bound to time and place. It is an abstraction from the flowing reality that we can never fully express in language. In opposition to the traditional conception of Truth as *what is* (what *is*, both now and forever), Truth becomes for Bergson and James each age's interpretation of *what is practical* or *what is useful* for its own time. Influenced by them, modernists like Edouard Le Roy argued that 'God does not exist but becomes. His becoming is our very progress, and like all progress, can be known only by lived intuition, not by conceptual analysis.'[9] Similarly, Alfred Loisy (like Le Roy, a pragmatist and a Bergsonian), suggested that truth 'evolves with [man], in him, and by him'.[10]

Alive to contemporary controversies in philosophy and theology, Eliot became familiar with modernism during the year he spent in Paris. Caught up in the Parisian mood, he became a Bergsonian – he later spoke of experiencing a conversion to Bergsonism at this time, describing it as his first *conversion* experience. He also recalled his year at the Collège de France as a time when the famous modernist 'Loisy enjoyed his somewhat scandalous distinction'.[11] Most modernists – like Lucien Laberthonnière (who found his books placed on the Index and who was eventually forbidden to publish) – submitted to Vatican authority in the face of the papal encyclical condemning modernism in 1907, but Loisy refused to yield and so became notorious. The controversial nature of Bergsonism and the immanental Catholic theology that borrowed from it could nowhere else have been brought home so clearly to Eliot.

Given his experiences in Paris, Eliot might well have approached books on Anglican modernism in the expectation of uncovering an immanental and pragmatic genealogy. His awareness of the intellectual energy invested in attacks upon and apologies for French modernism could explain his initial interest in reviewing books by English modernists. Did the same energy exist in the English version of the movement? Perhaps his awareness of Bergson's role in modernism ('over all [French intellectual life] swung the spider-like figure of Bergson'), and his own revised attitude toward Bergson in 1915, led him to scrutinize English modernism for the same pernicious influence.[12] Or reservations about pragmatism developed after his year in Paris might have brought him to Anglican modernism with a critical eye in this regard. In any event, he did not like what he found, and said so loudly and clearly – even eleven years after his first review: 'Modernism . . . is a mental blight which can afflict the whole of the intelligence of the time, whether within or without the Church'.[13]

Eliot discovered his antipathy towards the English version of modernism while reviewing *Conscience and Christ*, by Hastings Rashdall, one of the 'giants of Modernism'.[14] Eliot acknowledges Rashdall's stature: 'There is no one better qualified than Canon Rashdall for the task which he has set himself. . . . Dr. Rashdall is distinguished both as a Christian and as a moral philosopher.' The task that Rashdall sets himself is typically modern: 'What is the relation of conscience to authority? When must conscience appeal to the teaching of Jesus for justification, and how far is the teaching of Jesus justified by appeal to conscience?'[15] Like most modernists, Rashdall is concerned to raise personal religious experience above the claims of other religious authority – such as the Church or the Bible. And so he argues for the authority of conscience, poking fun, all the while, at the outraged Anglo-Catholic ('High-church') believer who acts, he writes, 'as if the admission that the human mind possessed any such activity [as an individual moral consciousness] would be fraught with the gravest disaster to Church and State.' The hostility of the Anglo-Catholics notwithstanding, Rashdall asserts that:

> The kind of authority which we can attribute to the teaching even of Christ Himself . . . must be determined by the impression which His teaching actually makes upon the moral consciousness of the *present*. And therefore we cannot in the *old-fashioned* way first examine the credentials of the Master's authority; and then, having done so . . . accept and act upon His precepts blindly.[16]

The grounding of authority in the self (and thereby in the present) was anathema to Eliot. Three years before circumscribing the individual talent of the eccentric artist by tradition, and seven years before characterizing pursuit of the 'inner voice' as the habit of soccer hooligans and 'palpitating Narcissi', Eliot practised upon Rashdall the irony that would announce these positions (SE, 27):

> Now it follows almost inevitably, if one holds a theory of conscience similar to Dr. Rashdall's, that conscience will consist in the usual structure of prejudices of the enlightened middle classes. To this middle-class conscience the teaching of Jesus is gradually assimilated.[17]

The argument that Eliot held up to scorn is found in the following passage:

> neither [Christ's] ideal nor His practice were world-renouncing in the sense of despising and condemning all ordinary pleasure – still less in the extremer sense of courting bodily pain. He . . . neither practised nor enjoyed fasting. He spent much of his time and energy in curing diseases of mind and body. He made little of bodily pleasures and satisfactions in comparison with higher

things. But he never condemned them. . . . And that really implies that in principle His ideal was not world-renouncing.[18]

Eliot excoriates Rashdall's pandering to 'the usual structure of prejudices of the enlightened middle classes':

> we learn that Christ was not ascetic, that he did not consider celibacy superior to marriage, that . . . Christ was not a socialist, and did not disapprove of private property. . . . All that is anarchic, or unsafe or disconcerting in what Jesus said and did is either denied, or boiled away.

In fact, the argument is merely Rashdall writ large: 'He proceeds, I believe, first to assimilate Christ's teaching to his own morality, then makes Christ the representative of this morality.'[19]

The witting or unwitting transposition of the human and the divine − here, Rashdall become Christ, in modernism generally, the human being become God − is what Eliot regarded as the fundamental error of modernism. This error also appears in the substitution of Christ's humanity for His divinity. Rashdall does not find Christ to be unique in kind: 'I do not believe that Jesus is the only man in whom the Word or Reason or Wisdom of God has dwelt.' At most, he is unique in degree: 'the unique appeal which Christ still makes to our conscience both by His teaching and by His life and death of self-sacrifice, . . . justifies us in saying that with Him the Logos was united in a supreme manner, that in Him God is most fully revealed to men.'[20] Although a supreme example of human being, Christ is no more than a human being.

Eliot recognized in his family's religion one of modernism's theological forbears: 'we find Dr. Rashdall taking up a position hardly different from Unitarianism.'[21] Eliot had suggested to the Harvard Philosophy Club that Unitarianism was the refuge of the 'intellectual drunkard'.[22] In flight from such a theology, he seems somewhat surprised and disappointed that it should be offered as the up-to-date version of Christianity: 'I am not sure, after reading modern theology, that the pale Galilean has conquered.'[23] He notes with amazement Rashdall's explanation of a good reason for Christian belief:

> A Christianity without Christ − or a Christianity in which Christ is not emphatically put above other masters − will always be maimed and *not very effective* Christianity. . . . I believe that

Jesus will always be *better followed* in a society which actually recognizes His unique position.

The question of whether or not Christ actually *is* the Son of God does not seem relevant to Rashdall. The criterion for belief is *effectiveness*:

> For ourselves the following of Christ is *made easier* by thinking of Him not only as the supreme Teacher and the supreme Example, but as the Being in whom that union of God and Man after which all ethical Religion aspires, is most fully accomplished.[24]

Quoting this passage, and underlining the words '*made easier*', Eliot ruefully notes that 'Certain saints found the following of Christ very hard, but modern methods have facilitated everything'.[25]

Eliot's suspicion of 'modern methods' is a suspicion of Modernism's pragmatism, whose catch phrases about belief he recognizes in Rashdall's book. According to James, '"The true" . . . is only the expedient in the way of our thinking, just as "the right" is only the expedient in the way of our behaving.'[26] Eliot recognizes in Rashdall's theology the claim that religious truth is only the expedient – a *making easier* – in the way of belief. Thus Rashdall's interest in grounding authority in individual religious experience – a pseudo-mysticism to be cultivated as an easy and effective facilitator of belief.

A few months before, in reviewing *Group Theories of Religion and the Religion of the Individual* by Clement C.J. Webb, another Modernist, Eliot had articulated his hostility toward pragmatism. Against Lévy-Bruhl and Durkheim, the 'French sociologists', Webb argues that their 'group theories of Religion . . . do not do justice to what we usually mean by individual or personal religion, and must inevitably end in a view of it as something illusory and destined to perish in proportion as genuine knowledge of the world increases.' He supplements their accounts of religion with an affirmation of the importance of individual religious experience – such as 'enjoyment of communion with God' – as the foundation of faith: 'if religious experience is not fundamentally illusory, this faith, too, must have substantial worth.'[27] Championing the role of individual religious experience in faith, Webb announces himself a modernist.

Lévy-Bruhl and Durkheim, in fact, often function for Webb as straw men ironically characterized as representing a point of view close to the neoscholastic theology of the Roman Catholic Church, with its insistence that faith is assent to dogma. Thus Webb's sarcastic reference to the Vatican as aligned with the anti-individualist spirit of the French sociologists:

> The champions of vigorous traditional orthodoxy (the Vatican, for example, in its condemnation of Roman Catholic Modernism) are in the right in their conviction that the spirit of free investigation is incompatible with that of the surrender to collective suggestion which is of the essence of Religion, and which may be fairly described by the old-fashioned names of 'faith' or 'belief', but not without great risk of confusion by the newfangled name of 'religious experience'.

Webb reinforces his parallel between the French sociologists and orthodoxy later in the book:

> The French sociologists have, indeed, done a service to the philosophy of religion by insisting on the evidence borne by history to the social character of religion. I find myself often in sympathy with them in certain criticisms which they are led by their point of view to make on some philosophical and psychological accounts of religion which abstract unduly from the historical facts of religious development. . . . [S]ometimes the orthodox have preserved better than liberal theologians of the type of Auguste Sabatier . . . 'the sense of necessities inherent in all religion'.[28]

Webb thus situates himself between the extremes of Vatican orthodoxy and the liberal Protestant theology of Auguste Sabatier.

That Eliot recognized both the nature of Webb's polemic and the inadequcy of it is indicated by his cryptic conclusion:

> Whoever wishes to understand just what the issue is should read Mr Webb's last two chapters, then M. Durkheim's last chapter. Then he ought to realize that the struggle of 'liberal' against 'orthodox' faith is out of date. The present conflict is far more momentous than that.

Webb's tilt with the Vatican is significant because of the spectacular way it misses the point. Eliot complains that 'When Mr Webb turns to deal with Durkheim, he confuses genuine issues with misinterpretation. . . . [H]is statement that "for sociologists religion, because it is a 'collective representation', misrepresents the world" is quite unfair to the author in question.'[29] Eliot's point is that Webb has missed Durkheim's pragmatism, his belief that religion and science – indeed, all aspects of a culture – are social constructions. The question of misrepresenting an objective world does not arise for Durkheim and so Webb confuses a genuine issue – the inadequacy of Durkheim's anthropology – by misinterpretation.

Webb does not recognize that pragmatism is the bogey in the 'momentous . . . present conflict'. Having summarized Durkheim's *Elementary Forms of the Religious Life* – 'The function of religion is to help us to live and act, the believer is *stronger* than the unbeliever. The view of both religion and science is pragmatic' – Eliot concludes with a 'wish that Mr Webb had attacked on this issue'.[30] Although Eliot does not explain what he finds after comparing the concluding chapters by Webb and Durkheim, his identification of Durkheim's pragmatism and Webb's blindness to it as the crux of the conflict is suggestive. In his last two chapters, Webb reveals himself to be something of a pragmatist: the faith that comes from 'enjoyment of communion with God' must have 'substantial worth'.[31] This attribution of substance to a state is what Eliot would characterize a few years later in his essay on Dante (1920) as 'quite in harmony with pragmatic doctrine, and with the tendencies of such a work as William James's *Varieties of Religious Experience*. The mystical experience is supposed to be valuable because it is a pleasant state of unique intensity' (SW, 170). Not only is Webb ineffective in countering Durkheim's claim that 'Religious forces are . . . human forces'; he unwittingly reinforces it by identifying nothing more than the force of individual human experience as the ground of faith.[32]

Eliot's riddling conclusion to his review of Webb's book marks the moment when he began to understand modernism as the fifth column in the 'momentous . . . present conflict'. He implies here what he made more explicit several months later in the review of Rashdall's book: the conflict is not between kinds of faith, but between faith and no faith, between Christianity and something not Christian. As in the case of Rashdall, it is not clear which side Webb is on. These are the sorts of modernists that Eliot recalled twelve years later when he characterized the age of modernism as 'a period of intellectual indistinctness' populated by 'a host of half-Christians and quarter-Christians'.[33]

The extent of Eliot's animation against pragmatism at this time is suggested by the toleration shown to points of view almost equally antipathetic to him in a book that implies a slight to pragmatism. The work of the modernist Arthur Clutton-Brock, *The Ultimate Belief*, passes largely unscathed because 'its thought is not daring, but its commonsense is sound'. Clutton-Brock's interest is in the education of boys; the philosophy upon which his recommendations are based is Croce's. The philosophy does not interest Eliot: 'The merit of the book does not lie in an original theory of value, but in its comments upon education.' The commonsense about education that Eliot finds in the book is Clutton-Brock's criticism of the pragmatic criterion of usefulness. Of Croce's four categories by which 'the human spirit' may be comprehended – truth, beauty, goodness and usefulness – Clutton-Brock extols the first three at the expense of the latter. As summarized by Eliot, the argument is that 'Boys should be taught to respect the values of truth, beauty and goodness for their own sake. . . . They should learn *why* knowledge is valuable, apart from purely practical success.'[34]

Fortunately for Clutton-Brock, Croce's celebration of the 'human spirit' as the somewhat Bergsonian vital impulse driving history is understated in the book – a fact that Eliot turns ironically in the book's favour: 'Mr Clutton Brock is a student of Croce, but his philosophical apparatus is unpretentious.'[35] Eliot's deprecations about the philosophy behind the book imply that had Clutton-Brock presented more pretentiously Croce's 'human spirit' as 'the ultimate belief' of the book's title, then he would have been forced to address here the same confusion between the human and the divine that he found in Rashdall. In another review, Eliot made his opinion of Croce quite clear: 'It is pleasant to find that Croce and Gentile are spoken of as "polluting" (at least *contaminando* [contaminating]) Hegel with Bergson.'[36] Eliot brings the Clutton-Brock review to the point at which he might have launched this kind of attack – summarizing Clutton-Brock's peroration: 'We must learn to love always, to exercise those disinterested passions of the spirit which are inexhaustible and permanently satisfying' – but he retreats, observing in the next sentence that 'The philosophical foundation of the book is adequate to its purpose.'[37] For the sake of the commonsense about education, Eliot pulls his punches about a metaphysics that transposes the human and the divine by attributing permanence to human passions.

That Eliot recognized unfinished metaphysical business remaining after this review is suggested by his review several months later of *Mens Creatrix* by the famous modernist William Temple. As though alluding to the review of Clutton-Brock's book, he ends his review of Temple's book with a nod toward the topic of the earlier review – commonsense on the subject of education: 'Mr Temple says many wise things by the way, especially in his chapter on Education.' Eliot's sly point in thus connecting the two books is to imply that Temple – like the less ambitious Clutton-Brock – might better have left metaphysics, aesthetics, ethics and theology alone in favour of education. But Eliot also identifies a connection between Clutton-Brock's book on 'the ultimate belief' and Temple's attempt 'to demonstrate that philosophy, art, morality, education and politics all aim at a completion which they never of themselves reach, and that they find this completion in Christianity.'[38] For Temple, Christianity is the ultimate belief.

The discussion of metaphysics disdained in connection with Clutton-Brock cannot be put off here. Eliot recognizes in Temple's 'compendious *Summa*' a sloppiness in the application of the pragmatic criterion of usefulness. It is this criterion that Eliot finds in Temple's analysis of 'social and individual ethics':

> In discussing the nature of the State, Mr Temple asserts that 'the nations . . . need some society that may include themselves, whose basis shall be a common purpose . . . arising out of loyalty to an all-inclusive Kingdom and a common Master'. And the problem of evil is stated in the form 'What is the good of evil?'

That something should be proven to exist by virtue of its having a good or being needed is to elevate usefulness from a criterion of value located in a philosophy with a particular history to an absolute outside of history. Hoisting this eminent modernist with his own pragmatic petard, Eliot asks 'might it not be maintained that religion, however poor our lives would be without it, is only one form of satisfaction among others, rather than the culminating satisfaction of all satisfactions?'[39]

One recognizes in this complaint about Temple the same complaint that Eliot makes a few years later about Valéry: modernists value religious experience as an experience of unique intensity – a pragmatic valuation according to the criterion of usefulness (SW, 170). Eliot plays upon this concept a decade later in his 'Journey of the Magi'. The magus observes of Christ's birth that 'it was (you may say) satisfactory' (CPP, 103). Ironically recalling the pragmatic exaltation of personal satisfaction to the position of ultimate satisfaction, Eliot portrays his Magus as a modernist witnessing one of the things discounted by modernism: the historical origin of Christianity. The ultimate satisfaction (the atonement for humankind's sins that Christ is born to perform) registers in the individual religious experience of the modern Magus only as 'satisfactory'. The Incarnation is 'satisfactory' in the sense of 'merely adequate'; it is evaluated as a satisfaction according to whether or not it answers the needs of the inquirer. Eliot's Magus thus betrays the self-centred criterion of modernism's pragmatists: God becomes the *individual's* satisfaction of all satisfactions.

Eliot's fullest criticism of pragmatism in theology emerges in related reviews later in 1917. As though to balance his reading in modernism, Eliot also reviewed books defending neoscholasticism – the revival in Catholic theology at the end of the nineteenth century of the work of Thomas Aquinas. The difference in tone is striking. Reviewing *A Manual of Modern Scholastic Philosophy* by Cardinal Mercier (who had crossed swords with the modernist George Tyrrel ten years before), Eliot argues that 'No student of contemporary philosophy can afford to neglect the neo-scholastic movement since 1879.' As though addressing the modernists whose work he had reviewed, he suggests that 'The reader who wishes to see how a modern philosopher is handled should turn to p. 381 for a refutation of Kant.'[40]

Familiarity with modernism has allowed Eliot to recognize that Kant is of the utmost importance – both for the modernists who would seek accommodation with him and for the neoscholastics who would refute him. Reviewing *Epistemology* by Father P. Coffey, therefore, and comparing his work to that of Cardinal Mercier and Father John Rickaby, Eliot begins the review by noting that although Coffey's work 'shows less familiarity with non-scholastic contemporary philosophy' than the work of the other two, 'there are certain sides of the problem, such as the Kantian criticism, which are here treated more fully than by either of the other works mentioned.'[41] As Gabriel Daly observes, 'Neo-scholastic theologians and philosophers frequently used the term "Kantian" as a pejorative label much as McCarthyite Americans used the word "communist". . . . Christianity is objective and absolute, while Kantianism is subjective and relativistic.'[42]

Eliot's allusion to 'Kantian criticism' acknowledges turn-of-the-century theological code. Eliot recognizes Kant as the site of the debate between modernists and neoscholastics about the death of metaphysics, the apparent outcome of Kant's argument that absolute truth, things in themselves, noumena are beyond human knowledge. Thus Eliot's surprise that Coffey 'overlooks Russell . . . and Bradley. . . . These two writers, between them, have nearly laid metaphysics in the grave', and thus his lack of surprise that Coffey 'handles Pragmatism boldly, and with effect'.[43] The pragmatists are foremost among the heirs of Kant in the argument against absolutes.

Eliot complains, however, that Coffey – like Clutton-Brock – 'has missed the point' about pragmatism. He wastes effort attacking 'its weaker sides rather than the central idea which is what makes pragmatism possible' – the central idea of truth as that which is expedient (useful or successful) in the way of thought:

> The conception of utility has been very loosely used by pragmatists. And of course we can always accuse the pragmatist of believing his own doctrine in a sense which is not pragmatic but absolute – in other words, of eating his cake and having it too. But the essential doctrine of Pragmatism is that truth is not a simple idea; that the 'truth' of any particular proposition *means* a number of other things, its consistency with other 'truths', its influence upon our behaviour, its success in leading to a desired end. The error of Pragmatism has often been to treat certain other concepts, like 'usefulness' or 'success', as if they had the absoluteness denied to truth.[44]

Eliot had made this point more obliquely in his review of Temple's book: by grounding faith not upon dogma but upon the ultimate satisfaction, Temple replaced God as absolute with the pragmatic concept of usefulness. In short, modernist pragmatism – a point of view occurring within human history – in practice acted as though it were an absolute point of view outside it.

In the course of these reviews of contemporary Anglican and Catholic theology, Eliot translates into a public forum the attitude toward pragmatism that he had formulated a few years before in an essay delivered to the Harvard Philosophy Club (of which he was president) just before he left America. The problem with pragmatists and pseudo-pragmatists like James and Bergson (and Nietzsche, for that matter), Eliot argued in 'The Relation Between Politics and Metaphysics' (a paper written in 1913 or 1914), is that they do not stop with the debunking of Truth; they proceed to set up something else in its place. In place of an absolute, they imagine a world of process, of movement, of perpetual change, and Eliot will not abandon himself to change: 'It is one thing to confess that all our theories, purposes, and reasons are founded on "irrational," or infrarational impulses . . . ; it is another thing to deny the reason and hypostasize the impulses' (Relation, 12). In the mysticism of modernism, in the celebration of individual religious experience, Eliot discovered the same hypostasization of impulses.

Like modernists, Bergson and James blur the distinction between the human and the divine. Eliot finds that Bergson denies the human, making everything part of a divine Life Force, and that pragmatists deny the divine, making everything a projection of human will:

> Bergson denies human values; for pragmatism man is the measure of all things. . . . You choose a point of view because you like it. You form certain plans because they express your character. Certain things are true because they are what you need; others, because they are what you want. . . . For Bergson history is a vitalistic process in which human purposes do not exist; for pragmatism a chaotic process in which human purposes are illusory. (Relation, 21)

The same argument appears in a similar political context twenty years later in a *Criterion* Commentary (1932):

> If the progress of mankind is to continue as long as man survives upon this earth, then . . . progress becomes merely change; for

the values of man will change, and a world of changed values is valueless to *us* – just as we, being a part of the past, will be valueless to *it*.[45]

The vehicle that transports the argument about process, progress and values from the 1913 essay into the essay of 1932 is Eliot's engagement with modernism. For modernists like Rashdall and Henry D. Major – the 'Apostle of English Modernism' – reality is process.[46] If reality is process, then the Incarnation cannot have been a discrete event; such a view is 'old-fashioned'. The Incarnation, for modernists, is a continuing process. As Rashdall argues, Christ was different not in kind, but in degree. According to Major, it is clear 'that the Incarnation process is not the mechanical addition of a Divine Personality to a human personality, but the *development of human consciousness until within the sphere of human limitations it may be said to coincide with the Divine consciousness*'.[47] For modernists, history as process becomes history as progress – progress toward divine consciousness.

As we have seen, Eliot's response was '*Ubi est* the pale Galilean'? His withering comment about Rashdall's 'modern methods' suggests his attitude toward modern progress. In fact, it recalls his comment about progress in his Harvard essay: 'as a man makes of Progress something independent of human need and human meaning, something upon which these rather are dependent – then he is losing his hold upon social reality, he is become an intellectual drunkard' (Relation, 11–12). Eliot's attack on the modernist theology of satisfaction originates here. Modernists make of satisfactions something independent of human need and meaning, losing hold upon divine reality.

In each case – in his Harvard essay on pragmatism, in his criticism of modernism, and in his comments about changing values in 1932 – the argument is the same: 'if *all* meaning is human meaning, then there is no meaning' (Relation, 19). Pragmatism is incomplete and needs to be supplemented:

> History . . . must be interpreted from a point of view which puts itself outside the process. . . . Philosophy *is* to fit a need. On the other hand we cannot tell *what* we need unless we philosophize. Pragmatism needs to be supplemented by a theory of the relation of human life to the world. And with this completion it would I think cease to be pragmatism. (Relation, 21)

Eliot develops this observation in his reviews of modernism in a Derridean way: the supplement both adds to and replaces that which it supplements. If modernism supplements belief with pragmatism, then usefulness becomes the absolute that replaces God. This is Eliot's point in his reviews of the books by Rashdall, Webb and Coffey. If modernism supplements pragmatism with belief, then pragmatism is incomplete and is replaced by 'a theory of the relation of human life to the world'. Modernism has not recognized that its pragmatism is always already supplemented by an *a priori* assumption about what Eliot calls here 'the relation of human life to the world'. As the papal encyclical of 1907 noted,

> For the Modernist Believer . . . it is an established fact that the divine reality does really exist in itself and quite independently of the person who believes in it. If you ask on what foundation this assertion of the Believer rests, they answer: In the *experience of the individual*.[48]

It is this circularity, this *a priori* assumption, that Eliot identifies by pointing out in his review of Temple's book that Christianity is not necessarily the satisfaction of all satisfactions.

Having reviewed Eliot's engagement with Modernism between 1915 and 1918, it is possible to return to Eliot's study of mysticism at Harvard and argue that his course of reading upon his return from France in 1911 is a response to his first acquaintance with Modernism. To read W.R. Inge's *Christian Mysticism* (Eliot made notes on it) is to encounter the claim by Anglican Modernists for the centrality of mysticism in the modern religious experience:

> It is not claimed that mysticism, even in its widest sense, is, or ever can be, the whole of Christianity. Every religion must have an institutional as well as a mystical element. . . . Still, at the present time, the greatest need seems to be that we should return to the fundamentals of spiritual religion. We cannot shut our eyes to the fact that both the old seats of authority, the infallible Church and the infallible book, are fiercely assailed, and that our faith needs reinforcements.[49]

Not surprisingly, Eliot's notes on Underhill's *Mysticism* in 1912 or shortly thereafter hint that both the issues and the language of the modernist controversy were known to him at this time. Of the first part of Underhill's study, he observes that 'The most important part is relation of m.[ysticism] to theological system' (Notes). He begins his note-taking, in fact, only with Chapter 5, 'Mysticism and Theology'. Underhill seems to respond in this chapter to the papal encyclical of 1907, *Pascendi Dominici Gregis* – a sweeping condemnation of modernism as 'the synthesis of all heresies'. Whereas *Pascendi* condemns modernism's celebration of individual religious experience as the foundation of faith as a 'pseudo-mysticism', Underhill writes in Chapter 5 a contra-*Pascendi*, affirming the value of mystical experience and dismissing the neoscholastic determination to equate dogma with divine truth.[50] Eliot's notes record her warning that 'Attempts to limit myst. truth – direct apprehension of the divine substance – are as futile as the attempts to identify a precious metal with the die which converts it into current coin' (Notes).[51]

Eliot's notes consistently reflect an awareness of the points at which Underhill's study of mysticism enters the modernist controversy. The first argument that he notes is Underhill's claim that 'the healthy mystic is generally an acceptor & not rejector of creeds' (Notes); he thereby records her attempt to address *Pascendi*'s characterization of modernism as 'the synthesis of all heresies'.[52] Eliot then quotes Underhill on the importance of dogma: 'The dogmas of Christianity, whether or not accepted on the scientific & historical plane, are necessary to an adequate description of (Western) mystical experience' (Notes).[53] She thereby reaffirms what the encyclical condemned – the separation of matters of science and history on the one hand, and faith on the other. Eliot also records that 'Immanence [is] apt to degenerate into pantheism' (Notes) – Underhill at this point addressing with regard to the 'extreme theory of Immanence, so fashionable amongst liberal theologians at the present time', precisely the concern about the theory articulated by *Pascendi* (*Mysticism*, 118).

Eliot's attention to *Underhill's* attention to the relationship between mysticism on the one hand, and theology, creeds and dogmas on the other, suggests that his awareness of the Loisy controversy in Paris introduced him both to the main concerns of the papal encyclical that condemned modernism and to mysticism's role as the modernist catchword. His wide reading and note-taking on the subject of mysticism may have been motivated by interest in the role of mysticism in the Modernist controversy. As Daly notes,

'Few words appear in modernist writing with greater frequency than "mysticism", "mystic", "mystical".'[54]

Underhill, in short, is the likely conduit by which Eliot was brought from his initial acquaintance with Roman Catholic modernism to the sequence of book reviews surveying writings by Anglican modernists. The continuing impact of her book is evident in a number of his reviews at the time of his modernist reading. In his review of George Saintsbury's book on Balzac (1919), he refers to the experience of 'the indestructible barriers between one human being and another' as 'a "mysticism" not to be extracted from Balzac, or even from Miss Underhill'.[55] His review of Wilhelm Wundt's *Elements of Folk Psychology* (1917) acknowledges Underhill's work more indirectly. Wundt baffles Eliot by ignoring mysticism: the latter complains that 'Mysticism is not even included in the index'.[56] If unpersuaded by modernists that mystical experience should be the foundation of faith, Eliot was nonetheless persuaded by Underhill's subtitle, 'A study in the nature and development of Man's spiritual consciousness', that mysticism must figure in a book like Wundt's with so similar an ambition announced in its substitle: 'Outlines of a psychological history of the development of mankind'.

Alerted to the importance of mysticism in modernism, Eliot generally refrained from using the word 'mysticism' itself in his writings about modernism. He was disappointed to find the term so abused. Bertrand Russell meant by 'mystical', among other things, those dyeing themselves druid blue and living on hips and hawes; Underhill and Webb meant those expressing 'the innate tendency of the human spirit towards complete harmony with the transcendental order' (*Mysticism*, x). Saintsbury meant Balzac's '*aura* of other-worldliness'. Of this aura, Eliot observes that it 'is easily called "mystical", but more truly "occult"'.[57] Not surprisingly, then, like Underhill and Spurgeon before him, Eliot eventually explodes, complaining about the vague use of the word. A book by E.B. Osborn on 'the lives of young men who have fallen in the great war' quotes a soldier's celebration of war: 'The fighting excitement vitalizes everything, every sight and word and action. One loves one's fellow-man so much more when one is bent on killing him.' Eliot's concern is that Osborn should call the soldier's attitude 'mystical': 'What is intolerable is Mr Osborn's comment:

"This, the mystical way of looking at war, is the right way for war is a form of mysticism in action." It may be the mystical way, for mystical may be almost anything.'[58]

Eliot's outburst is the culmination of his dissatisfaction with Osborn's attitude toward youth:

> We are a little wearied . . . by the solemnity with which Mr Osborn accepts the youthful mind and the youthful point of view. 'Youth knows more about the young', he says, 'than old age or middle age.' If this were so, civilization would be impossible, experience worthless. *Hommes de la trentaine, de la quarantaine* [men in your thirties, in your forties], assert yourselves. Sympathy with youth is life; but acceptance of youth at its own valuation is sentiment; it is indifference to serious living. It leads to a pose, a form . . . an idealization of actions and emotions, as contrasted with an interest in knowing what the world is like.[59]

His attention to the word 'mystical' in this context is no accident. It is part of a flood of similar observations about the mysticism with which he has become disenchanted. The opposition between youth and adulthood, sentiment and seriousness, emotion and knowledge, and action and stasis is repeated regularly in Eliot's reflections on creative evolution, progress and process – identifiable as his reflections on the mysticism of modernism, whether or not he uses the word 'mysticism' in the course of such reflections.

Commenting upon George Bernard Shaw's *Back to Methuselah* in 1921, Eliot repeats the substance of his attack on Osborn's 'mysticism' of youth, emotion, and action:

> the fact which makes Methuselah impressive is that the nature of the subject, the attempt to expose a panorama of human history 'as far as thought can reach' almost compels Mr Shaw to face ultimate questions. His creative evolution proceeds so far that the process ceases to be progress, and progress ceases to have any meaning. Even the author appears to be conscious of the question whether the beginning and the end are not the same, and whether, as Mr Bradley says, 'whatever you know, it is all one'. . . . [H]e has not realized that at the end he has only approached a beginning, that his end is only the starting point towards the knowledge of life. . . . Creative evolution

is a phrase that has lost both its stimulant and sedative virtues.
It is possible that an exasperated generation may find comfort
in admiring, even if without understanding, mathematics, may
suspect that precision and profundity are not incompatible, may
find maturity as interesting as adolescence, and permanence
more interesting than change.[60]

In this prose so reminiscent of the beginnings and ends of 'East
Coker', Eliot does not complain of Shaw's 'mysticism', but the
repetition of the argument from the Osborn review suggests that
Shaw suffers from the same sloppy thinking that Osborn's use of the
term exposes.

Furthermore, the return of the word 'mysticism' in Eliot's
review of Edmund Blunden's book on Henry Vaughan (1927)
makes it clear that the argument about youth, action and emotion
is indeed his anti-mystical argument:

> The mystical element in Vaughan which belongs to his poetry
> is there for any one to see; it is 'mysticism' only by a not
> uncommon extension of the term. . . . Vaughan is neither a great
> mystic nor a very great poet; but he has a peculiar kind of feeling
> which Mr Blunden is qualified to appreciate. . . . Mr Blunden
> appears to understand Vaughan so long as he confines himself to
> Vaughan; but the one comparison that he draws is by no means
> fortunate. . . . [H]e considers that Herbert is inferior to Vaughan.
> . . . [T]he emotion of Herbert is clear, definite, mature, and
> sustained; whereas the emotion of Vaughan is vague, adolescent,
> fitful, and retrogressive. This judgement is excessively harsh; but
> it is only as much as to say that Mr Blunden, like some persons
> of vague thinking and mild feeling, yearns towards a swooning
> ecstasy of pantheistic confusion.[61]

Shaw achieves the same 'pantheistic confusion' in which all
becomes one – beginning not distinct from end, one thing not
distinct from another, the divine not distinct from the human. Eliot
had been on the watch for this immanental form of mysticism since
1912 – 'Immanence [is] apt to degenerate into pantheism' – and
perhaps since 1910, when first made aware of Loisy, modernism
and the papal condemnation of the immanentism of the modern
'pseudo-mystics'.

The false mysticism to which Eliot alludes in his 1920 essay on

Dante is this 'swooning ecstasy' and 'pantheistic confusion' of the childish. Thus, implicitly commenting in 1927 on Wordsworth's observations about the mystical moments in his childhood – 'I was often unable to think of external things as having external existence, and I communed with all that I saw as something not apart from, but inherent in, my own immaterial nature' – Eliot scruples about the tendency to apply the word 'mysticism' to Wordsworth's 'Ode on the Intimations of Immortality': 'when Wordsworth's great Ode, which is simply great poetry based upon a fallacy, . . . is described as "mysticism", I cannot agree.'[62]

Later the same year, G.K. Chesterton is taken to task more severely for his version of the same fallacy. Noting Chesterton's complaint that contemporary literature suffers from 'an almost complete absence of joy', and that 'it is not childish enough to be cheerful', Eliot responds caustically:

> The modern world is . . . childish, and, like childhood, is rather anarchistic. . . . I should be very glad to be joyful, but I should not care for any joy to be obtained at the price of surrendering my life's experience. . . . There is one authoritative sense, to be respected, in which we are admonished to be like children. Mr Chesterton seems to think that we must execute these instructions by a romp. Hence his regular outbursts of heavy-weight Peter-Pantheism.[63]

The allusion to Christ's 'authoritative' admonition – 'Except ye be converted, and become as little children, ye shall not enter into the kingdom of heaven' – situates this rhetoric within the pattern of Eliot's resistance to modernism's attempt to replace the authority of the Bible and dogma with the mysticism of individual religious experience.[64] The mysticism of modernism – whether called mysticism, sentiment, childishness, immaturity, pantheism or Peter-Pantheism – is directly or indirectly a continuous focus of Eliot's criticism from 1912 onward.

Turning to Eliot's criticism of the first book that he reviewed for *The International Journal of Ethics*, A.J. Balfour's *Theism and Humanism*, we can see Eliot beginning as early as 1915 to formulate his attack on the conceptual foundations of the immanental mysticism of modernism as immature, unserious and impermanent. He summarizes Balfour's argument: 'if science is unable to explain the existence of value and of truth, we must find for them an origin "congruous with their character". This origin theism alone . . . can provide.' According to Eliot, 'The whole issue, in Mr Balfour's discussion of aesthetics and ethics, seems to owe its origin to a confusion between aesthetic and ethical values (i.e. feelings) and the values of the beliefs about these feelings.' The confusion arises from a complication in feelings: 'We enjoy the feeling, and we cannot rest content unless we can justify it by exhibiting its relation to the other parts of our life. Having made this attempt, we then enjoy the theory we have made.'[65] Different feelings (enjoyments) supplement the original feeling and in effect replace it. Eliot notes the logic of the Derridean supplement again: value and truth are both added to and replaced by our enjoyment of our theories about them.

Not himself a card-carrying modernist, Balfour nonetheless introduced to Eliot the strain of argument that he would encounter in the works by modernists that he would review over the next two years. From this review comes Eliot's transfer to theology of his analysis of sloppy pragmatism: it is a theory about truth as process that pragmatists enjoy so much that it becomes itself the truth – as a function of its usefulness as the satisfaction of all satisfactions. From this review comes Eliot's analysis of the mysticism of modernism: it is mistakenly preoccupied with the enjoyment of religious feelings – emotions, sentiments, swooning ecstasies – and its enjoyment of its theories about these feelings. An 'orgiastic mysticism', Eliot warns, is 'as fatal to values in morals . . . as any materialism can be.'[66]

Eliot's final thoughts about modernism recapitulate his arguments during the previous fifteen years. In a *Criterion* review (1927), quoting Hilaire Belloc's analysis of H.G. Wells's religious beliefs – 'Men like Mr Wells, who have ceased to believe that Our Blessed Lord was God, or even that He had Divine authority, cling desperately to the emotion which the old belief aroused – because they find those emotions pleasant' – Eliot observes that 'That is well said, and it applies to many persons in England besides Mr Wells', perhaps recalling that he had said as much himself years before about A.J. Balfour. A few lines later, he recalls his own phrase wielded against pragmatism ten years before and his suspicion even before that (in the Balfour review) of the over-enjoyment of theories about our values: 'Mr Wells merely panders to the general unthinking desire to have one's cake and eat it too, to have a religion without believing in anything except the latest theories of comparative anatomy, anthropology and psychology.'[67]

In 1928, Eliot's obituary review of Baron Friedrich von Hügel's *Selected Letters* functions simultaneously as an obituary of modernism. In some ways 'the Pope of Modernism', although never excommunicated like some French and English modernists, von Hügel was one of the driving forces behind the rehabilitation of mysticism within modern theology – Roman Catholic, Anglican and liberal Protestant.[68] Much of the modernism informing Underhill's work, for instance, came to her by way of von Hügel, a great influence on *Mysticism* and later Underhill's spiritual director.

Like most modernists, von Hügel believed in God's transcendence, but he argued that in a post-Kantian world our contact with the transcendent must be through the immanent – in effect, through the categories of human experience. Mystical experience represents the point of contact between the human and the divine. Intellect, he acknowledged, is fine for determining the truths of logic; but the truth of existence can only be determined by the vividness and fruitfulness of our experience. Mysticism, therefore, was his prescription for healing the sick soul of the modern world – the soul suffering what Eliot called a dissociation of sensibility, a separation of thought and feeling. Eliot found no cure for the sick soul in modernism – whether von Hügel's or anyone else's – but rather a symptom of the sickness:

> Modernists thought that they were trying to reconcile ancient feeling with modern thought and science. If that had been what they were trying to do, they might have been more successful; but they were really attempting something much more difficult – the reconciliation of antagonistic currents of feeling within themselves. This is the real issue; and they remain tragic not because some of them suffered in the world, or suffered excommunication by the Church: that is a slight matter compared to the division in their own hearts.[69]

In a *Criterion* Commentary later the same year, Eliot again pointed to modernism's confusion of points of view as 'a mental blight':

> Where you find clear thinking, you usually find that the thinker is either a Christian (if he is a European) or an atheist; where

you find muddy thinking you usually find that the thinker is something between the two, and such a person is in essentials a Modernist.[70]

Eliot makes clear that his obituary of von Hügel and Modernism is also an obituary of modernism's mysticism: 'I never met Baron von Hügel, and I have never read his greatest book, *The Mystical Element in Religion.* The latter defect I do not regret; it is easily repaired, though I am not sure that I shall ever repair it.' Of 'the Baron' and mysticism he writes:

His feelings were exact, but his ideas were often vague. And his mysticism is no longer the order of the day. He belongs to a past epoch, a period of intellectual indistinctness, in which he moved among a host of half-Christians and quarter Christians. The present age seems to me much more an age of black and white, without shadows. Mysticism – even the particular Christian mysticism studied by von Hügel – is not the issue of our time. We are able to quote with approval that remark of Bossuet of which Professor Babbitt has reminded us: 'true mysticism is so rare and unessential and false mysticism is so common and dangerous that one cannot oppose it too firmly.' We demand of religion some kind of *intellectual* satisfaction – both private and social – or we do not want it at all.[71]

By implication, Eliot defines the mysticism of modernism as a common and dangerous false mysticism. Similarly, by implication, he defines it as the vehicle of modernism's intellectual indistinctness, muddy thinking and antagonistic currents of feeling. Again, Eliot's complaints about immature emotion, sentiment and swooning ecstasy begin and end in reaction against the mysticism of modernism.

Yet there is more to this story of Eliot's reaction to Modernism than Eliot tells in his reviews and essays. For instance, although declaring himself an Anglo-Catholic in 1928 – and therefore of the party opposed to modernism – Eliot was baptized in 1927 by a modernist (his friend William Force Stead), had for one of his godfathers the modernist theologian of Queen's College, Oxford (B.H. Streeter), and was confirmed by a Bishop of Oxford sympathetic to modernism (Thomas Strong).[72] This surprising support group appropriately symbolizes the continuing influence of modernism upon the anti-modernist Eliot. As much as he disdained its methods as evidence of 'intellectual blight', he was sympathetic to its motivation. As he confessed in his review of *Group Theories of Religion and the Religion of the Individual*, 'Mr Webb has our sympathy in his stand for the rights of "individual" religion, though we may not sympathise with his demand for the personality of God or with his demand for individual immortality.'[73] Confessing to a dissociation between heart and head ('sympathy' and intellect, 'ancient feeling' and 'modern thought'), Eliot implies the need for a true modernism to redeem the modernism lost in 'antagonistic currents of feeling' – but one half of the dissociation.

'Mr Eliot's Sunday Morning Service' subtly expresses Eliot's residual sympathy for the modernist cause. Given the backdrop of modernist and neoscholastic book reviews against which Eliot wrote this poem late in 1917 or early in 1918, the setting of the poem and its pattern of allusions confirm for it a place in Eliot's struggle with modernism. Ernest Schanzer explains the setting: 'It is Sunday morning and a service is in progress in what must be either a High Anglican or a Roman Catholic church, for religious paintings are found within its walls.'[74] Invited by the title to read the poem at least in part biographically, one might be tempted to speculate that Eliot's aversion to modernism led him to attend the High Anglican church that the poem apparently recalls. Yet, curiously, the 'Mr Eliot' of the poem's title is no more sympathetic to what he finds in the High Anglican church than Eliot himself seems to be sympathetic to what he finds in modernism.

Schanzer reads the 'sutlers' drifting 'across the window-panes' as stained-glass images of early Church Fathers, which make the poem's Mr Eliot 'reflect on the ironic contrast between the word of God and the wordiness of the controversialists of the early Church' (CPP, 54). The paintings – one of the Baptism of Christ and the other of a scene in purgatory – suggest 'the true Christianity from which both the Alexandrian Fathers and the modern priests and congregation seem to the poet to have strayed'. The result is the poem's 'main satiric theme: the remoteness of the Alexandrian theology from simple Christian sentiment and belief' (one of modernism's greatest concerns).[75] Schanzer sees Sweeney as one of the elements in the poem remote from true Christianity. David Ward, however, marks the contrast 'between Sweeney's "hams" in the bath-water and Christ's "unoffending feet" in the river Jordan; and that between Sweeney's voluptuous wallowing in his hot bath and the tortures of the elect in the flames of purgatory.' He sees Sweeney as that from which the past 'masters of the subtle schools' and the present 'sable presbyters' have become remote:

> He is the ordinary sensual man, the focus of all metaphysical and theological problems; mortal in flesh, yet the figure without whom the thousands of years of debate about the spirit, the sacrifice of Christ, the elaborate theology of the Trinity, would all be meaningless.[76]

Here again is modernism's main theme.

From this point of view, the question for the poem's Mr Eliot is how the Church is to connect with Sweeney. Can connection with him be made by a return to the Origens/origins of Christianity? The pun is Eliot's, I believe. The reviews contemporaneous with the poem and patterns of reference in the poem itself make such a reading plausible. The phrase 'mensual turn of time' is an allusion to the philosophy of creative evolution so much a spur to modernism and so much a preoccupation of Eliot's in his reviews of modern theology, philosophy and politics: time is menstrual – changing, flowing, ready to make it new. The conservative theological response to the philosophy of creative evolution as it appeared in the modernist criticism of dogma was to emphasize the *origin* of faith in Biblical revelation. The ironies that the conjunction of a menstrual creative evolution and Origen/origin offer are manifold, and no accident. First, there is the little joke that creative evolution should have produced Origen – an individual become sterile through castration. Second, there is the more interesting irony that the evolution of Christian theology in general should have enervated Origen's theology. Finally, there is the most immediate irony that the evolution of Christian theology into modernism in particular should have enervated the historical origin of Christianity as the ground of faith.

Support for a reading of the poem in the terms of Eliot's contemporary reviews of modernist and neoscholastic books comes from the word 'superfetation'. Ward explains the word as representing the paradoxical theological culmination of the spiritual tension figured in the poem as a sexual tension between fertility and infertility: 'The Word is one with the Father and yet begotten by

Him; therefore by an inescapable logic begotten upon Himself.'[77] Schanzer suggests that 'The wordiness of some of the early theologians is described as a "superfetation", a second conception, of God, following upon the initial conception of the Word of God.'[78] B.C. Southam's explanation focuses more directly upon Origen:

> superfetation [is] . . . a biological term meaning multiple impregnation of an ovary, resulting in twins or larger multiple births. In the doctrine of Origen . . . this would refer to Christ: 'in relation to God this Logos or Son was a copy of the original and, as such, inferior.'[79]

Yet the word 'superfetation' – as opposed to anything in Christian theology that it might explain – was itself introduced into modernist theology at the turn of the century by Lucien Laberthonnière. Rejecting the traditional account of faith as an extrinsic process by which intellectual acknowledgement follows recognition of historical revelation, Laberthonnière focused – like other modernists – on an intrinsic, immanental process. As Daly explains, according to Laberthonnière, 'Something in us must correspond with extrinsic revelation, otherwise the revelatory process amounts to no more than a crude juxtapositioning of grace and nature – a process devoid of moral content.'[80] In such a Christianity, Christ is no different from the fabled being from another planet that arrives mysteriously on earth, imposing its will by the miracle of its strange powers: 'From this point of view, the supernatural, the revealed truths, all of Christianity appears therefore as a kind of superfetation [*superfétation*], something supererogatory with which we will be burdened, that will weigh on us and that will enslave us.'[81] Although Eliot was certainly aware of Laberthonnière in 1927, whether or not he directly or indirectly knew his work in 1917 or 1918 is not clear.[82] It is possible, however, that Eliot knew of Laberthonnière as early as 1911 through his friend Jean Verdenal. The latter wrote to Eliot from Paris in July of 1911 on the subject of Christianity in the modern world:

> While positivism (materialism poorly disguised) spreads downward through society, an aspiration towards the Idea can be seen growing daily stronger among the Elite. . . . It frequently takes the form of a return to Christianity, whether

Catholic or Galilean and evangelical. What value is there in the innumerable and varied works showing this feature? What differences appear, indeed, as soon as you think of a few names! (Verlaine, Huysmans, Barrès, Francis Jammes, Péguy, Bourget, Claudel, Le Cardonnel, etc.). . . . It would be appropriate to decide, in each case, how far various causes have operated: . . . sincere repentance, flawed intelligence, literal Catholic belief in the dogma, social attitudes (national, provincial, traditional, sectarian), . . . pragmatism, etc. But the main thing is to say, in the case of each, *how far he can influence our inner life towards the knowledge of the supreme good.* My dear fellow, I shall be here in September, and very pleased to see you again.[83]

Verdenal's sympathetic reference to 'our inner life' (*notre vie intérieure*) as the source of knowledge of the supreme good aligns him with the immanental epistemology of the modernists. He is clearly familiar with the positions in the debate within the Catholic church: literal belief in Catholic dogma versus pragmatism. He recognizes its role in the reaction against positivism. He implies its connection to the nationalist politics of a writer like Maurice Barrès. In the end, both the allusions and the phrases in his letter suggest awareness not just of the modernist controversy centred upon Loisy but also of Laberthonnière's books of 1911: *Positivisme et Catholicisme, à propos de 'l'Action française'* (Positivism and Catholicism, with Regard to the *Action française*) and *Autour de 'l'Action française'* (About *Action française*), each a criticism of the conservative, anti-modernist theologians supporting the nationalist *Action française*. His comment to Eliot – 'We'll talk about all this again some time, if you like' – suggests that modern Christianity and modern Catholicism had been subjects of conversation before between the two friends and that they might have been discussed again in September before Eliot returned to America. These shared interests of Verdenal and Eliot may be one of the reasons that the latter associated his year in Paris both with 'the memory of a friend coming across the Luxembourg Gardens' (Verdenal) and with the 'scandalous distinction' of the modernist Loisy at the Collège de France.[84]

The poem itself, however, constitutes evidence that Eliot had somehow come upon Laberthonnière's word and the point of view that it represents. The word 'superfetation' is applied to the 'masters of the subtle schools' by a 'Mr Eliot' who shares Laberthonnière's point of view. The Mr Eliot of the poem – like Eliot his creator – seems to have some sympathy for the rights of individual religion. First, the contrast between the masters of the subtle schools and the earthy Sweeney – apparently outside the communion of epicenic presbyters and castrated theologians this Sunday morning – undercuts the former. On the one hand, they are merely controversial and abstract; he is alive. This is the contrast between the schools (scholastics) and the life of modern human beings that modernism drew. On the other hand, Mr Eliot's patronizing conclusion that they are controversial (questionable) seems to follow immediately from his recollection of Sweeney – suggesting that for the poem's Mr Eliot the fact of Sweeney's existence is itself an argument to make one question the scholastics. Second, the poem's Mr Eliot seems to approve of Sweeney as a polymath. The word 'polymath' is used vocatively. This Mr Eliot may be addressing himself in an internal monologue, or he may be addressing the reader (as at the end of the first section of *The Waste Land*), but the concluding stanza's contrast between the substantiality of Sweeney and the insubstantiality of the schools supports the reading that Mr Eliot is addressing the absent Sweeney as 'polymath', for he is the one who knows more than the men of the schools.

Somewhat surprisingly, then, we meet a Mr Eliot who seems sympathetic to modernism. Less surprisingly, of course, one can also detect in the poem another Eliot – the anti-modernist Eliot uncomfortable with Rashdall's modernist interpretation of Christ as Rashdall writ large. The unattractive image of Sweeney as an entirely human version of the 'Baptized God' links this Mr Eliot's apparently approving interest in him to the modernist confusion between the human and the divine that Eliot castigated: the modern God is Sweeney! Yet more important than the unsurprising appearance of Eliot the anti-modernist in this poem is the appearance in Eliot's work at this time – however briefly – of Mr Eliot the modernist. He is a reminder of Eliot's sympathy for the rights of individual religion, a reminder that however unsavoury a Sweeney might be there is something in him that ought not to be thrown out with his bath water. The poem's Mr Eliot is a closet modernist, a secret admirer of Laberthonnière, who referred to himself as the one who had appealed 'to the concrete and alive method of the mystics against the abstract and purely logical method' of the scholastics 'more than anyone'.[85] Eliot's 'Mr Eliot' is an acknowledgement that the mysticism of modernism was offered as an answer – however inadequate – to a real question (against the background of positivism and scholasticism) about the role of individual religious experience in faith. As we shall see in readings of *The Waste Land* and The Clark Lectures, Eliot was no less interested in this question than his 'Mr Eliot'.

4

Mystical Personae

As we have seen, Eliot's experience of Bergsonian and Catholic modernist mysticism in Paris, his studies of mysticism and the occult at Harvard and his criticism of Anglican modernist mysticism in his book reviews of 1915 to 1918 are reflected in early poems like 'Rhapsody on a Windy Night' and 'Mr Eliot's Sunday Morning Service'. As evidence of the impact of his interest in mysticism upon his poetry, however, these poems represent no more than the tip of the iceberg. Written and revised over the course of 1919, 'Gerontion' is also informed by Eliot's interest – simultaneously sceptical and hopefully curious – in mysticism as a way of knowing and experiencing. In fact, 'Gerontion' can be seen as the third in a sequence of 'mystical' poems including 'The Death of Saint Narcissus' and 'Descent from the Cross'. Each explores the perils of a mysticism given to confusing human love with divine love. The would-be mystics Narcissus and the speaker in 'The Love Song of Saint Sebastian' confuse sensual ecstasy with divine ecstasy: Narcissus masturbates by metamorphosis; the speaker in 'The Love Song of Saint Sebastian' wears a hair shirt and flogs himself to gain entrance to a woman's bed. Gerontion – just as much a would-be mystic – is perhaps less in the grip of his senses, but it is not clear whether he has forsaken them or been forsaken by them (his metaphor for his mystical contemplation remains sexual: it is to 'Excite the membrane, when the sense has cooled') (CPP, 38).

'The Love Song of Saint Sebastian' – the first of the poems to be written – is part of a sequence of poems provisionally titled 'Descent from the Cross', which was to have included 'a mystical section'.[1] It is not certain that the fragments contained in Eliot's letter describing this sequence of poems to Conraid Aiken include the mystical section, but the part that begins 'Appearances appearances' may well represent the theme of the projected section – if not the section itself. The speaker in this fragment is fed up with 'dialectic ways' that lead always – despite 'restless nights and torpid days' – to 'the same unvaried / Interminable intolerable maze'.

Although it is not clear how his truth is won, he offers a true word beyond the ways of contradictory appearances:

> This word is true on all the paths you tread
> As true as truth need be (when all is said)
> That if you find no truth among the living
> You will not find much truth among the dead.
> No other time than now, no other place but here,
>   he said.[2]

Thirty years later, the same 'mystical' insight is offered in 'Little Gidding': 'There are other places / Which also are the world's end . . . / But this is the nearest, in place and time,/ Now and in England' (CP, 192).

Negative evidence can be offered to substantiate the claim that the 'mystical section' is part of the poetry that Eliot sent Aiken. In addition to 'The Love Song of Saint Sebastian', Eliot specifies the other parts of the projected poetic sequence:

> an Insane Section, and another love song (of a happier sort) and a recurring piece quite in the French style beginning
>
> > The married girl who lives across the street
> > Wraps her soul in orange-coloured robes of Chopinese
>
> — Then a mystical section — and a Fool-House section beginning
>
> > Let us go to the masquerade and dance!
> > I am going as St John among the Rocks
> > Attired in my underwear and socks.[3]

'Appearances appearances' is not the Insane Section, the other love song, the recurring piece in the French style or the Fool-House section. Of all the potential labels for it, the one that remains — 'mystical section' — is most appropriate.

'Appearances appearances' is a poetic response to Bradley's *Appearance and Reality*, which Eliot was no doubt studying in preparation for his work at Oxford in the fall. The speaker is not satisfied with Bradley's philosophy. Bradley argues that 'Ultimate reality is such that it does not contradict itself; here is an absolute criterion'. Reality is an absolute whole; appearance is a plural world of contradictions: 'Reality is one. It must be single, because plurality, taken as real, contradicts itself. Plurality implies relations, and, through its relations, it unwillingly asserts always a superior unity.'[4] We are confined to appearances, but aspire to reality. The result, Eliot's speaker complains, is a search for superior unity without the hope of encountering anything but contradiction:

Contradiction is the debt you would collect
And still with contradiction are you paid
And while you do not know what else you seek
You shall have nothing other to expect.[5]

In the end, 'Appearances appearances' succinctly summarizes the conclusions about knowledge and experience that become the theme of the dissertation: 'Appearances appearances he said / And nowise real; unreal, and yet true; / Untrue, but real – of what are you afraid?'[6] In fact, Eliot's programme for his dissertation is announced by the question 'of what are you afraid?'. The tension in this part of the poem is the main tension in the dissertation, the tension between the Real and the conventional. Eliot's project is to dispel anxiety on account of this tension. One ought not to fear the paradox that appearance is, on the one hand, true and unreal and, on the other, untrue and real. The dissertation concludes on a similar note. Reality is conventional – 'For a metaphysics to be accepted, good-will is essential. Two men must *intend* the same object, and *both* men must admit that the object intended is the same' (KE, 168) – but it is no less real for being, in the final analysis, a function of a convention that yields always and only an appearance of reality: 'A metaphysic may be accepted or rejected without our assuming that from the practical point of view it is either true or false' (KE, 169).

Bradley writes of being 'obliged to speak of philosophy as a satisfaction of what may be called the mystical side of our nature.' Thus his Absolute as the satisfaction of our yearning for the resolution of discord in wholeness: 'To know *how* the one and the many are united is beyond our powers. But in the Absolute somehow, we are convinced, the problem is resolved.'[7] It is with the mystical side of his nature that Eliot's speaker responds to Bradley's Absolute. Implying that it is transcendentally remote and nebulous, Eliot's speaker seeks a truth closer to home – not a transcendental truth in the keeping of 'the dead', but an immanent truth 'among the living' – 'No other time than now, no other place but here'.

The sensibility represented by such an assertion is akin to the pragmatic mystical sensibility of modernists. In fact, on the evidence both of its 'mystical section', in a 'theme to recur twice, in variations', and of 'The Love Song of Saint Sebastian', one can argue that 'Descent from the Cross' was to have been an exploration of the 'false mysticism' that Eliot encountered in philosophy and theology in the early years of the century.

'The Love Song of Saint Sebastian' is an example of such false mysticism. As though in justification of the tentative title for the sequence of poems, 'The Love Song of Saint Sebastian' traces from the crucifixion (the 'Cross') the descent – on the one hand suggesting lineage, but on the other suggesting 'fall', 'decline', 'sinking' – of Christ's passion as a model for Christians of the attitude to be taken toward suffering both in one's spiritual life and in one's everyday life. ('Cross' itself has come to stand for the trial or affliction that Christians are to endure with patience.)

The language in the first stanza is explicitly religious. As though his beloved were the Virgin Mary, the speaker aspires through 'hour on hour of prayer' to become the beloved's 'neophyte'.[8] The word 'neophyte' recalls the new converts to the early Christian Church. The devotional programme also includes self-flagellation and the wearing of 'a shirt of hair' – practices reminiscent of medieval asceticism at its most extreme. The first stanza thus traces the descent of these Christian practices from the crucifixion, but it does so against a background of sexuality that reveals their decline into sexual perversion.

The result is a contemporary version of the Song of Solomon: Eliot's 'when the morning came / Between your breasts should lie my head' derives from 'he shall lie all night betwixt my breasts'.[9] Traditionally interpreted allegorically as an example of God's love for his Church, the Song of Solomon received its 'fullest and most influential' exegesis in *Sermones in Canticum* where St Bernard 'equated the beloved with the individual soul seeking God and used the language and imagery of the Song to speak of the heart of the mystical life.'[10] Eliot had encountered precisely this tradition in his Harvard research on mysticism. He records in his notes on Inge's *Christian Mysticism* that 'The Romantic Side of Mysticism received the greatest stimulus fr. S Bernard. He recalled "devout

& loving contemplation to the image of the crucified Christ",
& founded "the worship of the saviour as the 'Bridegroom of
the Soul'" (Notes). St Bernard's employment of the Song of
Solomon imagery as metaphors for the mystical life of the soul led
Eliot almost fifteen years later to trace the 'Romantic Mysticism'
criticized in his Clark Lectures (1926) back to him. The first
stanza of 'The Love Song of Saint Sebastian' represents a stage in
Eliot's movement from his note-taking at Harvard to his anatomy
of mysticism in his Clark Lectures — revealing in the poem what
he would emphasize in the lectures: the potential in the spiritually
immature for misunderstanding St Bernard's metaphors.

The speaker — in a different time and place perhaps a Dante
infatuated with a Beatrice — descends even further from the Cross
in the second stanza into a type of Porphyria's lover. For Eliot's
speaker as much as for Browning's, the confusion of things of the
spirit with things of the flesh is complete when all that remains of
the beloved is a dead body. So complete is the substitution of the
body for the spirit that in anticipating the end of time — when, if
ever, his mind ought to be concentrated on the last things — the
speaker can imagine turning his thoughts to nothing but a part of
the body: 'When all the world shall melt in the sun / Melt or
freeze / I shall remember how your ears were curled.' On the one
hand an elaborate compliment to the beloved, it is on the other the
disastrous end of a false romantic mysticism descended almost as far
as possible from the Cross.

The two parts of 'Descent from the Cross' that exist (in addition
to a brief introduction) thus conspire to depict the mystical
sensibility that Eliot had encountered in the philosophy and
theology debated in Paris in 1910 and 1911. On the one hand,
'Appearances appearances' articulates this mystical sensibility in
terms of its philosophical register; on the other, 'The Love Song
of Saint Sebastian' articulates it in terms of its emotional register.
Each of the speakers in these sections is an aspect of the up-to-date
persona in the Introduction — a figure complaining of those who
would 'come between the singer and the song' and impatient with
those who are old-fashioned ('So confident on wrinkled ways of
wrong'). The latter condemn the former as those who 'blow
against the wind and spit against the rain' and confute them with
a rhetorical question that focuses on the last things: 'what could
be more real than sweat and dust and sun / And what more sure

than night and death and sleep?' Most sure for the persona in the Introduction is human experience, and so he depicts as those who truly descend from the Cross those 'who seek to measure joy and pain' – that is, in one of their manifestations with which Eliot was familiar, the pragmatic pseudo-mystics of modernism.

'The Death of Saint Narcissus', written late in 1914 or at the beginning of the next year, might be the other 'love song (of a happier sort)' to which Eliot refers in his outline of the projected sections of 'Descent from the Cross'. Happier to the extent that Narcissus is ultimately 'satisfied', though not necessarily less morbid, 'The Death of Saint Narcissus' is linked to 'The Love Song of Saint Sebastian' by the depiction of Narcissus as 'struck down' by a love of the body as profound as that of the speaker in the earlier poem (CPP, 605). The connection is made explicit in the description of Narcissus as 'in love with the burning arrows' (CPP, 606). Narcissus is thereby revealed as the Saint Sebastian missing from 'The Love Song of Saint Sebastian', for Eliot becomes in the writing of 'The Death of Saint Narcissus' the equivalent of the painters of the Saint Sebastians that he admired: 'I have studied S. Sebastians – why should anyone paint a beautiful youth and stick him full of pins (or arrows) unless he felt a little as the hero of my verse?'[11] For Eliot subsequently to stick Narcissus full of arrows is to identify himself retrospectively with the speaker of 'The Love Song of Saint Sebastian'. Hay hits the nail on the head when she implies that 'The Death of Saint Narcissus' and 'The Love Song of Saint Sebastian' articulate both Eliot's interest in diseased forms of spirituality and his fear of his personal liability to the same.[12]

'The Death of Saint Narcissus' surveys a wider range of human sexuality than 'The Love Song of Saint Sebastian'. There is the 'young girl / Caught in the woods by a drunken old man' (CPP, 605); there is the homosexual dimension to the penetrant arrows (despite Eliot's avowal that 'there's nothing homosexual about this', he went on to observe: 'but no one ever painted a female Sebastian, did they?'); there is the masturbatory dimension to the imagery associated with Narcissus's enjoyment of himself.[13] He imagines himself a fish 'With slippery white belly held tight in his own fingers, / Writhing in his own clutch, his ancient beauty / Caught fast in the pink tips of his new beauty' (CPP, 605). Eliot may have drawn the connection between Narcissus and masturbation from

Ovid's description of Narcissus as *se deprendere* ('clasping himself'
or 'laying hold of himself'):

> Unwittingly he desires himself; he praises, and is himself what
> he praises; and while he seeks, is sought; equally he kindles love
> and burns with love. How often did he offer vain kisses on the
> elusive pool? How often did he plunge his arms into the water
> seeking to clasp the neck he sees there, but did not clasp himself
> in them![14]

The self-love that Ovid's story and Eliot's poem depict is for Eliot
the diseased spirituality that Hay remarks. As Gordon notes, it also
symbolizes the literary romanticism that Eliot would excoriate in
his early criticism.[15] But that narcissism is for Eliot far more than a
figure for diseased spirituality and sloppy romanticism is suggested
by connections between 'The Death of Saint Narcissus' and the
dissertation.

By the beginning of 1915 (by which point both 'The Death of
Saint Narcissus' and 'The Love Song of Saint Sebastian' had been
written), Eliot had completed the first draft of his dissertation and
was setting out to 'turn it into a criticism and valuation of the
Bradleian metaphysic' after his 'difficulty, even agony, with the
first draft, owing to [his] attempt to reach a positive conclusion.'[16]
It is this turn against Bradley that leads in the first chapter of the
final draft of the dissertation to Eliot's deconstruction of the self
as a point of view from which to observe Bradley's 'immediate
experience': 'We have no right, except in the most provisional
way, to speak of *my* experience, since the I is a construction out
of experience, an abstraction from it' (KE, 19). Eliot anticipates
here his dismissal of solipsism later in the work: 'The self, we
find, seems to depend upon a world which in turn depends upon
it; and nowhere, I repeat, can we find anything original or ultimate'
(KE, 146).

'The Death of Saint Narcissus' was written at the same time –
according to Gordon, 'at the end of 1914 or beginning of 1915'.[17]
In its own way, the poem is as much about the insubstantiality
of the self – as much about the self's inadequacy as a ground of
absolute experience – as the dissertation. In it, Eliot demonstrates
the same awareness that the 'I' is not a stable identity, for he depicts
the 'I' of Narcissus as having metamorphosed many times: 'First he
was sure that he had been a tree. . . . / Then he knew that he had

been a fish. . . . / Then he had been a young girl' (CPP, 605). Eliot articulates in the poem an insight similar to the one achieved at the same time in the dissertation:

> for Bradley the finite centre, (or what I call the point of view), is not identical with the soul. We may think provisionally of finite centres as the units of soul life . . . we vary by passing from one point of view to another . . . we vary by self-transcendence. The point of view (or finite centre) has for its object one consistent world, and accordingly no finite centre can be self-sufficient, for the life of a soul does not consist in the contemplation of one consistent world but in the painful task of unifying (to a greater or less extent) jarring and incompatible ones, and passing, when possible, from two or more discordant viewpoints to a higher which shall somehow include and transmute them. The soul is so far from being a monad that we have not only to interpret other souls to ourself but to interpret ourself to ourself. (KE, 147–8)

Narcissus intuits his lack of self-sufficiency – oscillating between the feeling of self-induced sexual ecstasy and the feeling of post-climactic exhaustion ('he felt drunken and old' (CPP, 606)).

Simultaneously searching for more variety and disappointed by the variety within himself that he has already experienced, Narcissus turns toward God. But Narcissus is not shown to be conscious of his insufficiency. The poet, however, alludes by means of his word 'So' – a conjunction meaning 'for that reason' or 'therefore' – to the dissertation-like logic that has turned Narcissus from the unrecognized experience of his insufficiency toward the being who is self-sufficient: '*So* he became a dancer to God' (CPP, 606, emphasis added). The turn to God is the result of a logic that at least the narrator perceives. As in the dissertation, then, the metamorphosis of self-transcendence is the proof of the lack of self-sufficiency, and so (for Eliot) proof against solipsism. The poem can be interpreted, therefore, not just as evidence of Eliot's quarrel with romantic self-absorption and inadequate spirituality, and not just as evidence of his own sexual tensions, but also as evidence of his quarrel with any post-Cartesian metaphysics that depends upon a substantial self.

In the end, Narcissus and the speakers in 'Descent from the Cross' are trapped in the blind alley of self. Their recognition of the Other is frustrated by an epistemology that turns their love back upon themselves. It is left to Gerontion to recognize this problem and try another mystical ladder of escape.

That the contemplation of the false mystical sensibility in 'Descent from the Cross' and 'The Death of Saint Narcissus' is related to 'Gerontion' (written five years later) is suggested by the repetition of a phrase: Narcissus comes to know the joy and pain of his own body and is 'Struck down by such knowledge' (CPP, 605); Gerontion knows the story of Christ but is not struck down by such knowledge: 'After such knowledge, what forgiveness?' (CPP, 38).[18] The 'knowledge' is in each case different, but the implied question is the same: what is the knowledge that saves?

The pseudo-mystical sensibilities of Narcissus and the speakers in 'Descent from the Cross' locate truth by means of an immanental epistemology. They locate truth within themselves. Gerontion attempts to do the same, but by means of a more intellectual discipline. Having attained the age 'when the sense has cooled', he is not prone to overvalue his own experiences as a body. Neither is he persuaded that mind – through 'a thousand small deliberations' – can supplement personal experience in such a way as to gain access to truth. Like the speaker in 'Appearances appearances' lost in an 'Interminable intolerable maze', Gerontion finds himself 'In a wilderness of mirrors'. Yet although confused by appearances, like the former, Gerontion's image of this confusion – 'a wilderness of mirrors' – suggests that he has recognized (as neither Narcissus nor the speakers in 'Descent from the Cross' ever do) that the reflection back to him of his own image in every direction that he looks is a big part of the problem.

As Gordon observes, 'In the figure of Gerontion, Eliot brought back the disappointed religious candidate but made him into a contemporary, postwar character.'[19] One of Gerontion's distinctive features as contemporary figure – in addition to his awareness of the word 'estaminet' ('a French word for café, brought into English by soldiers returning from France and Belgium during the First World War'), and in addition to his allusion to the Polish Corridor contrived by the Treaty of Versaille in 1919 – is his modernist sensibility.[20] Written after Eliot's reviews of Anglican modernist theology and Catholic neoscholasticism, the poem is not surprisingly more thoroughly informed than the earlier poems by the awareness of the 'momentous . . . present conflict' that Eliot recognized at the root of modernism.[21] Like Eliot himself, Gerontion is aware of the seductiveness of a theology that would ground belief in personal religious experience. He is concerned that he was not present when history occurred:

> I was neither at the hot gates
> Nor fought in the warm rain
> Nor knee deep in the salt marsh, heaving a cutlass,
> Bitten by flies, fought.

Also like Eliot, however, he recognizes that Christianity depends upon historical facts. In his review of R.G. Collingwood's *Religion and Philosophy* in 1917, Eliot asserts that 'Christianity − orthodox Christianity − must base itself upon a unique fact: that Jesus was born of a virgin: a proposition which is either true or false, its terms having a fixed meaning'.[22] It is to this fact − the 'word, / Swaddled with darkness' − that Gerontion turns. The poem, in short, wrestles with the modernist problem: the disjunction between knowledge of 'History' and a more intimate knowledge of God. It explores the temptation toward mysticism experienced by such a sensibility as Gerontion's until − attempting the first stage of mystical contemplation − Gerontion falls asleep.

Like Eliot's Magus nine years later, Gerontion is a modernist contemplating the life of Christ and its resonance as authoritative historical fact in the modern world. The poem overflows with direct and indirect allusions to the Incarnation, many of which are couched in the terms of Lancelot Andrewes. Much of the second stanza: 'Signs are taken for wonders. "We would see a sign!" / The word within a word, unable to speak a word' − is taken directly from Andrewes' Nativity Sermon of 1618: 'Signs are taken for wonders. "Master, we would fain see a sign". . . . *Verbum infans* [the Word as infant], the Word without a word; the eternal word not able to speak a word.'[23] Furthermore, like Andrewes, Gerontion invokes the Christian calendar to link the Incarnation to the Sacrament (Eucharist). As Andrewes explains,

> Christ in the sacrament is not altogether unlike Christ in the cratch. To the cratch we may well liken the husk or outward symbols of it. Outwardly it seems of little worth but it is rich of contents, as was the crib this day with Christ in it. . . . [I]n them

we find Christ. Even as they did this day . . . 'in the beasts' crib
the food of Angels'; which very food our signs both represent,
and present unto us. . . . Either of these of itself apart, but
together much more. For the Sacrament, that comes at other
times; the day, but once a year.[24]

The poem moves from the Incarnation on Christmas day, 'In the
juvescence of the year', to 'depraved May'. We have entered the
time corrupted by Judas (the tree upon which he supposedly
hanged himself now flowers). Christ is crucified. And yet he
continues to live and die, not only symbolically each year in the
Christian calendar, but also both symbolically and actually in the
communion service, where the echo of the Incarnation endures:
'In the juvescence of the year / Came Christ the tiger. . . . / To
be eaten, to be divided, to be drunk / Among whispers.'

Andrewes' sermon on signs provides an appropriate scaffolding
for Gerontion's concerns about the relationship between knowledge and forgiveness, for each is concerned with the authority
and the interpretation of signs. Andrewes criticizes those who
cannot cope with the disjunction between signifiers and what
they signify:

> we, if we admit a conference with flesh and blood, when we
> lay together the sign, and of Whom it is the sign; we find to our
> thinking a great disparagement, and I know not how, thoughts
> arise in our hearts, as if some better sign would have done better.
> The meaning is, we would find Christ fain, but we would find
> Him in some better place. Half Jews we are all in this point; we
> would have a Messias in state.[25]

Gerontion is one of those who would see a sign – but a better
sign than what he has been offered, either in his own life or by
means of history. Gerontion's reference to the 'Jew [who] squats
of the window sill' is instructive. Smith suggests that 'Eliot's Jew in
"Gerontion" . . . may be linked with Christ, though sarcastically.'[26]
Gerontion refuses to attribute anything but parodic significance to
'the Jew . . . / Spawned in some estaminet of Antwerp'. It is as
though by way of distinction from the pathetic Jew 'patched and
peeled in London' that Gerontion introduces the grander Jew,
'Christ the tiger'. Gerontion is in Andrewes' terms 'Half Jew'
because of this attitude: 'If His sign be no better, as good lost as

found. . . . for no good news thus to find Him.'[27] Ironically, then, Gerontion himself is the Jew who owns his 'decayed house' – he is himself the non-Christian resident within. Expecting 'some kind of proportion . . . between *signum* [sign or signifier] and *signatum* [signified]. . . . A chief Person in a chief place, a Lord and Saviour something Lord and Saviour-like', Gerontion cannot acknowledge the presence of Christ – actually or symbolically – in the depraved modern world.[28]

Andrewes' sermon also helps to explain Gerontion's cryptic comments about 'Virtues' and 'Unnatural vices' in stanza four. Gerontion seems to align himself here with the Augustinian Adam and Eve of Andrewes' sermon and thereby acknowledges his own culpability in the disjunction between *signum* and *signatum*. According to Andrewes, the disparity between the cratch as signifier and Christ as signified is explained by the sin of pride – both the pride of those who refuse to countenance the idea of Christ in a cratch and the pride of Adam and Eve in daring to compare themselves with God. As remedy for this sin, Christ comes in humility:

> if it be *signum vobis* [a sign for you] to some, it is for others *signum contra vos* [a sign against you]; and that is the proud. For the word of God . . . shews us the malignity of the disease of pride, for the cure whereof this so profound humility was requisite in Christ.

In 'Gerontion', as in the Garden of Eden, the 'heroism' that produces 'Unnatural vices' is spiritual pride. Andrewes loathes 'this vice that laid this so great a disgrace as we count it upon the Son of God'. That 'Virtues / Are forced upon us' is the consequence of heroism, redefined as 'our impudent crimes'. Heroism is robbery: for Adam and Eve 'To make themselves equal with God is plain robbery. . . . For that robbery of theirs was the Son of God robbed, as I might say, and quite spoiled of His glory.'[29]

What it means for virtues to be 'forced upon us' is not immediately clear. In the Augustinian theology upon which Andrewes' sermon depends, however, human beings since the fall are capable of virtue only by the grace of God:

> But this part of the human race to which God has promised pardon and a share in his eternal kingdom, can they be restored through the merit of their own works? God forbid. For what

good work can a lost man perform, except so far as he has been delivered from perdition? Can they do anything by the free determination of their own will? Again I say, God forbid. For it was by the evil use of his free-will that man destroyed both it and himself. . . . And hence he will not be free to do right, until, being freed from sin, he shall begin to be the servant of righteousness. And this is true liberty, for he has pleasure in the righteous deed; and it is at the same time a holy bondage, for he is obedient to the will of God.[30]

Virtues are forced upon us in the state of holy bondage. Gerontion plays with the idea of the fortunate fall (as much in Andrewes as in Augustine), acknowledging the paradoxical recovery of freedom through slavery and grace through sin.

In these most difficult of lines, Gerontion sums up the Incarnational theology of Andrewes and Augustine, moving from the impudent and criminal heroism of the Fall to the redemption and the paradoxically 'forced' virtues of holy bondage. Gerontion has 'shaken' these tearful reflections 'from the wrath-bearing tree' – an image appropriately concluding so concentrated a presentation of history by concentrating within itself both the tree of knowledge and the rood or cross, respectively the cause and consequence of the spiritual pride that Gerontion bemoans.

The question of the effect of such knowledge remains. Having acknowledged that Christianity began with Christ's birth (a definite historical event) and that it has developed to the point of embracing the variety of cultures represented by Mr Silvero, Hakagawa, Madame de Tornquist and Fräulein von Kulp (the result of a historical process), and having acknowledged his own general sense of his remoteness from the things that constitute history in his own day, Gerontion is left to contemplate the implications of his remoteness from the moment when the eternal entered time.

Knowledge mediated by history is apparently unreliable: 'History has many cunning passages, contrived corridors / And issues, deceives with whispering ambitions, / Guides us by vanities.' It is especially unreliable insofar as questions of faith are concerned: history 'Gives too late / What's not believed in, or if still believed, / In memory only, reconsidered passion.' What has been given to Gerontion is knowledge of the Passion, but 'such knowledge'

is no longer sufficient. It is temporally remote from the event –
emphasized by the prefix 're' in 'reconsidered'. It arrives 'too late'
in the sense that it comes to Gerontion in an age not predisposed
toward belief. Its authority as evidence has been compromised by
the nineteenth-century biblical criticism of scholars like David
Friedrich Strauss. To borrow the terms of 'Mr Eliot's Sunday
Morning Service' from the year before, too much time and
interpretation have intervened between the twentieth-century
Christian and Christ. Passion considered – let alone *re*considered
– is a different thing from Passion witnessed. (The same gap is
realized later in 'Gerontion' in the difference between 'delirium'
and 'deliberations' – the latter apparently arising only after the
former is 'chilled'.) For Gerontion, remoteness in time from the
Passion is remoteness from the ground of faith: there is a gap
between knowledge of a historical fact (an enervate origin) and
living belief. History gives only knowledge *that* something (the
Passion) is true, whereas Gerontion craves to experience its truth
himself, and so 'the giving famishes the craving' by stimulating the
hunger for truth without even beginning to satisfy it.

In the sermons of which we know that Eliot had taken note by
1919 (the Nativity Sermons of 1617 and 1622), Andrewes is at
pains to emphasize the adequacy of the Bible as ground of faith
in the absence of signs like the cratch in which Christ was found
and the star that led the Magi: 'the cratch is gone many years ago.
What is our sign now? Why, what was the sign of? . . . Humility,
then: we shall find him by that sign. . . . This day it is not possible
to keep off of this theme . . . it is so woven into every text there
is no avoiding it'; 'We cannot say *vidimus stellam* [we have seen a
star]; the star is gone long since, not now to be seen. . . . It will
be the more acceptable, if not seeing it we worship though. It is
enough we read of it in the text; we see it there.'[31] Similarly, in
his Nativity Sermon of 1607 on Hebrews 1.1–3 ('God, who at
sundry times and in divers manners spake in time past unto the
fathers by the prophets, Hath in these last days spoken unto us by
his Son'), Andrewes celebrates the word of God that we hear today
as incomparably beyond any other and celebrates Christmas as 'the
beginning of this dignity to us, wherein God gave His Son to speak
viva voce [with a living voice] unto us, to purge our sins, and to
exalt us to His throne on high.' Andrewes' conclusion again brings
forward the claim that this voice endures in the New Testament:

The same flesh that cleansed our sins, the same now sitteth on the throne. . . . The same blood is the blood of Sacrifice for remission of sins, and the blood of the New Testament for the passing to us the bequest, which is the right of His purchase for which He was made Heir.[32]

The efficacy of the New Testament as sign is an assumption that Andrewes and fellow divines cannot doubt.

Gerontion does. The fear to which he alludes in stanza four seems to arise as a result of his inability to accept the New Testament as ground of faith. It is his and his day's inability to accept the New Testament bequest of Christ's purchase that Gerontion acknowledges in lines from stanza four that we have not yet considered: history 'Gives too soon / Into weak hands, what's thought can be dispensed with / Till the refusal propagates a fear'. What has been given too soon is knowledge; what has been refused is forgiveness. As further reading in Hebrews makes clear, recognition of this fact propagates a fear.

Perhaps led to read further in Hebrews by the text of Andrewes 1607 sermon (or quotations in other sermons from the same book of the New Testament), Eliot relies on Hebrews almost as much as he relies on Andrewes for ideas, images and words that permeate 'Gerontion'. The fear that arises in consequence of the refusal of Christ's New Testament bequest is explained later in a text that overlaps the Andrewes sermon quoted in stanza two:

3 How shall we escape, if we neglect so great salvation; which at the first began to be spoken by the Lord, and was confirmed unto us by them that heard *him*;
4 God also bearing *them* witness, both with signs and wonders?[33]

Thus, not only does Hebrews address the very question that preoccupies Gerontion about the relationship between the knowledge offered as history by the New Testament and salvation or forgiveness, but it also contains words and images that Gerontion uses.

There is the metaphor of the house:

4 Every house is builded by some *man*; but he that built all things *is* God.

5 And Moses verily *was* faithful in all his house, as a servant, for a testimony of those things to be spoken after;

6 But Christ as a son over his own house; whose house we are. (Hebrews 3.4–6)

Thus Gerontion's 'house' as 'decayed house' and 'the Jew . . . the owner'. There is the 'fear' in stanza four that comes of hearing the New Testament without faith:

1 Let us therefore fear, lest, a promise being left *us* of entering into his rest, any of you should seem to come short of it.

2 For unto us was the gospel preached, as well as unto them: but the word preached did not profit them, not being mixed with faith in them that heard *it*. (Hebrews 4.1–2)

There are the 'weak hands' and the 'refusal' that lead to this fear:

12 Wherefore lift up the hands that hang down, and the feeble knees. . . .

25 See that ye refuse not him that speaketh. For if they escaped not who refused him that spake on earth, much more *shall not* we *escape*, if we turn away from him that *speaketh* from heaven. (Hebrews 12.12, 25)

And there is the disjunction between knowledge and forgiveness with which stanza four begins: 'if we sin wilfully after that we have received the knowledge of the truth, there remaineth no more sacrifice for sins' (Hebrews 10.26). In other words, 'After such knowledge, what forgiveness?' The epistle implies that history gave too soon to the Hebrews what the poem implies that history gave too soon to Gerontion – a knowledge that was not appreciated.

Before leaving stanza four, it is important to note that Eliot recognizes that Gerontion is also remote from the moment when the eternal entered time in the same way that Narcissus and the speaker in 'The Love Song of Saint Sebastian' are remote from it: they have all substituted things of the flesh for things of the spirit. Gerontion has apparently succumbed to the temptation to 'Stiffen in a rented house' – in one of several possible readings, the stiffening representing an erection, the rented house representing the 'cunning passages' of a prostitute's body. And so, however much of Andrewes and Augustine is to be found in stanza four, there is also a good deal of Eliot's earlier poems, 'The Love Song of Saint Sebastian' and 'The Death of Saint Narcissus'. This is also to say that however much of a spiritual dimension there is to these lines in stanza four, there is also a sexual dimension.

The sexual subtext in this stanza is flagged by such words as 'She' for history (she of the 'cunning passages'), 'passion', 'propagates' and 'fathered' (not to mention the less directly sexual potential of such words as 'Unnatural vices', 'Virtues' and 'impudent crimes'). 'The Death of Saint Narcissus' is recalled by the phrase 'such knowledge', which, as Smith observes, 'seems to connote more than intellectual accomplishment'.[34] The speaker in 'The Love Song of Saint Sebastian' is recalled indirectly by the word 'heroism'. In Eliot's letter about the poem, the speaker is described as 'the hero of my verse'.[35] Although Eliot presumably means 'protagonist', his flippant tone suggests that he may also mean (although ironically) one who performs superhuman sexual deeds: masochistic suicide and cold-blooded murder.

The 'heroism' that breeds 'Unnatural vices' in 'Gerontion' is thus subtly related to the heroism of the earlier poems. Narcissus heroically abandons the world: 'He could not live men's ways' and therefore became a hermit devoted to the unnatural vice of the love of his own flesh and blood. The speaker in 'The Love Song of Saint Sebastian' heroically triumphs over human sexuality – but again, viciously. In each case, heroism produces an unnatural vice: the morbid self-love of Narcissus, the fantasies of sado-masochistic suicide and murder entertained by the speaker of 'The Love Song of Saint Sebastian', and Gerontion's apparent whoremongering. Heroism also fathers death, just as Milton's hero Satan fathers Death by Sin. Narcissus has achieved death; Gerontion and the speaker in 'The Love Song of Saint Sebastian' anticipate it. In each case the heroism and the vice are one: a spiritual pride that would substitute what satisfies the self for what satisfies God.

As Eliot had noted in his Harvard study of St Bernard's mystical metaphors, passion and Passion are inextricably related in a certain false mystical tradition. The caricatures in 'Descent from the Cross' and 'The Death of Saint Narcissus' of the sensibility prone to confusing the two is replaced in 'Gerontion' with a sympathetic portrait of a person in the turmoil of contemplating final things. There is a forsaking of passion and a yearning for Passion. Yet the next move is not clear. The conjunction of questions about the relationship between history and belief with a reference to 'passion' in stanza four recalls Eliot's concerns about modernism's devaluation of the gospel accounts of Christ's life as a basis for faith: 'I am not sure, after reading modern theology, that the pale Galilean has conquered.'[36] Hebrews and 'Gerontion' alike offer faith as the middle term that will lead from knowledge to forgiveness. 'Neither fear nor courage saves us' because it is by faith that we are rewarded. But Gerontion remains without faith. He is aware that Andrewes and Hebrews locate its ground in the Bible, but he seeks something more.

Against the combined background of Gerontion's modernist awareness of the gap between historical origin and present religious experience, on the one hand, and his growing awareness of the dangers lurking in a religious sensibility prone to confuse the human and the divine, on the other, one can appreciate the mystical turn that occurs in stanza five. In the grip of the modernist's question – whence faith: from history (the Bible and dogmatic theology) or from one's own experience? – Gerontion arrives at a possible ground for belief in the depths of his own experience. He experiences a mystical moment, but misses its meaning.

George Williamson believes that the person addressed in stanza five is Christ.[37] Smith believes that the person is a woman.[38] Given that Christ 'the tiger' devours 'us', Christ is distinct from 'us' and presumably from the 'we' in the next line. There is no reason to assume that the 'you' addressed later is not one of those who apparently make up the 'we' – the poet and at least one other person, who is not Christ. Williamson's reading goes against the grain of the pronouns; Smith's does not. Furthermore, Smith's reading of stanza five is in keeping with the dynamic in stanza four in which Gerontion opposes himself to a force that is marked as feminine.

Gerontion seems to be addressing a woman in stanza five (she need not be present) in an insensitive – if not cruel – declaration of something approaching celibacy. On the one hand, the phrase 'stiffen in a rented house' can be interpreted as an allusion to Gerontion's death: in the decayed house that he has rented, his body will experience rigor mortis. On the other hand, the phrase is also – and more insistently – sexual, for it involves two people: '*We* have not reached conclusion, when I / Stiffen in a rented house' (emphasis added). As noted above, the stiffening is perhaps an erection, and the rented house is perhaps a brothel or the body of a prostitute. If the stiffening is rigor mortis, it is not clear how Gerontion can understand his relationship with his companion as *not* having reached conclusion, yet if the stiffening is symbolic of sexual activity, Gerontion can argue that he and his companion have not reached conclusion, despite such a consummation of their relationship, because of his own conclusion that there is more to life than sex. He has learned that 'Nature' (the word in the original draft of the poem that was replaced by 'History') is as untrustworthy as history.[39]

These lines imply that Gerontion is far from impotent – as Smith, for instance, assumes.[40] He has performed sexually ('made this show' of stiffening) such that the act of intercourse has 'reached conclusion'. He pointedly denies, however, that he has simply lapsed into the lustful behaviour of earlier days (what he calls a hypothetical 'concitation / Of the backward devils'). Rather, he has 'made this show' purposefully. The phrase 'to make a show' also means 'to pretend'; it may be that Gerontion is pretending to be passionate in order to show that appearances are deceptive. The false show of sexual interest is ironically the pretext for honesty – 'I would meet you upon this honestly'. He is confessing his loss of sexual interest in his companion despite what his 'show' or arousal might suggest. In an even deeper sexual irony, then, he would meet her 'honestly' in the sense of 'in chastity'. In the poem's present, Gerontion sits twice removed from her love: 'I that was near your heart was removed therefrom / To lose beauty in terror, terror in inquisition.'

The experience that Gerontion outlines in these cryptic lines is glossed by Eliot in his discussion – in an article written in the same month (May 1919) that he was writing 'Gerontion' – of 'the inevitable inadequacy of actual living to the passionate capacity':

> The surface of existence coagulates into lumps which look like important simple feelings, which are identified by names as feelings, which the patient analyst disintegrates into more complex and trifling, but ultimately if he goes far enough, into various canalizations of something again simple, terrible, and unknown.[41]

Eliot's language is Bergsonian, but his conclusion about the Absolute is not as cheerful as Bergson's or Bradley's. As in his dissertation, Eliot concludes that the end of our speculative journey is 'annihilation and utter night' (KE, 31). Rather than cordial acceptance of this fact, however, Eliot now alludes to terror – as does Gerontion.

In 'Gerontion', the essay's disintegration of feeling into the terrible and unknown becomes the disintegration of passion into terror. The despair in the essay of any simple, pure feeling becomes in the poem the despair of any simple, pure passion: 'I have lost my passion: why should I need to keep it / Since what is kept must be adulterated?' In the context of a discussion of the failure of the sexual relationship between two people, the use of the word 'adulterated' suggests that Gerontion feels betrayed – not so much by his partner as by passion itself.[42] The essay speaks of 'the awful separation between potential passion and any actualization possible in life'. Eliot immediately links this separation to 'the indestructible barriers between one human being and another'.[43] Gerontion makes the same turn from passion compromised to people inevitably separated: 'I have lost my sight, smell, hearing, taste and touch: / How should I use them for your closer contact?' The question is rhetorical: Gerontion is as certain as Eliot that the barrier is 'indestructible'. The same point is made in 'Whispers of Immortality': 'No contact possible to flesh / Allayed the fever of the bone' (CPP, 52).

Terror, however, is lost in inquisition, and this is a greater loss than the beauty lost in terror, for Eliot locates the possibility of contact with the Other not in the passion for human beauty or the detachment of inquisition but rather in the abyss of terror.

Gerontion's inquisition – represented by the questions in stanzas four, five and six – is his response to the loss of passion. The inquisition concerning passion ('why should I need to keep it?') leads to his inquisition concerning the Passion ('After such knowledge, what forgiveness?') and so seems to lead in the direction of the Other. The poem turns from Gerontion's former passion and from the passion of Narcissus and the speaker in 'The Love Song of Saint Sebastian' to the Passion. We have not reached conclusion in sexual passion because it is merely a prelude, as Dante knew, to the Passion. Furthermore, in token of the fact that the dead end reached in passion can become the first step toward the Passion, Eliot allows Gerontion's inquisition concerning the senses ('I have lost my sight, smell, hearing, taste and touch: / How should I use them for your closer contact?') to double as a petition to God through its echo of Newman's sermon on Divine Calls: 'Let us beg and pray Him day by day to reveal Himself to our souls more fully, to quicken our senses, to give us sight and hearing, taste and touch of the world to come.'[44] Yet Gerontion pointedly remains unaware that his rhetorical question about himself and his human powers might become a real question to be put to God as a petition for the employment of His powers.

The experience of terror acknowledged in stanza five – the experience that presumably gives rise to the thoughts that constitute the poem – is explained more fully in Eliot's essay. Acknowledging an alliance between terror and truth, Eliot concludes his description of 'the awful separation between potential passion and any actualization possible in life' and 'the indestructible barriers between one human being and another' with the observation that 'This is a "mysticism" not to be extracted . . . even from Miss Underhill'.[45] In the experience of 'something . . . simple, terrible and unknown' resides the possibility of contact with something Other.

Reading the essay as a gloss upon the poem allows one to interpret the experience represented in stanza five as a mystical experience. Yet although Gerontion has had the mystical experience in question, he has missed the meaning, for the meaning is in the terror, not in the inquisition that displaces it. Stanzas two to five show Gerontion's first tentative steps up the mystical ladder of contemplation by means of meditation or recollection – according to Underhill, the first stage of contemplation, involving 'the deliberate consideration of and dwelling upon one aspect of Reality . . . one of the names or attributes of God, a fragment of Scripture, an incident of the life Christ.' Focusing upon the Incarnation and the Passion, Gerontion's meditation is successful – to a point:

> The self, concentrated upon this image or idea, dwelling on it more than thinking about it . . . falls gradually and insensibly into the condition of reverie; and, protected by this holy day-dream from the more distracting dream of life, sinks into itself, and becomes . . . 'recollected' or gathered together. (*Mysticism*, 375–6)

Gerontion arrives at revery, but not recollection. He has not so much dwelt lovingly upon the Incarnation and the Passion as *thought* about them: 'Think now', 'Think now', 'Think', 'Think at last', 'Think at last'. Thought, as the Bergsonian language in Eliot's essay suggests, causes feeling to disintegrate. Passion reconsidered is passion adulterated. Delirium chilled is canalized as 'a thousand small deliberations'. Gerontion's thoughts – the referent of the pronoun 'These' – serve only to 'multiply variety / In a wilderness of mirrors'. The delirium that has chilled into deliberation is the terror that has been lost in inquisition: thought would protract the profit of the mystical experience but is no more satisfying than the protracted excitement of 'the membrane, when the sense has cooled'.

The incapacitatingly ratiocinative dimension of Gerontion's character can be illuminated by reference to another of Eliot's essays written in May of 1919, 'A Sceptical Patrician' – a review of *The Education of Henry Adams*. Eliot depicts Adams as a gerontion or little old man: 'we are acutely, painfully aware of an elderly man approaching a new subject of study with "This will be good for me"!' Whereas Gerontion has no faith, Adams has only doubt; their problem is the same: 'extreme sensitiveness to all the suggestions which dampen enthusiasm or dispel conviction.' Furthermore, like Gerontion, Adams is without passion: 'He had attended to everything, respectfully, had accumulated masses of information . . . ; but he was unaware that education . . . is a by-product of being interested, passionately absorbed.' In the end, Eliot judges Adams to be immature:

> It is probable that men ripen best through experiences which are at once sensuous and intellectual; certainly many men will admit that their keenest ideas have come to them with the quality of a sense-perception; and that their keenest sensuous experience has been 'as if the body thought'. There is nothing to indicate that Adams's senses either flowered or fruited: he remains little Paul Dombey asking questions.[46]

Eliot's verdict on Gerontion is similar: he remains a little old man asking questions.

With 'Gerontion', Eliot moves from his criticism in 'Descent from the Cross' and 'The Death of Saint Narcissus' of mystical personae with an excess of feeling to criticism of a mystical persona with an excess of thought. These mystical personae combine to identify the mystical experience closest to Eliot's own – the experience of 'the awful separation between potential passion and any actualization possible in life' and 'the indestructible barriers between one human being and another'.[47] Yet they cannot meditate in a healthy way upon the terror that might ground a mysticism because of their excessive foregrounding of the self. The speaker in 'The Love Song of Saint Sebastian' insists on either the exclusive attention of the other to himself or the exclusive possession of the other by himself. Narcissus would assume the whole world by metamorphosis and incorporate everything within himself. Gerontion moves beyond egotism of this sort, yet after finding himself freed from his passion and senses he becomes a hostage of his own self-centred thoughts and thereby becomes lost in the 'wilderness of mirrors' that traps all three mystical personae.

In the end, Gerontion is mystically immature. He cannot escape the distracting dream of life. Like the perfume from a dress that causes Prufrock to digress from his overwhelming question, the 'pungent sauces' of Gerontion's deliberate inquisition lead him away from his glimpse of 'something . . . simple, terrible and unknown' to 'a sleepy corner' and an unholy day-dream of a world in flux without end: 'De Bailhache, Fresca, Mrs Cammel, whirled / Beyond the circuit of the shuddering Bear / In fractured atoms'. Ernest Rutherford having published in June of 1919 his work on the disintegration of the nitrogen atom, Gerontion is an up-to-date Adams: 'Wherever this man stepped, the ground did not simply give way, it flew into particles.'[48] The 'something . . . simple, terrible and unknown' that Gerontion has glimpsed in the abyss between people is fragmented into the 'thousand small deliberations' that constitute what Gerontion knows. In such knowledge there is no forgiveness. Nonetheless, the '"mysticism" not to be extracted . . . from Miss Underhill' can be extracted indirectly from 'Gerontion'. It is to be found in the terror somewhere between passion and thought, and it is to be found in the maturity somewhere between Peter-pantheism and Gerontological reconsideration. In the unified sensibility for which Eliot is nostalgic, ripeness is all, and 'It is probable that men ripen best through experiences which are at once sensuous and intellectual.'[49]

5

The Waste Land's Mystical Void

Contemplating the publication of *The Waste Land*, Eliot once considered 'printing Gerontion as prelude in book or pamphlet form'.[1] Ezra Pound nixed the idea: 'I do *not* advise printing Gerontion as preface. One dont miss it AȚ all as the thing now stands. To be more lucid still, let me say that I advise you *NOT* to print Gerontion as prelude.'[2] Long before the correspondence between Eliot and Pound concerning revisions to *The Waste Land* became known, readers noted many of the connections between the two poems that might have justified linking them. By its fragmentary narrative style, its Jacobean dramatic speech rhythms, its imagery of desiccation, its expression of post-war despair, 'Gerontion' anticipates *The Waste Land*. Unremarked, however, is one of the most important ways in which the former anticipates the latter: through its mysticism of the void in human relations. 'Gerontion' introduces the experience of the absolute void between one human being and another – the only absolute experienced in *The Waste Land* and as such the foundation of the poem's mystical moments.

There are four such moments in *The Waste Land*, each involving a contemplation of this void. The first occurs in the section recalling the 'hyacinth girl'. The second occurs in the conversation between the man and the woman at the beginning of 'A Game of Chess'. The third involves the Thames daughters in 'The Fire Sermon'. The fourth and final mystical moment consists of the concluding contemplation of the Thunder's message in 'What the Thunder said'.

Reading the poem biographically, Lyndall Gordon assumes that the hyacinth girl is Emily Hale, a Boston acquaintance of Eliot's towards whom he was romantically inclined. Counteracting his 'fierce disgust for the flesh', Eliot revealed an 'incipient feeling of reverence' for it 'in response to the radiant young Emily Hale with her long, shining hair. Eliot's imagination dwelt on a beloved woman's hair, the light of it in "La Figlia" (1912), wet in *The Waste Land* (1922), loosened in *Ash-Wednesday*.' She is 'the model for

silent, ethereal women in Eliot's poetry, La Figlia, the hyacinth
girl, the Lady, who all elevate the poet's spirit.'[3] This mystical
moment, however, does not function quite as Gordon suggests it
does. The image of the hyacinth girl does not elevate the poet's
spirit by simply leading it to recognize the sympathy between her
beauty and divine beauty. As the speaker looks back on events in
the hyacinth garden, he begins to understand the elevation of his
spirit in the presence of the hyacinth girl as in part a reaction
against her image. The speaker interprets her retrospectively, I
would suggest, as the first person by whom he is introduced to
the void between people. At a considerable remove in time and
space from the hyacinth garden, the speaker reconsiders his passion
for the hyacinth girl and makes her the focus of his sense of 'the
indestructible barriers between one human being and another . . . a
"mysticism" not to be extracted . . . even from Miss Underhill.'[4]

The scene in the hyacinth garden begins not with the words
of the hyacinth girl herself but with the quotation from Wagner's
Tristan und Isolde. On a ship at sea, Wagner's sailor remembers his
beloved 'Irisch Kind' (Irish beloved, or Irish child) waiting for
him in 'Der Heimat' (the homeland) (CPP, 61–2, ll. 32–3).[5] The
connection between these lines about separation and the events
in the hyacinth garden is made in the first draft of 'What the
Thunder said'. Here the speaker seems to recall this scene from
Tristan und Isolde in three lines that Eliot considered for the
Damyata section of the conclusion: 'You over on the shore'; 'I
left without you'; 'There I leave you.'[6] The emphasis in each case
is upon the separation of a man and a woman by water. Reading
biographically, one cannot help but see these abandoned lines as
addressing the abandoned Emily Hale, the one remaining in the
homeland when Eliot travelled to Europe in 1914. She thus appears
as the figure behind both the 'hyacinth girl' and the 'Irisch Kind'
and so serves as the missing narrative link between *Tristan und Isolde*
and the hyacinth garden. Each scene symbolizes the separation of
Eliot and Hale.

The lines from *Tristan und Isolde*, furthermore, establish the
tableau repeated in each of the mystical moments: on the one side
a man; on the other side a woman; between them a void – literal sea
or sea of silence. The scene in the hyacinth garden reveals the latter,
for the evening with the hyacinth girl culminates in 'silence' (41).
The language is conventionally mystical – hinting at a dark night

of the senses, claiming a paradoxical suspension between life and death, pretending to a naughting of the self and an experience of illumination. Yet accompanying the suggestion that there is great spiritual potential in this moment is an emphasis upon the actual failure of the human relationship that has led to such a moment. The speaker's attitude is not clear: is the failure of the relationship to be regretted or to be celebrated?

The relationship fails in large part because the hyacinth girl and the poem's speaker alike fail to communicate. Her words – 'You gave me hyacinths first a year ago; / They called me the hyacinth girl' – were apparently spoken in the hyacinth garden upon receipt of a *second* bunch of hyacinths from the speaker one year after he gave her the 'first' bunch (35–6). These words are recalled in the poem's present, a time at some distance from the event and a time in which the speaker and the hyacinth girl are separated by a sea: 'Oed' und leer das Meer [Waste and empty is the sea]' (42). The words remembered by the speaker reinforce the sense of separation. They constituted an invitation to intimacy that the speaker declined. By calling attention to the length of their relationship and to the fact that their evening together was an anniversary of sorts, the words of the hyacinth girl establish a romantic mood. Yet despite her words, and despite the inviting language that the speaker attributes retrospectively to her body ('Your arms full, and your hair wet' (39)), he could not communicate with her: 'I could not / Speak, and my eyes failed' (38–9). The speaker thus identifies the separation that he experiences in the poem's present as beginning not with his voyage across the sea but with his refusal of the hyacinth girl's invitation. He seems nostalgic for a time when their relationship might have succeeded.

At the same time, he explains his failure in this relationship as important to a success elsewhere: he implies that he perceived through the beauty of the hyacinth girl intimations of a perfect beauty beyond her. As Dominic Manganiello points out, 'The protagonist's eyes fail as he gazes into the heart of light, or heavenly city, just as Dante's eyes fail when he encounters Beatrice in the earthly paradise, or when he gazes at the beatific vision.'[7] A Beatrice of the hyacinth garden, the hyacinth girl led the speaker where Beatrice led Dante: to the 'heart of light' (41). His incapacitation as earthly lover is explained by the intimation of perfect beauty. Such an illumination – whether occurring to the mystic or the prisoner in Plato's cave – is bound to produce a stumbling and a stammering in the face of mundane affairs. The speaker thus explains his experience in the hyacinth garden as part of an evolution by which he is led from earthly beauty to divine beauty. Like Dante, the speaker apparently recognizes no hostility between the earthly beloved and 'the heart of light'.

Yet between the lines of the hyacinth garden passage one can also read another result of the speaker's reflections upon the double event in the hyacinth garden. Just beginning to take shape is the conclusion that the failure of the human relationship was a necessary prerequisite to whatever divine success was achieved. From this point of view, the hyacinth girl and 'the heart of light' are indeed antithetical. Meaning 'nevertheless' or 'in spite of that', the speaker's 'Yet' ('Yet when we came back, late, from the hyacinth garden' (37)) suggests on the one hand his awareness of the extent to which his silence before the hyacinth girl was a contradiction on his part of both her words and her body: in spite of her invitation to some sort of romantic intimacy, he failed to seize the moment. On the other hand, it hints at an awareness of a more general contradiction between things physical and things spiritual: in spite of her invitation to some sort of romantic intimacy, he achieved spiritual vision. The dash reinforces this hint of a gap between the physical and the spiritual: on the one side of the dash is the physical world; on the other side is the spiritual world. The dash represents the speaker's understanding of the necessity of the gap between himself and the hyacinth girl. It not only represents the separation that *was* between them; it also effects the separation once more. According to Calvin Bedient, 'The dash before "Yet" rescinds (recuts) the protagonist's tie with the hyacinth girl. A mark of pure alienation, a sudden straitening, it divides the two inexorably.'[8] Unlike the presumably unconscious standoffishness of the speaker upon his return from the hyacinth garden so long ago, the separation between the speaker and the hyacinth girl in the poem's present is effected with the speaker's awareness of and assent to its necessity.

Perhaps interpreted on that long ago evening as an intimation of the divine, the hyacinth girl's value as beauty incarnate is compromised as the speaker's distance from that moment increases. The words used in the poem's present to describe this past event suggest a growing awareness of the danger in the hyacinth girl's invitation to a potentially physical intimacy. This awareness is further suggested by an allusion to *The Divine Comedy*. The speaker describes his reaction to the hyacinth girl's words and appearance by means of Dante's words upon confronting Dis, or Lucifer, in the last circle of Hell:

> How frozen and how faint I then became,
> Ask me not, reader! for I write it not;
> Since words would fail to tell thee of my state.
> I was not dead nor living.[9]

The Waste Land's lines 'I could not / Speak' (38–9) and 'I was neither / Living nor dead' (39–40) recall Dante's reaction before Dis. Although the hyacinth girl initially appears to the speaker as a Beatrice figure leading to 'the heart of light', the speaker's phrases suggest that in retrospect he has also interpreted her as a type of Satan. The hyacinth girl may not represent an evil as gigantic as Satan, but she figures as something fundamentally antithetical to the speaker's spiritual fulfilment. She is made the representative of the material world, calling the speaker to the merely physical passions that can be actualized within it.

The hyacinth girl is also positioned as the material siren of *The Waste Land* by a more local intertextuality, for the word 'silence' invokes Eliot's poem of the same name written twelve years before. Gordon has focused upon this poem as evidence of Eliot's own mystical experience. The speaker notes a silence in the middle of a bustling city. It is a moment for which he has waited – a moment providing through stillness and silence a hint of the ultimate meaning of life. Mixed with the feeling of peace, however, is the feeling of terror – a terror that comes of the awareness that nothing else matters beside this silence.[10] And so the question that the word 'silence' insinuates into *The Waste Land* – insofar as it introduces the concerns of the earlier poem – is whether, since the hyacinth girl cannot be all, she ought to be for the speaker anything. After all, there is nothing else besides silence. Following the word 'silence' in *The Waste Land*, Wagner's words 'Waste and empty the sea' reprise the earlier poem 'Silence': in each case, the speaker's conclusion is that talk is nothing and that silence is all.

Hay suggests that 'Silence' is evidence that 'the Buddhist peace of emptiness and negation was already more real to [Eliot] than

Christian peace, however terrifying that emptiness seemed to him at the time.'[11] Appreciation of the void, however, proves to be as important to Eliot's Christianity as to any form of Buddhism that he might have embraced at Harvard or during the writing of *The Waste Land*. Writing to his spiritual mentor Paul Elmer More in the early 1930s, Eliot refers to 'the void that I find in the middle of all human happiness and all human relations, and which there is only one thing to fill'.[12] Whether understood ultimately in Christian or Buddhist terms, however, Eliot's experience of the void in the middle of human relations is better understood initially as the basis of his mysticism – from 'Silence' to *The Waste Land*, and beyond.

His speaker's experience with the hyacinth girl is explicable in these terms. By the speaker's recollection of the double dimension of events in the hyacinth garden – on the one side human beings, on the other side the divine 'heart of light' – he begins to confront and acknowledge 'the awful separation between potential passion and any actualization possible in life.'[13] Whither the hyacinth girl, if she is but a hint of a higher passion? The point at which the speaker in *The Waste Land* has arrived is the contemplation of the void at the centre of all human relationships (one of the meanings of the word *leer* that Wagner uses to describe the sea between lovers is 'void'). As though glossing the double potential of the moment in the hyacinth garden, Eliot confessed to More: 'I am one of those whom the sense of void tends to drive towards asceticism or sensuality, and only Christianity helps to reconcile me to life which is otherwise disgusting.'[14] The hyacinth girl offers sensuality; the speaker chooses asceticism.

Despite initial appearances to the contrary, the speaker is no Tristan waiting for Isolde. The incidental separation in time and space that is a part of the history of the relationship between the speaker and the hyacinth girl symbolizes a more 'awful separation' that cannot be overcome by crossing a physical space – whether that space be the distance made by a sea or the distance made by the fact that we are all separated by the bodies that we inhabit. The experience of this radical separation between human beings is the ground of the mystical moments in *The Waste Land*. In the words of Eliot's 1919 essay, this experience of separation leads to a glimpse of something 'simple, terrible and unknown'.[15]

The occasion of this mystical experience of the indestructible barriers between people seems to be woman. She is just as much the focus of the second mystical moment in *The Waste Land* as she was the first. The second moment occurs during the conversation between the man and the woman in 'A Game of Chess'. We meet this woman first through the gaze of her male partner – a gaze that quickly elides the distinction between woman and the water beyond which the hyacinth girl resides: the speaker relates that her 'liquid' 'perfumes' 'drowned the sense in odours' (88, 87, 89). Madame Sosostris's warning – 'Fear death by water' (55) – takes on a new meaning against this background: she is saying, 'Fear death by woman.'

Eliot's assurance that 'all the women are one woman' is not necessary for us to recognize that the woman at the beginning of 'A Game of Chess' is continuous with the dangerous hyacinth girl of 'The Burial of the Dead' (CPP, 78). Each is Belladonna. The latter is not just literally 'beautiful lady' – with a suggestion in the Italian name of epithets in Italian for the Virgin Mary – but also symbolically 'Deadly Nightshade', a poisonous plant. Similarly, the hyacinth girl provides hints through her beauty of a divine beauty, yet she also seems to be connected in the speaker's mind to Satan. The woman at the beginning of 'A Game of Chess' is just as much Belladonna, 'the Lady of the Rocks' (49). Although she may have belladonna in her vials of cosmetics (it brightens the eyes), she is more directly linked to Belladonna as 'Lady of the Rocks' by her 'jewels' ('From satin cases poured in rich profusion'), for *rocks* was from Eliot's time American slang for diamonds and jewels (85). Like the hyacinth girl and Belladonna, this Lady of the Rocks is beautiful, but dangerous – something to be feared.

This sort of connection is not the only thing that makes it necessary to understand the conversation between the man and the woman in 'A Game of Chess' as a repetition of and development from events in the hyacinth garden. Consider other textual echoes. As though responding to the man's 'I could not / Speak' in the hyacinth garden, the woman implores her companion to speak: 'Speak to me. Why do you never speak. Speak' (112). As though familiar with the 'I knew nothing' and 'my eyes failed' posture in the hyacinth garden, she asks 'Do / You know nothing? Do you see nothing?' (121–2). Confirming the thematic link between the two scenes, the original draft follows the woman's question 'Do you remember / Nothing?' with the response, 'I remember

/ The hyacinth garden.'[16] Cancelling this reference to the hyacinth garden in the published version of the poem, Eliot seems to have reconsidered the matter of the connection between the two scenes when the time came to compose his notes. His note to the revised lines – 'I remember / Those are pearls that were his eyes' – reads 'Cf. Part I, l. 37, 48' (CPP, 77). L. 48 is the same line about 'pearls' and 'eyes' quoted from *The Tempest*; l. 37 is the line about coming back late 'from the hyacinth garden'. The note remembers the hyacinth garden, even if the line in the poem no longer does, and thus reinvigorates a connection between the two scenes in danger of being muted by the revision of the poem.

The speaker in 'A Game of Chess' seems to have concluded that the danger represented by woman can be avoided by avoiding communication. The speaker's reaction by accident in the hyacinth garden – he fails to communicate and so becomes silent – thus becomes the reaction by choice in the bedroom – he refuses to communicate and so remains silent. The man in 'A Game of Chess' refuses to converse with the woman despite five different conversational gambits on her part: 'Speak to me'; 'What is that noise?'; 'Do / You know nothing?'; 'Are you alive, or not?'; 'What shall I do now?' (112, 117, 121–2, 126, 131). Yet his internal, unvoiced responses to her questions tell us a good deal about his view of their relationship and the lesson that he has taken from it.

As in 'Gerontion', the speaker raises the issue of sexual performance. Whereas Gerontion can 'stiffen', however, the speaker in 'A Game of Chess' cannot. His cryptic response to the question about what he is thinking is suggestive: 'I think we are in rats' alley / Where the dead men lost their bones' (115–16). In British and American slang, *bone* has long meant 'the erect penis'. Appearing here in the context of a collapsing relationship, the word cannot escape this sexual dimension: the speaker is confessing to a loss of physical desire for the woman, if not to a more general impotence. Unlike Gerontion, the speaker cannot even make a show of sexual passion. The lack of physical connection between the man and the woman is emphasized by the woman's suggestion that she will walk the streets in her night attire: 'I shall rush out as I am, and walk the street / With my hair down, so' (132–3). Her threat to present herself as prostitute parodies the invitation to intimacy expressed by the hyacinth girl – the body language represented by hair figuring the invitation to sexual behaviour in each case. The man in 'A

Game of Chess' has rejected this invitation just as the man in the hyacinth garden did.

Although the woman at the beginning of 'A Game of Chess' is not equated with Satan, she seems to the speaker to be such a threat that he aligns her with so dangerous a figure as the murderer in Webster's *The White Devil*. Whereas the woman in 'A Game of Chess' asks her companion, 'What are you thinking of? what thinking?', Webster's murderer asks his victim, 'What dost thou think on?' (113).[17] The speaker's internal response to the question about what the wind is doing – 'Nothing again nothing' – duplicates the victim's answer in *The White Devil* to the murderer's question about what he is thinking: 'Nothing; of nothing. . . . I remember nothing' (120).[18] At the beginning of 'A Game of Chess', therefore, the man is the victim and the woman is the potential murderer: she is poisonous; she drowns the senses.

The associations that lead to the speaker's next thought – 'I remember / Those are pearls that were his eyes' – are manifold and yet manifestly continuous with the theme of the mystical potential in experience of the void at the centre of human relations. This line from *The Tempest* is appropriate enough as an allusion in a scene in which the speaker depicts himself as a potential victim of a murderer and in a poem whose epigraph states, 'I want to die.' The line also recalls the Tarot reading by Madame Sosostris, and, as we have seen, Eliot's note for 'A Game of Chess' refers readers to the the speaker's recollection of this very line during that Tarot reading. Eliot's note also refers readers to the hyacinth garden scene, implying a link between this scene and the line from *The Tempest* (a link acknowledged at this point in Part II of the original draft by the line, 'I remember / The hyacinth garden'). The link is through the 'nothings' that these two scenes share: the woman's questions – 'Do / You know nothing? Do you see nothing? Do you remember / Nothing?' (121–3) – recall the line from the hyacinth garden scene, 'I knew nothing.' The states of nothingness experienced by the speaker in the hyacinth garden and by the speaker in 'A Game of Chess' are related: both mark the end of a relationship with another person.

The line from *The Tempest* is about the rich and strange transformation that paradoxically comes out of the nothingness of death. It serves in 'A Game of Chess' to introduce again the speaker's suspicion that something can come of the nothingness in the middle of human relations. The line's recollection of simultaneously watery death and beautiful renewal must be read against the background of Madame Sosostris's warning to 'Fear death by water' and the speaker's identification of woman with water (her perfumes drown the senses). We then find in the line the speaker's ambivalent attitude toward 'death by water'. Should he ever die by succumbing to an invitation like that proffered by the hyacinth girl and the woman at the beginning of 'A Game of Chess' – that is, should he ever die by succumbing Prufrock-like to perfumes – his death would indeed be fearful, for it would in his eyes lead to distraction by physical passion from the 'simple, terrible and unknown'. It would be the death of his spirit. Should he die in a different sense – dying out of the world of physical passion rather than into it – then such a death would be a consummation devoutly to be wished. The tongue-lashings of the woman that prompt thoughts of rich and strange development from the nothingness of a failed relationship have perhaps caused a 'death by water' of this sort. They have extinguished desire and ironically proven the spur to recognition of the 'indestructible barriers' between people and recognition of the 'void' at the centre of human relationships.

The many dimensions of the speaker's thoughts in this part of the poem are summed up in his response to his companion's question about what they will do tomorrow. First, his ambiguous attitude toward water (symbolically woman) reappears: water that need not be feared is represented by the 'hot water at ten'; water that should be feared is represented by rain that would necessitate a 'closed car at four' (135–6). Next, his fear of seduction is represented by reference to 'a game of chess' (137). Eliot's note about this line reads: 'Cf. the game of chess in Middleton's *Women beware Women*' (CP, 77). In the play, the game of chess is played by a mother-in-law against the accomplice of a man who is seducing the woman's daughter-in-law in another room. Checkmate in the one game equals successful seduction in the other. Eliot reverses both the roles of the genders and the result of the game in *The Waste Land*, as the man staves off mate by staving off his mate. Finally, the death into a new life that both the speaker in 'A Game of Chess' and the speaker in the hyacinth garden scene glimpse as a possibility of this refusal of mate is anticipated in the suggestion that the speaker is 'waiting for a knock upon the door' (138). Although in the original draft of Part II of *The Waste Land* the speaker seems to anticipate the knock of the chambermaid, the muting of this context in the published poem brings into greater relief the allusion to Christ's words in Revelation: 'Behold, I stand at the door, and knock: if any man hear my voice, and open the door, I will come in to him.'[19] In *The Waste Land*, the experience of the void in the middle of human relations leads always to a glimpse of something other and beyond.

Although it might seem that the important mystical moment in the speaker's life occurred long ago in the hyacinth garden with the glimpse of the heart of light, the reflections upon the scene in the hyacinth garden that occur first in Part I of the poem (when the events in the hyacinth garden are recalled) and then in the bedroom conversation in Part II (when the events in the hyacinth garden are repeated) are in Eliot's terms the true mystical moments. In them, the speaker perceives 'the indestructible barriers between one human being and another' through the void at the centre of his relationships with women. The result is mysticism and misogyny. Eliot is not shy about acknowledging that his mysticism depends upon a certain hatred. As we have seen in his letter to More, for Eliot perception of the void in human relations is bound up with a 'disgust' for life that only Christianity can help him to overcome. Similarly, in 'Cyril Tourneur' (1930), he seems to have this experience of the void in mind when he writes that 'the loathing and horror of life itself . . . the hatred of life is an important phase – even, if you like, a mystical experience in life itself' (SE, 190). The mystical moments in *The Waste Land* spring from such hatred of life, yet this hatred of life locates itself at this time in a more particular phenomenon: the hatred of women.

Woman, in fact, is the symbol upon which the Eliotic speaker grounds his mysticism of loathing and hatred – not just in *The Waste Land*, but also in 'The Love Song of J. Alfred Prufrock', 'The Love Song of Saint Sebastian', 'The Death of Saint Narcissus', and 'Gerontion'. She is depicted according to the extreme stereotypes of the patriarchal imagination: woman as monstrous whore and woman as blessed virgin. The temptation to locate the speaker's misogyny in Eliot himself is almost overwhelming. Fear and hatred of women is recognizable in many of his portraits of women – from the woman in 'Hysteria' (1915) by whom the speaker is swallowed, to the woman in 'Ode' described as a 'Succuba eviscerate'.[20] His muse and succuba in one, Vivien Eliot is presumably the model for most of these women, and Eliot's fear and hatred of Vivien is presumably a large part of the fear and hatred directed towards these women in the poems. Perhaps surprisingly, then, one finds that *The Waste Land* also articulates a point of view other than these – an alternative point of view first introduced in 'A Game of Chess', an alternative point of view that makes sense of Eliot's consideration in 'The Fire Sermon' of mystical loathing and horror of life from a woman's perspective.

'A Game of Chess' urges alongside its misogyny the more subtle argument that men and women are alike victims – in different ways and to varying degrees – of a patriarchal history that has distorted their relationship. This argument permeates all of 'A Game of Chess' but comes into relief with the shift of the speaker's gaze from the woman to the room that contains both her and her gazing partner. Eliot's very long and apparently important (but actually quite silly) note about the word 'laquearia' (92) brings attention to the room's ceiling and walls. Upon these ceilings and walls are the culture's stories – what Cleanth Brooks takes to be nostalgic allusions to past glories, but what the poem itself marks more ambiguously as the 'withered stumps of time / . . . told upon the walls' (104–5).[21] The phallic image of the stump acknowledges the masculine sexual impulse so much a part of the stories told on the walls: the story of Cleopatra and Antony, the story of Dido and Aeneas, the story of Eve and Adam, the story of Philomel and Tereus. Yet this image of the phallus is also an image of a castrated phallus – it recalls Prufrock's word for his own life story, 'butt-ends' (CPP, 15) – and so acknowledges that although 'still the world pursues' such a story, it is no longer a viable one (102). These stories of destructive relationships between men and women literally shape the room in which the man and the woman at the beginning of 'A Game of Chess' reside as surely as they shape symbolically the socialized space in which Albert and Lil reside. Implying a certain claustrophobia, the speaker notes that 'staring forms / Leaned out, leaning, hushing the room enclosed' (105–6). The perpetuation of these 'withered stumps of time' in the modern world is the force that wastes the land: 'we are in rat's alley / Where the dead men lost their bones' (115–16). Only Lil and the speaker seem to have begun to reconcile themselves to a world without 'bones'; Lil's friend and the nervous woman still pursue them, not recognizing that they are now but 'withered stumps'.

This aspect of 'A Game of Chess' makes less surprising the mystical moment in 'The Fire Sermon'. In the voice of a woman – to be precise, in the three voices of women identified in the Notes as 'the (three) Thames Daughters' – Eliot presents the moment between the hyacinth garden of Part I and the bedroom of Part II (CPP, 78). That is, his Thames Daughters between them manage to depict a seduction such as might have followed the moment in the hyacinth garden and such as might have initiated the ill-fated relationship that appears in the first part of 'A Game of Chess'. 'The Fire Sermon' is largely about seduction or attempted seduction – of the 'nymphs' by the 'loitering heirs of City directors', of the speaker by Mr Eugenides, and of the typist by the 'young man carbuncular' (CPP, 175, 180, 231). Only the Thames Daughters, however, have reflected upon the matter and judged it.

The first Thames Daughter is aligned by Eliot's note with Pia de Tolomei in Dante's *Purgatorio*, a woman murdered by her husband. Imitating the diction in Dante's lines, the Thames Daughter indicates not that she has been unmade, but that she has been undone – 'Richmond and Kew / Undid me' (293–4) – a word meaning 'to ruin by seduction'. The posture of raised knees that she assumed 'Supine on the floor of a narrow canoe' was the prelude to sexual intercourse (295). The next Thames Daughter – mysteriously and supinely continuous with the first, and so participating in the same sexual exercise – speaks 'After the event' (297). Whether or not the sexual event was physically consummated is not clear, but that the male partner should have 'wept' and 'promised "a new start"' suggests that the event was unfulfilling in some way – and devastatingly so, for him (298). The Thames Daughter's response to the event is very different. It replicates that of the male speaker in the hyacinth garden and that of the partner of the nervous woman in the bedroom: 'I made no comment' (299). Here the woman – not the man – is the unspeaking spectator within the relationship, and here the woman – not the man – is presented as the one being harmed. Yet she has observed the same thing: an unbridgeable gap between man and woman in relationship. Her rhetorical question – 'What should I resent?' – suggests a despair that the relationship could ever be fulfilling (299). She implies that if she did not anticipate the particular failure that she contemplates, then she ought to have anticipated failure in general. Whatever the failure, it could not have been resented, for nothing else could have been expected.

To the third Thames Daughter is left the task of articulating the recognition of 'the void . . . in the middle of all human happiness and all human relations' to which the experience in the canoe leads. Like the speaker in the hyacinth garden, and like the partner of the nervous woman in the bedroom, the third Thames Daughter encounters 'nothing': 'I can connect / Nothing with nothing' (301–2). Her consciousness is fragmented. Popping into it first is the memory of the 'dirty hands' of her seducer (303). Into it next comes a recollection of her humble background: 'My people humble people who expect / Nothing' (304–5). Ironically, then, her suggestion that she cannot connect anything with anything else is belied by the sequence of recollections that rounds to a close on this word 'Nothing'. Far from confessing here to an inability to connect one thing with another, the third Thames Daughter is explaining to herself the sequence of cause and effect in her life. The 'Nothing' from her past is connected to the 'nothing' in her present by more than the coincidence of the word that is used to describe both states. Her humble background has led her to make contact with the sort of man who has 'dirty hands' – part and parcel of the men with 'dirty ears' and 'Exploring hands' who populate the poem (303, 103, 240). Brought up to expect nothing, she has entered a relationship that amounts to nothing.

Following another instance of a failed relationship between a man and a woman, the apparent emphasis on the inability to connect is appropriate, but the lines 'I can connect / Nothing with nothing' are ambiguous. Breaking the line where he does – 'I can connect' – Eliot allows it a positive dimension. In fact, this affirmative phrase combines with our tendency to understand 'nothing' as something – whether metaphysically, mathematically, psychologically, or grammatically – to encourage a reading by which the speaker seems to be declaring that she has learned how to connect one kind of nothing with another kind of nothing. Like the man recalling the line from *The Tempest* in 'A Game of Chess', the Thames daughter is at the point of failure in human relationship when something might be made out of nothing.

The something that the Thames daughters would make turns out to be a kind of nothing. Singing with one voice again as of line 307 ('la la'), the Thames Daughters conclude their song with the expression of a desire to escape desire. They sing fragments of St Augustine's *Confessions* and the Buddha's Fire Sermon and thereby insinuate into Part III an ascetic response to the previous scenes of seduction. Eliot's Notes assert that 'The collocation of these two representatives of eastern and western asceticism, as the culmination of this part of the poem, is not an accident' (CPP, 79). The experience of the nothingness at the centre of human relationships leads to nothing through naughting – the asceticism with which Part III concludes. Neither is it an accident that Part III should conclude with a suggestion of oscillation between a burning with desire for created things and a burning away of desire as in a purging flame, for Eliot later confessed to More that he was 'one of those whom the sense of void tends to drive towards asceticism or sensuality.'[22] Whether in *The Waste Land* or 'The Love Song of Saint Sebastian', asceticism and sensuality are alike responses to the 'something . . . simple, terrible and unknown' glimpsed through the void between people.

The fourth mystical moment in *The Waste Land* occurs in response to the DA spoken by the Thunder. In an almost meta-mystical moment, the speaker reconsiders each of the mystical moments of loathing and horror introduced in Parts I, II and III. *Datta*, the injunction to 'give', recalls the hyacinth garden – recalls both the flowers *given* in the past and, a year later, the response to be *given* to the woman's invitation. *Dayadhvam* – commanding 'sympathise' – recalls the woman's plea for sympathy at the beginning of 'A Game of Chess'. The command to 'control' – *Damyata* – recalls both the loss of control by the man weeping after the event in the canoe and the demonstration of control by the man in the hyacinth garden scene before the inviting words and image of the hyacinth girl, by the man in 'A Game of Chess' before the nervous woman and by the Thames daughters before the weeping man.

   The mystical moment begins with another symbolically significant semantic oscillation between sensuality and asceticism. With the question 'what have we given?' the speaker recalls his giving of hyacinths to a girl once and his later failure to give her anything more. As in 'The Burial of the Dead', the speaker might be understood here to regret this failure, implying that only in a 'blood shaking' surrender of the heart to a person such as the hyacinth girl is existence to be found: 'The awful daring of a moment's surrender / Which an age of prudence can never retract / By this, and this only, we have existed' (402, 403-405). On this reading, the speaker implies that there was an actual surrender to which he can compare the failure to surrender in the hyacinth garden – presumably the surrender in the canoe or the surrender that preceded the relationship revealed in the bedroom in 'A Game of Chess'. Smith, however, understands the speaker to be confessing that this actual surrender 'has involved no acceptance of love, of the demands of life, but a yielding to lust.' The speaker and his partner have lived by a 'craven surrender to a tyranny of the blood'. Smith implies that this is what the speaker means when he says that 'By this, and this only, we have existed': there has been nothing in the relationship but lust. A sensuality redeemed from lust, however, can fill the emptiness: such is the import of the injunction to 'give'.[23]

Such a reading – possible, and also popular – goes against the grain of the ascetic sensibility revealed in the previous mystical experiences of loathing and horror before life. In these mystical moments, surrender to another person is resisted in the name of the divine 'heart of light', the divine 'knock upon the door', and a divine plucking out. Even to speak to one's companion would be too great a concession to the sensual claims of the other human being. Emphasizing the speaker's undiminished sense of the void at the centre of human happiness and human relations, Eliot's note to these lines identifies another allusion to Webster's *The White Devil*:

>   – o Men
> That lye upon your death-beds, and are haunted
> With howling wives, neere trust them, they'le re-marry
> Ere the worme pierce your winding sheete: ere the Spider
> Make a thinne curtaine for your Epitaphes.[24]

The allusion suggests that salvation does not lie in human relationships. As Bedient argues,

> By what logic or superiority to logic should one human being 'surrender' himself irrevocably to another? What was the hyacinth girl that she could command such a gift? The notions of giving and surrender are – outside of the mists of romanticism –

terrible and radical ones, and scandalous in any context but the supernatural. Clearly the protagonist finds 'giving' awesome and clearly the supernatural is the largest and final and determining context here – the one that decides the real, the existent.[25]

The life recounted in obituary and epitaph does not matter; the dispersal of material property by means of a will does not matter. Furthermore, emphasizing the ascetic spirit, the speaker suggests that the rooms are empty, so that there may be little to disperse. Thus the language of sensuality is in the end displaced by the language of asceticism here just as it is in the hyacinth garden, the bedroom and the canoe. Like St Bernard, Eliot's speaker has employed the language of earthly love – 'blood shaking my heart' – as a strategy for describing the desire for divine love (402).

The reference to having 'heard the key / Turn in the door' (411–12) recalls the conclusion of the non-conversation between the man and the woman in 'A Game of Chess' in a 'waiting for a knock upon the door'. The prison from which the speaker would escape is thus defined as the world in which the men and women of 'A Game of Chess' find themselves claustrophobically enclosed – and, worse, in which they find themselves violently intertwined. The folly of seeking salvation through relationship with another human being is suggested not just by this recollection of socialized violence between men and women but also by Eliot's note citing Bradley's *Appearance and Reality* on the question of the remoteness of our experiences from those of our fellow human beings:

> My external sensations are no less private to my self than are my thoughts or my feelings. In either case my experience falls within my own circle, a circle closed on the outside; and, with all its elements alike, every sphere is opaque to the others which surround it . . . . In brief, regarded as an existence which appears in a soul, the whole world for each is peculiar and private to that soul. (CPP, 80)

Although Jewel Spears Brooker emphasizes that neither Bradley in writing this passage nor Eliot in quoting it accepts solipsism – for Bradley, 'it is simply impossible to think of a self unless one has simultaneously in his mind an idea of a not-self' – the passage that Eliot introduces in his Notes reinforces the sense of the unbridgeable gap between people that is so much a part of the poem's mystical moments.[26] The point is not whether others exist, but to what extent connection with them *can* be and *ought* to be made.

Coriolanus is introduced here as a type of the figures in *The Waste Land* who are undone by their connections with other people. Shakespeare's play explores the tensions between the individual and society, depicting in Coriolanus a man whom pride sets so far apart from society as to make him an exile. Like the speaker in the hyacinth garden, the man in the bedroom and the woman in the canoe, Coriolanus eventually recognizes that his only defence against compromising connections with others is silence. Fed up with his own country, Coriolanus would admit no discourse with it were it not for his mother. At the approach of this person, the woman against whom he is defenceless, he identifies the way to his salvation: 'out, affection! / All bond and privilege of nature, break!'[27] His natural bonds unbroken, however, Coriolanus admits conversation with his mother − ambassador of Rome − and so is himself broken. From this point of view, the 'broken Coriolanus' (416) of *The Waste Land* is the man who has admitted 'affection' for mother, wife and country − against his better judgement.

Revival can come to such a broken figure (and is seen to do so throughout *The Waste Land*) only from 'aethereal rumours' heard in the depths of one's brokenness (415). A 'broken' Coriolanus − as sexually broken as the bridegroom in 'Ode' − will not revive physically. Not for him Gerontion's purposeful show. A dead man who has lost his bone, the speaker is trapped in a relationship with another human being − a relationship similar to that described at the beginning of 'A Game of Chess'. Waiting behind a locked door (Eliot's note about the door refers readers to Dante's *Inferno*, in which Count Ugolino hears the tower door below him being locked), the speaker is continuous with the speaker in 'A Game of Chess' who is trapped in the claustrophobic room with the nervous woman and waiting for a knock upon the door. As suggested by lines in the 'The Death of the Duchess' − much of which was to be transformed into Part II of *The Waste Land* − the key that the speaker has heard 'Turn in the door once and turn once only' is the key by which he has been locked in another's heart (412):

Under the brush her hair
Spread out in fiery points of will

Glowed into words, then was suddenly still.

'You have cause to love me, I did enter you in my heart
Before ever you vouchsafed to ask for the key.'[28]

Placed here in the mouth of the woman, this quotation from
Webster's *The White Devil* marks keys, doors, rooms and hearts in
the poem as the symbol of confinement within a relationship. 'The
Death of the Duchess' makes clear – and all too autobiographically,
no doubt – that the relationship between the man and the woman
in 'The Death of the Duchess' and 'A Game of Chess' constitutes
a prison:

It is terrible to be alone with another person. . . .

And if I said 'I love you' should we breathe
Hear music, go a-hunting as before?
The hands relax, and the brush proceed?
Tomorrow when we open to the chambermaid
When we open the door
Could we address her or should we be afraid?
If it is terrible alone, it is sordid with one more.

If I said 'I do not love you' we should breathe
The hands relax, and the brush proceed?
How terrible that it should be the same![29]

The repetition in this context of the word 'terrible' – it is 'terrible'
to be alone with another person, and it is 'terrible' that a declaration
of love or lack of love should have so little impact – echoes
the *Athenaeum* essay a few years before in which Eliot refers to
'something . . . simple, terrible and unknown' that can be glimpsed
in the mystical experience of 'the indestructible barriers between
one human being and another'.[30] 'The Death of the Duchess', the
beginning of 'A Game of Chess' and the *Dayadhvam* section of
'What the Thunder said' thus take up residence in the void at the
centre of human relationships in which only 'aethereal rumours'
provide hope and from which only a plucking can save.

In the *Damyata* section of 'What the Thunder said', the speaker
returns for a final time to a contemplation of the moment in the
hyacinth garden. The sailing imagery invoked by the quotations
from *Tristan und Isolde* is recalled by references to 'boat', 'sail and
oar'. The sea subsequently to separate speaker and hyacinth girl is

recalled as 'calm' (418–20). There is no mention of the garden, but the evening's aura of lost romantic opportunity is recalled. This recollection emphasizes that there was never a moment of 'blood shaking' surrender of the speaker's heart to the human heart of the girl in the hyacinth garden. The hyacinth girl's heart 'would have responded', but it was never 'invited' to do so (420–1). The original draft refers even more explicitly to the evening's romantic failure: 'You over on the shore [alternatively 'I left without you' or 'There I leave you'] / Clasping empty hands'.[31] The recollection of the moment's mystical dimension, however, is notably absent. The 'heart of light' is replaced by the memory of the hyacinth girl's human heart. Its humanness, and the human emotion that concerns the speaker in his final reference to the moment, is emphasized by his observation that the girl's heart was then as open to the control of his hands as was the sailboat. Like the woman in 'The Death of the Duchess', she seems to have entered him in her heart before he ever vouchsafed to ask for the key.

With this concluding recollection of the hyacinth girl, the poem's sequence of mystical moments comes full circle. As in Part I, we might read this passage as suggesting a regret for the failure in the garden: if only the speaker had invited her heart to respond! Yet the intertextual echoes of imprisoning keys and hearts in Part V function to introduce once more the speaker's suspicion – despite his nostalgia for the garden – that all such human relationships are dangerous. The question implied by the similarity of the posture of the heart of the nervous woman in Part II (as recollected in the *Dayadhvam* section of Part V) and the posture of the heart of the hyacinth girl in Part I (as set out most fully in the *Damyata* section of Part V) is whether having been entered into the hyacinth girl's heart would not in time have resulted in the same imprisonment for the speaker that came of being entered into the nervous woman's heart. According to Gordon's reconstruction of Eliot's romantic life, such was indeed Eliot's conclusion when years later he finally terminated his relationship with Emily Hale, the hyacinth girl.[32]

From the *Datta* of mystical surrender to the *Dayadhvam* of mistaken sympathy for the nervous woman and the *Damyata* of the speaker's wonder at his control of his human heart in the face of the hyacinth girl, the concluding mystical moment focuses upon the nothings that have shaped the speaker's mystical experience: the unexpected nothing offered to the hyacinth girl (left 'Clasping empty hands'), the mutually acknowledged nothing between the man and woman at the beginning of 'A Game of Chess' and the nothing that might be chosen by the awful surrender of oneself not to another but to something other. The speaker thus traces to the experience of 'nothing' in the hyacinth garden his first intimation of the void at the centre of human relationships – the void by which arises for him the opportunity to glimpse a 'simple, terrible and unknown' something beyond it.

6

A Broken Coriolanus

In reading 'Gerontion' and *The Waste Land* for evidence of Eliot's mysticism, I have focused on his personae's experience – as a result of the breakdown of their implicitly sexual relationships with other people – of something 'simple, terrible and unknown'. In his 1919 essay 'Beyle and Balzac', Eliot approves of novelists like Beyle, Flaubert, Dostoyevsky and perhaps even Turgenev; they have glimpsed this very thing and 'indicate . . . the indestructible barriers between one human being and another'. This experience is 'a "mysticism" not to be extracted from Balzac, or even from Miss Underhill'. In 1935, Eliot seems to describe the same experience – but this time with a sense of the salvation from isolation possible through his Christian faith:

> There are moments, perhaps not known to everyone, when a man may be nearly crushed by the terrible awareness of his isolation from every other human being; and I pity him if he finds himself only alone with himself and his meanness and futility, alone without God. It is after these moments, alone *with* God and aware of our worthiness, but for Grace, of nothing but damnation, that we turn with most thankfulness and appreciation to the awareness of our *membership*: for we appreciate and are thankful for nothing fully until we see where it begins and where it ends.[1]

This terrible awareness of isolation grounds in both 'Gerontion' and *The Waste Land* the mystical aspiration for the something 'simple, terrible and unknown' beyond the void at the centre of human relations. Following St John of the Cross, Eliot called this form of mysticism 'the way of dispossession' in 'East Coker' (CPP, 181). In a letter to his confessor William Force Stead in 1930, he described in very similar terms the experiences that presumably lie behind the poems and the essays of the 1918–22 period: he revealed that Stead's poem 'The House on the Wold' represented for him 'an emotional state that I know but have never seen so well expressed. This sense of dispossession I have known twice, at Marlow [1918] and at Périgueux [1919].'[2]

Ronald Schuchard traces to these horrific moments the inspiration for Eliot's depiction in *The Waste Land* of his horror before life in general and his horror before sex in particular.[3] The experience of dispossession at Périgueux occurred during a walking vacation in the south of France with Ezra Pound during the last three weeks of August 1919. Eliot took 'Gerontion' along with him, entreating a friend to return his early draft so that he could do so: '*Please* send *Gerontion* back to me at once. I leave Saturday night, and I must revise it in France.'[4] Gerontion's dispossession – 'I have lost my sight, smell, hearing, taste and touch' – no doubt symbolizes Eliot's own. Yet I suspect that it symbolizes what happened at Marlow more than it symbolizes what happened at Périgueux. 'Gerontion' is undoubtedly a poetic record of Eliot's feelings of isolation behind what he calls in contemporaneous prose the indestructible barriers between people. Yet he is writing of these things several months before his vacation and has completed the unrevised 'Gerontion' at least a week before leaving for Périgueux. Eliot's experience a year before at Marlow, that is, seems to have been the initial cause of the horror of life and human relations that came to plague him and to work its way into his poems, essays and letters. If I am correct in asserting in Chapter 4 that Gerontion is announcing a turn away from sex, and that Gerontion's announcement is symbolically Eliot's announcement of a similar turn away from Vivien, then I would guess that the experience at Périgueux is an echo of what happened at Marlow, where such a turn was first contemplated – 'Gerontion' functioning as the Trojan horse by which the most devastating of Eliot's experiences of dispossession was taken with him to Périgueux, there to be lived again in all its mystical intensity.

As Schuchard explains, what happened at Marlow is not entirely clear – and yet neither is it completely indecipherable:

> The nature of Eliot's professed dispossession at Marlow is unknown, but we do know that he had begun to live out, on a banal scale, a Jacobean nightmare of sexual mortality, compounded by his probable knowledge of the exploits of Bertrand Russell, who provided the cottage in Marlow [where the Eliots lived for the summer of 1918]. . . . Russell wrote to

his mistress, Lady Constance Malleson, that he began having sexual relations with Vivien in the autumn of 1917, and Eliot's intimation or discovery of this double infidelity may have been the cause of his spiritual devastation. He certainly knew that Russell had disturbed Vivien; early in 1919 he forbade her to answer Russell's letters and made his own difficult break with Russell. He later wrote to Ottoline Morrell that Russell had committed evil and that this 'spectacle' had been a significant factor in Eliot's eventual conversion.[5]

My readings of 'Gerontion' and *The Waste Land* suggest that it is from this experience of the void at the centre of his most intimate of human relations that Eliot appeals for a glimpse of 'the heart of light' and a hint of the plucking out that would eventually save him.

I have deferred discussion of Eliot's reaction to events at Marlow until after my discussion of 'Gerontion' and *The Waste Land* because it is only after publishing these poems that Eliot begins to doubt the whispers of immortality that he hears in mystical moments like the ones represented in these poems – mystical moments, that is, like the one at Marlow. His inclination to endow this mystical experience with absolute spiritual significance eventually leads him in The Clark Lectures and related essays and poems to scrutinize suspiciously the nature of his own mysticism. As we shall see in the chapters to follow, Eliot came to suspect – much to his own surprise and disappointment – that in his reactions to the feeling of dispossession at Marlow he was no less narcissistic a mystic than the degenerate figures in 'The Love Song of Saint Sebastian' and 'The Death of Saint Narcissus'. In The Clark Lectures, Eliot implicitly acknowledges the extent to which his mystical hatred of life in general and of women in particular is a function of his own emotional history.

To make this point most effectively, however, I will again have to defy publishing chronology in the interest of a chronology that better reflects the doublings-back so much a part of Eliot's spiritual development. Although The Clark Lectures – researched in 1925, but delivered at the beginning of 1926 – dismantle what Eliot had built up from his experience at Marlow, before examining them we must review Eliot's reinterpretation in the 1930s of his relation to D.H. Lawrence. This reinterpretation begins in The

Clark Lectures, and it is no coincidence that Eliot's reconsideration of his mysticism occurs alongside his reconsideration of Lawrence, for Lawrence comes to serve Eliot as a surrogate for his own mystical mistakes. But what is merely a Lawrentian subtext in The Clark Lectures is set out more clearly in prose and poetry written after The Clark Lectures. Here one can follow Eliot's awkward relationship with Lawrence and demonstrate his conclusion that each is a broken Coriolanus. In the light of this conclusion, one can return to the experience at Marlow and trace within it – as Eliot himself seems to have done – a history of mystical mistakes that only a broken Coriolanus could have made.

As I have suggested, the reconsideration of mysticism that Eliot undertakes in The Clark Lectures can be seen to be part of his response to the mysticism of Lawrence: 'There is always some type of mysticism about, whether that of Mr Russell, or Mr Lawrence, or Mr Murry; the number of types is limited, and it is possible and useful to distinguish them' (*Varieties*, 100). Murry and Russell are linked with Lawrence as examples of romantic mystics – according to Eliot, mystics given to confusing the human and the divine. Eliot amplifies his suggestion that Murry and Russell are mystics in essays written in the following year. Murry is criticized by Eliot for his 'depreciation of intelligence on the one hand, and . . . exaltation of intuition on the other.' It 'leads Mr Murry into making mistakes about his own intuitions.'[6] Russell's 'Non-Christianity is merely a variety of Low Church sentiment'. Eliot implies that although Russell's religion 'rests entirely upon emotional grounds', he mistakes the 'unreasoning prejudice' behind his views for reasoned argumentation.[7] Such confusion of human emotion with absolute truth is the kind of mysticism that Eliot finds it useful to distinguish because one can thereby more easily avoid it.

Eliot's disapproval of Lawrence's mysticism, however, took some time to surface. He was for a long time a fan of Lawrence's fiction. Writing in August of 1922, he confessed: 'in my opinion, the most interesting novelist in England . . . is Mr D.H. Lawrence.'[8] Similarly, later in the same year, he included high praise of Lawrence in a letter to his brother: 'there is certainly no contemporary novelist except D.H. Lawrence and of course Joyce in his way, whom I care to read.'[9] He knew his work well enough by 1919 to compare his earlier work with the most recent:

'What I have seen of [D.H.] Lawrence lately makes me think him thoroughly *dégringolé* [run down or in decline].'[10] The aspect of Lawrence that Eliot singles out for disapproval is his tendency to shift from description to explanation:

> Mr Lawrence has progressed – by fits and starts, it is true; for he has perhaps done nothing as good as a whole as *Sons and Lovers*. He has never yet, I think, quite surrendered himself to his work. He still theorizes at times when he should merely see. His theory has not yet reached the point at which it is no longer a theory, he still requires (at the end of *Aaron's Rod*) the mouthpiece for an harangue. But there is one scene in this book – a dialogue between an Italian and several Englishmen, in which one feels that the whole is governed by a creator who is purely creator, with the terrifying disinterestedness of the true creator. And for that we can forgive Mr Lawrence his subsequent lapse into a theory of human relationships.[11]

The harangue to which Eliot refers (the word 'harangue' is Lawrence's) is delivered to Aaron in the concluding chapter by his friend Lilly:

> Remember this, my boy: you've never got to deny the Holy Ghost which is inside you, your own soul's self. . . . You thought there was something outside, to justify you: God, or a creed, or a prescription. But remember, your soul inside you is your only Godhead. . . .
>
> But the mode of our being is such that we can only live and have our being whilst we are implicit in one of the great dynamic modes. We *must* either love, or rule. And once the love-mode changes, as change it must, for we are worn out and becoming evil in its persistence, then the other mode will take place in us. And there will be profound, profound obedience in place of this love-crying, obedience to the incalculable power-urge. And men must submit to the greater soul in a man, for their guidance: and women must submit to the positive power-soul in man, for their being.[12]

Lawrence's harangues, like Eliot's mystical experiences, are always concerned with human relationships. Although Eliot would later label Lawrence a heretic because of what he found in 'all of the relations of Lawrence's men and women: the absence of any moral or social sense', his objection in 1922 was against Lawrence's impure art, and not against the content of his theories: 'In the work of D.H. Lawrence, especially in his last book *Aaron's Rod*, is found the profoundest research into human nature, as well as the most erratic and uneven writing, by any writer of our generation.'[13]

In retrospect, one can see why Eliot sympathized with Lawrence. Each was intent on exposing the inadequacy of the 'love-mode' in human relationships. The foregrounding of the failure of human relationships in poems like 'Gerontion' and *The Waste Land* demonstrates Eliot's agreement with Lawrence's claim in virtually all of his fiction up to 1922 that something had gone wrong with the 'love-mode'. Eliot's depiction of the hyacinth girl as somewhat Dis-like implies that his speaker agrees with Lawrence that there is even something evil in its persistence. Eliot certainly shares with Lawrence the hope of getting beyond the stage of 'love-crying'. Furthermore, each locates his mystical moment somewhere beyond the failure of this mode of human relationship.

And yet one can also see why the sympathy could not last. Whereas Lawrence advocates a new mode of human love relationship (elevating the role of the body even beyond that which it served in the old 'love-mode'), Eliot would move beyond human relationship altogether – giving up sensuality for asceticism. Not surprisingly, then, even in this largely positive review of Lawrence's work in 1922 one can see hints of Eliot's later construction of Lawrence as a failed mystic. Borrowing the language of his earlier essay on 'Dante', he recognizes that Lawrence, like Dante, has the potential to 'see'. Yet whereas in Dante 'We are not . . . studying the philosophy, we *see* it, as part of the ordered world', in Lawrence 'theory has not yet reached the point at which it is no longer a theory' (SW, 170). Dante is a 'true mystic', and Lawrence is not – at least not yet. He is one of the moderns whose vision Eliot finds 'comparatively restricted' (SW, 171).

Eliot was seduced into his tolerant attitude toward Lawrence's mysticism by the coincidence of their similar psychological histories. He recognized *Sons and Lovers* to be as much his own story as Lawrence's and so he mistook Lawrence's fiction for 'the profoundest research into human nature . . . by any writer of our generation.' He did not at first recognize that the human nature that Lawrence was exploring was merely his and Eliot's own. When he came to suspect Lawrence – and thereby himself

– of this narcissism, he began to see the dangers of Lawrence's mysticism everywhere: as much in the committed Lawrentians like Murry as in the one-time Lawrentians like Russell, alike mistakers of their own intuition and their own 'unreasoning prejudice' for truth. For Eliot, disentangling his own psychological history (and the mysticism consequent upon it) from Lawrence's psychological history (and the mysticism consequent upon it) thus becomes an important subtext of The Clark Lectures.

Such a disentangling is the main goal of his 1931 review of *Son of Woman: The Story of D.H. Lawrence*, by John Middleton Murry. The review represents a self-conscious retraction of his tolerant attitude toward Lawrence of ten years before. Whereas he could once 'forgive' the sort of theorizing in which Lawrence defined the Holy Ghost for his own purposes, Eliot draws attention in 1931 to the intolerable nature of the very harangue that he had tolerated in 1922:

> a peculiarity which to me is both objectionable and unintelligible . . . is using the terminology of Christian faith to set forth some philosophy or religion which is fundamentally non-Christian or anti-Christian. It is a habit towards which Mr Lawrence has inclined his two principal disciples, Mr Murry himself and Mr Aldous Huxley. The variety of costumes into which these three talented artists have huddled the Father, the Son, and the Holy Ghost, in their various charades, is to me offensive. Perhaps if I had been brought up in the shadowy Protestant underworld within which they all seem gracefully to move, I might have more sympathy and understanding; I was brought up outside the Christian fold, in Unitarianism; and in the form of Unitarianism in which I was instructed, things were either black or white. The Son and the Holy Ghost were not believed in, certainly; but they were entitled to respect as entities in which many other people believed, and they were not to be employed as convenient phrases to embody any cloudy private religion. I mention this autobiographical detail simply to indicate that it is possible for unbelievers as well as believers to consider this sort of loose talk to be, at the best, in bad taste.[14]

In 1922, curiously, the then unbelieving Eliot had not thought the harangue at the end of *Aaron's Rod* to be in bad taste at all. Yet the terms of his argument nine years later suggest that he *ought* to have found it to be in bad taste. After all, Eliot explains his recourse to 'autobiographical detail' as necessary to present himself as an example of an 'unbeliever' who had indeed found it possible *when he was an unbeliever* to consider Lawrence's 'loose talk to be, at the best, in bad taste'. The combination here of an echo of the passage that he could 'forgive' in 1922 (despite its costuming of the Holy Ghost in such strange garb) and the 'autobiographical detail' that directs attention to Eliot's pre-conversion reaction to Lawrence's harangues suggests that Eliot feels the perverse need in 1931 both to acknowledge his earlier tolerance and to deny that it ever existed.

The harangue at the end of *Aaron's Rod* and Eliot's 1922 analysis of it are recalled once more in the assessment of Lawrence in the next paragraph of the review:

> a fault which corrupts his whole philosophy of human relations – which is hardly anything *but* a philosophy of human relations and unrelations – is his hopeless attempt to find some mode in which two persons – of the opposite sex, and then as a venture of despair, of the same sex – may be spiritually united.[15]

The word 'mode' is from the concluding harangue about the 'love-mode' in Lawrence's novel. The phrase 'philosophy of human relations' is similar to the 1922 phrase 'theory of human relationships'. Otherwise, this passage represents a reversal of the assessment in 1922: what was then just a 'lapse' into theory for which Lawrence might be forgiven is by 1931 regarded as always having been the predominant feature of Lawrence's fiction. Eliot implies in 1922 that although 'His theory has not yet reached the point at which it is no longer a theory', Lawrence is apparently very near the point. Yet he implies in 1931 that Lawrence never came close to the point in question: his philosophy of human relations 'is hardly anything *but* a philosophy of human relations and unrelations'. It is never merely seen, or observed 'with the terrifying disinterestedness of the true creator'.[16] Again, in 1931, Eliot rewrites what he wrote in 1922 as what he now feels that he ought to have written in 1922: Lawrence's failure is not so much an aesthetic failure as a spiritual failure.

On the one hand criticizing Lawrence harshly, Eliot hints on the other that he recognizes that he and Lawrence share the problem of a 'mother-complex' – encouraging biographical speculation in this direction: 'It is a definitive work of critical biography . . . so well done that it gives me the creeps. . . . [A]ny author still living might shudder to think of the possibility of such a book of destructive criticism being written about him after he is dead.' In the review, Eliot seems not only to have been thinking of the possibility of such a biography about himself, but also to have begun an autobiographical apology in anticipation of such a biography. First, he attempts to lessen the stigma associated with such a complex – distinguishing it from the 'Oedipus Complex': 'the common designation of "Oedipus Complex"' is 'inappropriate'. Second, he naturalizes the complex by marking it as omnipresent in human history: 'the "mother-complex" of Lawrence does not seem to me in itself a sign of the times. I find it difficult to believe that a family life like that of Lawrence's parents is peculiar either to a particular class or to a particular age.' Third, he ennobles the complex by making it a sign of 'a sensitive child': 'Such family life, with such consequences to a sensitive child, can hardly have taken place only in the latter part of the nineteenth century.' Finally, he argues that the problems that come of Lawrence's mother-complex are the result not so much of the complex itself as of Lawrence's reaction to it:

> I do not think that the unfortunate initial experience of Lawrence's life led *necessarily* to the consequences that came. He would probably have been always an unhappy man in this world; there is nothing unusual about that; many people have to be unhappy in this world, to do without things which seem essential and a matter of course to the majority; and some learn not to make a fuss about it, and to gain, or at least to strive towards, a kind of peace which Lawrence never knew.[17]

It is difficult not to suspect that Eliot includes himself in the category of those who have learned not to make a fuss about the mother-complex and the disappointments in life that may come one's way because of it.

The exercise of disentangling his own story from that of Lawrence is thus made necessary both by the impulse to identify with Lawrence that Eliot felt as late as 1922 and by the similarity of their early experiences, which Eliot acknowledges here. In arguing that Lawrence's problem does not reside in the experience of the mother-complex, but rather in his response to it, Eliot limits his own task to the disentangling of Lawrence's response to the mother-complex from his own response to it. When he focuses upon Lawrence's response to this complex, Eliot once again points to himself at the same time as he points to Lawrence:

> Mr Murry quotes a sentence of Gourmont which I have quoted myself: *ériger en lois ses impressions personelles, c'est le grand effort d'un homme s'il est sincère* [it is the great endeavour of every man, if he is sincere, to establish his personal sensations as a law]. Well, Lawrence tried to do that, certainly, but to my mind he failed completely.

Whereas Eliot can handle his '*impressions personelles*', Lawrence 'could neither leave his sensations alone and accept them simply as they came, nor could he generalize them correctly.' Lawrence fails 'by the adoption of a crazy theory to deal with the facts'.[18] Eliot presumably does not.

Yet the fear that animates the review – the fear that Eliot has been and perhaps remains closer to Lawrence than he would wish – is not allayed. The first and last paragraphs combine both to bracket the review and to bracket Eliot and Lawrence together within it. Eliot closes his first paragraph with a compliment to Murry on his 'definitive work of critical biography': 'no one but Mr Murry could have done it; and I doubt whether Mr Murry himself could do it to anyone but Lawrence. The victim and the sacrificial knife are perfectly adapted to each other.'[19] Eliot recalls this metaphor from his own review of Murry's work, *Cinnamon and Angelica: A Play* (1920): 'It is . . . a real pleasure, an exceptional pleasure, to have a patient like Mr Murry extended on the operating table; we need our sharpest instruments, and steadiest nerves, if we are to do him justice.'[20] The redeployment of this metaphor in 1931 establishes ratios of relationship amongst all three figures. The 1931 version presents Murry as a surrogate for Lawrence: he is a type of the sword-wielding priestly rival who would replace his victim, the Priest at Nemi. The 1920 version presents Murry as an ironic surrogate for Eliot. The latter attributes to himself the same role of sword-wielding acolyte that he later attributes to Murry *vis-à-vis* Lawrence. Murry and Eliot are rivals in the service of poetic drama, and Eliot is doing Murry justice by doing him in: 'we cannot say that Mr Murry has given himself away . . . , for his "close-knit intertexture" is a maze of such subtilized and elusive feelings as will hardly be threaded by any but those whom he would be willing to admit.'[21] Eliot has penetrated to the inner sanctum of Murry's meaning and discovered that poetic drama needs a new priest. The intertextual dimension of the metaphor in 1931 combines the function by which Murry is a surrogate for Eliot with the function by which Murry is a surrogate for Lawrence so as to infuse the review with a fear that through their common surrogate Eliot and Lawrence are related.

Each of these ratios is demonstrated in the review. First, Eliot introduces Murry as a little Lawrence – respectfully carving up his precursor. Then, less directly, he introduces Murry as an earlier version of himself. Remembering his rivalry with Murry in priestly service of a modern aesthetic, Eliot imputes to Murry an interest in impure art: 'I wonder . . . whether, had Lawrence been a success in this sense [as a pure artist] instead of a failure, Mr Murry would have been so interested in him.' Eliot thereby simultaneously forgets and remembers his own interest in 1922 in Lawrence the impure artist who could not 'see' his theory but was nonetheless interesting as a keen explorer of human nature. Murry is a lesser Eliot – a whipping-boy who has inherited punishment for another's indiscretions. Finally, Eliot introduces Murry as the intermediary between himself and Lawrence. Thus, in the face of a passage from *Lady Chatterly's Lover* demonstrating what he calls the 'complacent egotism' of 'a very sick soul', Eliot writes, 'I should like to be sure that it shocked Mr Murry, as a confession, as deeply as it shocks me.' Eliot insults Murry by implying that his soul is as sick as Lawrence's, yet at the same time he reveals his worry that Murry remains sufficiently an Eliot-surrogate for Murry's shocked reaction to be required as a reinforcing supplement to his own. Eliot would thus banish the influence of Lawrence and Murry alike:

> Unwillingly in part, I admit that this is a great tragic figure, a waste of great powers of understanding and tenderness. We may feel poisoned by the atmosphere of his world, and quit it with relief; but we cannot deny our homage as we retire. A fateful influence he must have been upon those who experienced his power; I cannot help wondering whether Mr Murry was not

compelled to write his book in order to expel the demon from himself; and if so, I wonder whether Mr Murry has succeeded.[22]

There is more homage to Lawrence than Eliot recognizes in his review, and there is sufficient evidence of Lawrence's fateful influence upon Eliot both in this review and in earlier prose to invite one to read lines about Murry as self-reflexive: one must wonder if Eliot wrote his review in order to expel the demon of Lawrence from himself, and if so, whether he succeeded.

Eliot's worries about his relation to Lawrence are brought into focus by his 1931 poem, 'Coriolan'. Written after his review of Murry's book, 'Coriolan' incorporates Lawrence and his mother-complex within a trope that Eliot had been exploring in his poetry for thirteen years. Lawrence was aware of his mother-complex: '[Murry] makes clear that Lawrence was pretty well aware of what was wrong.'[23] Eliot uses Murry and Lawrence to show that he, too, was aware of his own mother-complex – and not just in 1931, but also as early as 1918, for through Murry's account of Lawrence, Eliot finds a label for an experience that he had been exploring in his poetry at least since 'Ode' (1918).

Coriolanus figures for Eliot not so much the tragedy consequent upon pride as the Lawrentian tragedy consequent upon 'the emotional dislocation of a "mother-complex"'.[24] In 'Coriolan', Eliot emphasizes the importance of Coriolanus's mother in her son's life. In *Coriolanus*, the First Citizen argues that what Coriolanus has 'done famously' he did 'to please his mother and to be partly proud.'[25] Volumnia recalls for her son his own acknowledgement of this fact and asks him to please her by ignoring his own will and submitting to hers:

> I prithee now, sweet son, as thou hast said
> My praises made thee first a soldier, so,
> To have my praise for this, perform a part
> Thou hast not done before. (3.2.107–10)

According to Ackroyd, the Coriolanus that Eliot recalls in his poem 'is a man raised and then destroyed by his mother, as he becomes impaled upon the emotions which spring from his devotion to her.'[26] Having yielded to his mother's fatal request that he not press his advantage against Rome, Coriolanus explains what will come of this devotion to his mother:

> O mother, mother!
> What have you done? Behold, the heavens do ope,
> The gods look down, and this unnatural scene
> They laugh at. O my mother, mother! O!
> You have won a happy victory to Rome;
> But for your son – believe it, O believe it! –
> Most dangerously you have with him prevailed,
> If not most mortal to him. (5.3.182–9)

In Eliot's poem, the same plaintive cry occurs in the less glorious but equally political context of failure in the twentieth century:

> A commission is appointed
> To confer with a Volscian commission
> About perpetual peace. . . .
> What shall I cry?
> Mother mother. . . .
> Mother
> May we not be sometime, almost now, together.
> (CPP, 129–30)

Eliot's shift from the traditional focus on Coriolanus's pride to his desire to 'be sometime, almost now, together' with his mother is facilitated by Murry's description of Lawrence's life story as 'an appalling narrative of spiritual pride'.[27] For Murry, the mother-complex and spiritual pride are part of the same story. Eliot not only makes the same connection in 'Coriolan', but makes it with Lawrence's help. The 'Mother mother' cry of Eliot's Coriolanus is conflated both with the 'mother, mother' cry of Shakespeare's Coriolanus and with the 'Mother . . . mother' cry of Paul Morel at the end of *Sons and Lovers*:

> 'Mother!' he whispered – 'mother!'
> She was the only thing that held him up, himself, amid all this. And she was gone. . . . He wanted her to touch him, have him alongside with her.[28]

Written in the same year that he wrote his review of Murry's biography of Lawrence, 'Coriolan' suggests that Eliot had by 1931 come to · understand at least his own Coriolanus – if

not Shakespeare's Coriolanus – as suffering from a Lawrentian
mother-complex.

By this development in the 1930s of the Coriolanus figure
present in his work since 1918, Eliot mandates a retrospective
survey of the development of this figure. Has he superimposed
upon this figure in 1931 an association with the mother-complex
not present in earlier instances of the figure? Or has he finally
labelled as 'mother-complex' a psychological phenomenon all
along a part of this figure's significance for him? The question
is important in this study, for Eliot also makes clear in 1931 that
'Coriolan' is part of his reconsideration of mysticism. In a 1931
letter to none other than Murry himself, Eliot describes 'Coriolan'
as potentially a four-part poem, the fourth part – about which
he is least confident – deriving from St John of the Cross.[29] Is
Coriolanus's role in Eliot's engagement with mysticism new in
1931, or is this a role that the Coriolanus figure has always played?

As we have seen, the reference to Coriolanus in *The Waste Land*
plays its part in the poem's mysticism: it continues the poem's focus
on connection between people and constitutes a warning about its
dangers. Eliot also employs an allusion to Coriolanus in his earlier
poem 'Ode' (1918). 'Ode' depicts the morning after a honeymoon
night, presenting a bridegroom contemplating the blood left upon
the bed by a 'Succuba eviscerate' and indignant at the sordidly
abrupt end of the sexual activity the night before.[30] The epigraph
quotes the lines in which Coriolanus identifies himself to his rival
Aufidius as one who has done 'To you particularly, and to all the
Volscians / Great hurt and mischief'.[31] Gordon speculates that
the poem is about Eliot's own honeymoon and a problem with
premature ejaculation.[32] Ackroyd speculates that the extinction
of desire emphasized in the poem is due to Vivien Eliot, who
'wished for male devotion but did not particularly enjoy any
physical expression of it.'[33] Spender sees in 'Ode' the 'secret of
a method' that 'will later explode in *The Waste Land*. The key
idea is that the private failure of the sacrifice and sacrament, which
is ritual between bride and bridegroom, is the result of the public
failure of creativity within the civilization.'[34]

In these readings, the connection between 'Ode' and *Coriolanus*
is not clear. Smith implies that Coriolanus is invoked because the
speaker is in the end 'vanquished, like Coriolanus'.[35] Reading

'Ode' in the light of 'Coriolan', however, allows one to argue that Eliot's autobiographical persona in 'Ode' – the sexually dysfunctional man of the twentieth century – is placed beside one of his classical forebears because they share a mother-complex, a mother-complex in each case dislocated (to use Eliot's word from the 1931 review) into military affairs.

The subtitle of the poem – 'on Independence Day, July 4th 1918' – introduces the military motif and the theme of divided allegiances that the allusion to *Coriolanus* takes up. The reference to Independence Day identifies the writing of the poem as in part a response to the feelings of patriotism aroused in Eliot upon American entry into the European War in 1917. Setbacks for the Allied Forces and the United States (an Associated Power) in the spring of 1918, Independence Day celebrations in London in July, and the frequency with which Eliot was being asked questions about baseball (because of the visibility of American and Canadian soldiers playing the game in London at the time) seem to have prompted Eliot to rethink his role as American in Britain. (In July, he began seriously to pursue opportunities to join the American army.) As Ackroyd observes, Eliot's attitude towards his own nationality was at this time ambiguous: 'Although he referred to Americans as "us" in a letter to John Quinn, he was also in the same year referring to the English as "we".'[36] In short, he was in the position of Coriolanus – experiencing allegiances to two countries (the Britain in which his new home was based, and the America in which he was born). The epigraph complements this aspect of the poem's biographical origin by locating Coriolanus at the moment when he breaks with Rome and offers his services to the Volscians.

Although the obscure poem that follows title and epigraph hardly seems related to either, 'Ode' constitutes a review of the reasons why Eliot had not returned to America upon completion of the Harvard fellowship that had taken him to Oxford, and so the poem's content actually coheres with a title and epigraph that conspire to insinuate into the poem the theme of national allegiance. Letters on Eliot's behalf by his friends suggest that his reasons for forsaking his American home and family and staying in England were his poetry and his marriage. Two days after Eliot's marriage, Pound wrote to Eliot's father on the subject of his son's prospects in London as a poet: 'Your son asked me to write this letter, I think he expects me to send you some sort of apologia for the literary life in general, and for London literary life in particular.'[37] The next year, Bertrand Russell wrote of Eliot's prospects as poet to J.H. Woods, the supervisor at Harvard of Eliot's doctoral work: 'My view is that he is right to live in Europe because the atmosphere of Europe is better for that sort of work; and that is the sort of work he ought to aim at doing.'[38] The first section of 'Ode' reviews Eliot's career as poet from the perspective of the events of 1918: the speaker is a poet – tired, uninspired and misunderstood, contemplating retirement. His being tired and uninspired echoes Eliot's letter to John Quinn earlier in the year: 'I have only written half a dozen small poems in the last year, and the last I have been unable to finish. . . . The cause has been chiefly the simple reason of lack of time, and in the second place I have been too tired to do any original work.'[39] In this stanza, mocking laughter (so much a part of Eliot's poetry) marks the absence of poetic inspiration – from the sacred wood (a similar phrase in the poem anticipating the title of Eliot's first collection of criticism) to the river of inspiration that is now noxiously uninspired. The first stanza's transition from actually tired poet to potentially retired poet is thus less shocking: retirement as poet in order to join the American armed services is not the loss it once might have seemed.

Unacknowledged in the poem but for the indirections of the subtitle and epigraph is the extent to which this poetic retirement complicates a Coriolanean desire on Eliot's part to please his mother. Eliot's letters to Quinn explain another of the contexts in which the poem was written. He begins by mentioning the book for which he would soon write 'Ode': 'I wish that I had enough material for a volume of suitable size for the American public.'[40] The American public that Eliot wished to please by means of such a book consisted largely of his parents:

> I am not at all proud of the book. . . . But it is important to me that it should be published for private reasons. I am coming to America to visit my family some time within the summer or autumn, and I should particularly like to have it appear first. You see I settled over here in the face of strong family opposition, on the claim that I found the environment more favourable to the production of literature. This book is all I have to show for my claim – it would go toward making my parents contented with

conditions – and towards satisfying them that I have not made a mess of my life, as they are inclined to believe.[41]

Later in the month, after the death of his father, Eliot emphasized that it was his mother that he was out to please:

> I explained to you when I wrote last how important it was to me for family reasons to get something in the way of a book published in America. Since then my father has died, but this does not weaken the need for a book at all – it really reinforces it – my mother is still alive.[42]

Against this background, 'Ode' can be seen in a double light: on the one hand, it as an attempt to add a poem to a book that will justify to his mother Eliot's decision to stay in England; on the other hand, it is both a confession that the grounds for the decision have eroded and a signal that he is symbolically returning to America (via its army) as his mother had all along urged.

Eliot's other important reason for staying in England was his marriage. As Ackroyd observes, 'When the family learned of his decision not to leave England they were greatly disappointed and blamed Vivien.'[43] Vivien later confessed in a letter to Richard Aldington that she was indeed an important factor in Eliot's decision: 'once I fought like mad to keep Tom here and stopped his going back to America. I thought I could not marry him unless I was able to keep him here, in England.'[44] This reason for staying in England is also undercut in 'Ode'. In at least one respect – its physical aspect – the marriage seems to have come to an end shortly after it started. The second stanza of 'Ode' introduces the theme of sexual disgust in its attention to a bridegroom recomposing himself against the background of blood on a bed. An allusion to Catullus' 'Hymen o Hymenaee' and to Whitman's 'O Hymen! O Hymenee! why do you tantalize me thus? / O why sting me for a swift moment only?' prolongs the stanza's focus on the blood and adds to disgust the theme of sexual exasperation.[45] The victim here is not clear. On the one hand it is the bridegroom, tortured by his desire for the hymeneal succuba. Yet the blood is literally the woman's, and she is the one who is eviscerated. In the end, both the 'succuba' and the bridegroom seem tortured. As in *The Waste Land*, each is a victim and a victimizer.

The final section of the poem follows the allusion to Catullus back to the classical mythological context established with the first section's references to a sacred wood and a once-inspiring river. This section translates the tableau implied in the second section – bridegroom lying beside succuba in bed – into the story of Perseus, Andromeda and the monster in Ovid's *Metamorphoses*. Although Smith argues that the third section of the poem depicts 'the happy union of Andromeda and her transformed dragon, who, after the petulant departure of Perseus in Laforgue's story, make off together from her island prison', this section of the poem (which Smith finds 'a little perplexing') makes more sense if read in terms of the traditional myth.[46] The bridegroom becomes the dragon of the myth. Sailing toward the naked Andromeda chained to the rocks, 'parting the waves with the impact of his breast', the monster suddenly finds the shadow of Perseus interposed between himself and Andromeda, 'and the monster attacked that shadow in a fury'.[47] Here is the resentful, deluded dragon of 'Ode'. The dragon's vanquishing at the hand of Perseus, the child of Danae, 'whom Jupiter made pregnant with his fertile gold', enters the poem as a golden apocalypse.[48] The dragon's extinguished desire when about to ravish Andromeda symbolizes the bridegroom's sexual failure at a similar point during the honeymoon. Stabbed repeatedly by the sword of Perseus, the dragon 'spat out waves dyed red with blood' until finally killed by Perseus.[49] Through the similar image of the dragon in 'Ode' – lying in his own blood – the blood in section two is made symbolically the bridegroom's blood in section three. Like Saint Narcissus and the speaker in 'The Love Song of Saint Sebastian', the dragon suffers the assault on his body that provides the final satisfaction of sexual desire.

In this biographical reading, the bridegroom and dragon are Eliot, and the succuba and Andromeda are Vivien Eliot. The most likely candidate for Perseus is Bertrand Russell. As Schuchard suggests, late in 1917 Russell and Vivien seem to have consummated physically what until then was merely a platonic relationship. Like Schuchard, Ackroyd suggests that Eliot probably knew about or came to suspect what had happened 'but preferred to "forget" . . . and to remain silent'.[50] 'Ode' is a breaking of this silence, and an articulation of his suspicion. Ackroyd dates it as likely written in whole or in part in July of 1918 when the Eliots were staying 'at a cottage in Marlow, Buckinghamshire, in which Bertrand Russell had a financial stake'.[51] Apparently alone with his wife

at Marlow, but in another sense still confronted by the shadow
of his sexual rival, Eliot is prompted to include in 'Ode' as an
explanation of his marriage's failure an allusion to an 'arrangement'
with Russell/Perseus – whether that be the loan of the cottage at
Marlow, the Eliots' sharing of a flat in London with Russell, or
Vivien's holiday alone with Russell in Torquay – that resulted in
the appearance of the shadow between the dragon and Andromeda.
The laughter with which 'Ode' begins provides internal evidence
in support of this biographical speculation, for it marks the return
of Mr Apollinax – Eliot's poetic incarnation of Bertrand Russell.
In 'Mr Apollinax', this Priapus-like figure's disconcerting sexual
energy is located in his laugh: 'His laughter was submarine and
profound' (CPP 31). The 'Subterrene' laughter of the 'Ode'
written at Marlow comes from the owner of the property.

The extent to which Eliot's mother is a part of the sexual
problems catalogued in the poem is suggested by Eliot's attempts
to prevent her from reading it. Writing to his brother Henry about
Ara Vos Prec, Eliot confessed: 'I have not sent this to Mother or
told her about it. I thought of cutting out the page on which
occurs a poem called "Ode" and sending the book as if there
had been an error and an extra page put in.'[52] 'Ode' – which
Eliot imagined to be his last poem before entering the American
armed forces – would be misunderstood by her. More likely, its
sexual preoccupation would be too well understood:

> Do you think that 'Sweeney Erect' will shock her? Some of
> the new poems, the Sweeney ones, especially 'Among the
> Nightingales'[,] and 'Burbank'[,] are intensely serious. . . . But
> even here I am considered by the ordinary Newspaper critic as
> a Wit or satirist, and in America I suppose I shall be thought
> merely disgusting.[53]

Not allowing 'Ode' to be printed in Poems (the American edition
of Ara Vos Prec), and never allowing the poem to be reprinted, Eliot
confirms the extent to which his mother serves as the censorious
element in his own mind on matters relating to women and
sexuality. Eliot's mother and America are one: they would regard
the poem as disgusting. Ironically, although the disgusting poem is
an apology to both mother and America (for making a mess of his
life and for not returning home), it is an apology simultaneously
effected and cancelled by Eliot's suppression of it. Suppression of

the poem is a private mark of respect for the mother who resides within him as censor, yet suppression of the poem also hides from her both Eliot's acknowledgement in the poem of the mess that he has indeed made of his life (as she all along suspected) *and* his symbolic return to her and America through his retirement as poet and his determination to join the American armed services (if not the Harvard philosophy department).

Given Eliot's indirect acknowledgement of his own mother-complex in his review of Murry's book, and given the attribution of a mother-complex to Coriolanus in 'Coriolan', it is possible to read the allusion to *Coriolanus* in the epigraph to 'Ode' as a disguised – perhaps unconscious – acknowledgement of the role of something like a mother-complex in Eliot's explanation to his mother via 'Ode' of his failures as poet and husband. Like Coriolanus, what he has 'done famously' he did 'to please his mother and to be partly proud'.

Eliot's notorious essay on *Hamlet* (1919) confirms this reading of Eliot's state of mind at the time of the composition of 'Ode' and also links the experience of the mother-complex to his mystical experiences. The essay obliquely draws the connections between Shakespeare's Coriolanus, the mother-complex and Eliot's own relationships with women – the connections to be drawn more fully twelve years later in the review of Murry's book and in 'Coriolan'. Reviewing J.M. Robertson's *The Problem of Hamlet*, Eliot accepts that Gertrude's sexuality is at the heart of Hamlet's problems – 'the essential emotion of the play is the feeling of a son towards a guilty mother' (SE, 144). He quotes Robertson to the effect that Hamlet is 'one who has suffered tortures on the score of his mother's degradation', but argues that 'This . . . is by no means the whole story' (SE, 144). The pattern of argument here is similar to that in his review of the Lawrence biography twelve years later: 'What Mr Murry shows, and demonstrates with a terrible perti-nacity throughout Lawrence's work, is the emotional dislocation of a "mother-complex". (It should show also how inappropriate is the common designation of "Oedipus complex".)'[54] The Oedipus complex, in other words, is by no means the whole story. Eliot's complaint in 'Hamlet' is that so much of the rest of the story of Hamlet is untold: 'We find Shakespeare's *Hamlet* not in the action, not in any quotations that we might select, so much as in an unmistakable tone which is unmistakably not in the earlier [Hamlet] play' (SE, 145). As Davidson explains, 'Because Hamlet's emotion, according to Eliot, seems out of proportion to the events of the play, we are led to speculate about his inner state, and the play becomes a psychological problem, not art.'[55]

Eliot does not object that the story of the 'guilt of a mother' should have been told, and he does not deny that 'tortures on the score of . . . [a] mother's degradation' can become a psychological complex. The problem is that the psychological complex and the untold story in Hamlet remain Shakespeare's and are never made Hamlet's. That the play's untold story is Shakespeare's is hinted at first by Eliot's ambiguous reference to a 'period of crisis' in Shakespeare's career that Hamlet represents: was the crisis psychological or aesthetic (SE, 144)? Eliot's subsequent allusions to Shakespeare's sonnets locate the crisis in Shakespeare's life and confirm the hint that Hamlet provides that the crisis involves Shakespeare's most intimate relationships: 'Hamlet, like the sonnets, is full of some stuff that the writer could not drag to light, contemplate, or manipulate into art. And when we search for this feeling, we find it, as in the sonnets, very difficult to localize' (SE, 144). Eliot seems to assume, like Wordsworth, that in his sonnets Shakespeare unlocked his heart and that therefore the torturous devotion, suspicion, and infatuation described in the sonnets have their origin in Shakespeare's own experiences.[56] We cannot understand Hamlet without knowing such experiences: 'under compulsion of what experience he attempted to express the inexpressibly horrible, we cannot ever know. We need a great many facts in his biography. . . . We should have to understand things which Shakespeare did not understand' (SE, 146). And that is why the play is aesthetically a failure. Shakespeare projected his own psychological complex and his own (understandable) mystification before it onto his fictional character – a projection that Eliot can understand psychologically but not forgive aesthetically, for Shakespeare is entitled to his complex, whereas Hamlet is not.

Eliot attempts to isolate Shakespeare's psychological state from Hamlet's: 'the supposed identity of Hamlet with his author is genuine to this point: that Hamlet's bafflement at the absence of objective equivalent to his feelings is a prolongation of the bafflement of his creator in the face of his artistic problem' (SE, 145). Insofar as he is willing to speculate upon Shakespeare's psychological state, Eliot sanitizes it. Whereas Hamlet is subject to an implictly sexual disgust – 'Hamlet is up against the difficulty that his disgust is occasioned by his mother, but that his mother is not an adequate equivalent for it; his disgust envelops and exceeds her' (SE, 145) – Shakespeare is subject to a less obviously sexual phenomenon, 'intense feeling': 'The intense feeling, ecstatic or terrible, without an object or exceeding its object, is something which every person of sensibility has known; it is doubtless a subject of study for pathologists' (SE, 146). Yet the recovery of the intertextual resonances of this passage throughout Eliot's prose confirms that Shakespeare's feeling is Hamlet's feeling, and that Hamlet's feeling is Eliot's feeling – which is a very confused feeling, as much ecstatically and terribly mystical as sexual.

The 'intense feeling' in question is clearly known to Eliot; it is 'something which every person of sensibility has known'. It is 'the loathing and horror of life itself' to which he refers in 'Cyril Tourneur' (1930) – 'the hatred of life [that] is an important phase – even, if you like, a mystical experience – in life itself' (SE, 190). For the Eliot of 1919, this mystical feeling derives from experience of 'the indestructible barriers between one human being and another'.[57] As we have seen in analysis of *The Waste Land*, 'Gerontion', and 'The Love Song of Saint Sebastian', this feeling is more particularly located in the experience of the indestructible barriers between men and women. Given that woman is never the objective correlative for the intense feeling aroused by her, Eliot's explanation in 'Hamlet' of Shakespeare's problem as an artist and Hamlet's problem as a man proves not surprisingly to be an explanation of his own problems as an artist and as a man:

> it must be noticed that the very nature of the *données* of the problem precludes objective equivalence. To have heightened the criminality of Gertrude would have been to provide the formula for a totally different emotion in Hamlet; it is just *because* her character is so negative and insignificant that she arouses in Hamlet the feeling which she is incapable of representing. (SE, 145–6)

And so, just as Goethe, Coleridge and Laforgue have their own *Hamlet*, so does Eliot. His Prince Hamlet is Prufrock, the 'overwhelming question' for each aroused by a woman who cannot objectify it for them. Eliot's prose conspires to reveal about him what his analysis of *Hamlet* reveals about Shakespeare – the problem of mystical moments aroused in the author's life by relationships with women, mystical moments that prove unrepresentable by an objective correlative in art.

Against this background, the brief discussion of *Coriolanus* in 'Hamlet' is suggestive. Whereas *Hamlet* 'is most certainly an artistic failure', *Coriolanus* is 'Shakespeare's most assured artistic success' (SE, 143–4). Ostensibly distinguishing between the plays by contrast, Eliot implies that he has done so because they are connected in terms of similar biographical origins, for they represent the beginning and the end of Shakespeare's attempt to deal with the psychological crisis that Eliot imputes to him: 'We are surely justified in attributing the play [*Hamlet*] . . . to a period of crisis, after which follow the tragic successes which culminate in *Coriolanus*' (SE, 144). Eliot's argument is not necessarily of the *post hoc ergo propter hoc* sort; he is not necessarily arguing that *Coriolanus* is possible because the crisis in question is resolved. As the aesthetic opposite of *Hamlet* – that is, as an instance of artistic success *versus* an instance of artistic failure – *Coriolanus* represents not necessarily the successful resolution of Shakespeare's psychological crisis, but rather the successful resolution of his aesthetic crisis. In *Coriolanus* one finds the successful creation of an objective correlative: 'the pride of Coriolanus . . . [is] expanded into a tragedy . . . intelligible, self-complete, in the sunlight' (SE, 144).

Yet because of the similar preoccupations of Hamlet and Coriolanus with their mothers, one must entertain the possibility that Eliot perceived in *Coriolanus* as early as 1918 and 1919 what he had demonstrably perceived in the play by 1931: the successful creation of the particular objective correlative that *Hamlet* lacked – that is, the aesthetic objectification of the whole story of the mother-complex. And if Eliot had by 1919 perceived in *Coriolanus* the explanantion of Hamlet's emotional dislocation when confronting women and sexuality, one must ask whether Eliot had similarly perceived in the play by this time the explanation of his own emotional dislocation when confronting women and sexuality.

The result of Eliot's engagement with the figure of Coriolanus is the development within him of the double perspective that animates Part II of *The Waste Land*. On the one hand, Eliot experiences the mysticism that comes of the hatred of life that expresses itself as his misogyny. On the other hand, he recognizes this mysticism as a function of his mother-complex – the equivalent for him of the claustrophobic room from which the staring forms of the past impress the men and women in 'A Game of Chess'. My conclusion that Eliot uses the figure of Coriolanus to mark his growing awareness of the extent to which his mystical moments are a function not so much of contact with the divine as of involvement in his own mother-complex allows one to locate in Eliot's writing of the late 1910s and early 1920s the first hints of his growing awareness of the extent to which his own mysticism involves the same confusion of the human and the divine that he had criticized earlier in Bergsonism, pragmatism and modernism and that he would criticize even more vigorously in The Clark Lectures.

7

The Confidential Clark Lectures

The text through which Eliot focuses his concerns about the potentially psychopathological explanation of his own mysticism (an explanation enabled by his sense of Lawrence's psychological history) is The Clark Lectures – the most important development in his engagement with mysticism in the 1920s. Having reached by the end of his course of book reviews on theology and philosophy in 1918 the point of debunking most modern mysticisms as 'weakling', Eliot might be forgiven for assuming that such a catharsis would leave him immune to the mysticisms that he disdained. Like the great novelists Beyle and Flaubert that he celebrates in his 1919 review, Eliot has perceived 'something . . . simple, terrible and unknown'. This phenomenon, we recall, 'is a "mysticism" not to be extracted from Balzac, or even from Miss Underhill'. Balzac's failure in this regard is all the more regrettable for the opportunity wasted. In the story by Balzac to which Eliot refers, 'Adieu', there is the very lack of interest in marriage and resistance to entanglement in relationships with others that for Eliot grounds the mysticism unrecorded by Underhill. Unlike Balzac, who proceeds no further in his investigation of this experience, Eliot follows Beyle and Flaubert into a mysticism of 'the awful separation between potential passion and any actualization possible in life' and 'the indestructible barriers between one human being and another' – especially in 'Gerontion' and *The Waste Land*.[1]

As late as *Sweeney Agonistes*, abandoned at the end of 1924 or early in 1925, Eliot implies that he still considers experience of dispossession in confronting the void at the centre of human relations to be a potential mysticism. One of the play's epigraphs suggests that Sweeney's misogynistic project to 'do a girl in' – the misogynistic project that the play takes over from *The Waste Land* – is aligned with St John of the Cross's mysticism of dispossession: 'Hence the soul cannot be possessed of the divine union, until it has divested itself of the love of created beings' (CP, 124, 115). By the end of 1925, however, Eliot begins to express in his Clark Lectures the doubt that the 'something . . . simple, terrible and unknown' that he acknowledged in 1919 as lying beyond the apparently simple feelings that bind one human being to another can ground the mysticism not to be found in Balzac or Underhill.

The question for Eliot is whether he is like the great writers, willing like Beyle and Flaubert to strip away misconceptions about his motives and emotions until the simple, terrible, unknowable thing is encountered, or whether he is a facile Balzac, pursuing the explanation of his motive and emotion no further than his apparently simple feeling of revulsion before other human beings – particularly his wife. The Clark Lectures are written in response to his suspicion that he has so far been no more than the latter. They can be read, that is, not only as a discussion of poetry but also as the beginning of a project by which Eliot puts upon European intellectual, emotional and literary history a story of love and religious experience that is more his own than Europe's.

For instance, a simultaneously intellectual and biographical context for the lectures was the increasingly *ad hominem* debate between Eliot and Murry on the respective merits of romanticism and classicism. In 'The Function of Criticism' (1923), Eliot quarrels with an essay by Murry written earlier the same year in which Murry celebrates the romantic temperament and its respect for the authority of the 'inner voice' (SE, 27). Contrasting the romantic's journey into the self with that of Catholic mystics who wrote 'several handbooks . . . on its practice', Eliot marks Murry as a heretical pantheist – one of the 'palpitating Narcissi' who believes 'that God and himself [are] identical' (SE, 27–8). For his part, Eliot promotes the values of classicism, which he characterizes as a belief 'that men cannot get on without giving allegiance to something outside themselves' (SE, 26). These very terms reappear in the third of Eliot's lectures during his most extensive discussion of mysticism:

> I wish to draw as sharply as possible the difference between [the] mysticism of Richard of St Victor, which is the mysticism also of St Thomas Aquinas and of Dante, and the mysticism of the Spaniards. . . . The Aristotelian-Victorine-Dantesque mysticism is ontological; the Spanish mysticism is psychological. The first is what I call classical, the second romantic. (*Varieties*, 104)

For those following the debates in the prominent literary journals of the day, no reference to Murry was necessary here to confirm

that Eliot's lectures played a part in his continuing debate with
Murry about classicism and romanticism, on the one hand, and
about the nature of Murry's own mysticism, on the other.

Nonetheless, Eliot refers to Murry in the next paragraph. He
defends himself against the latter's charge – in an essay that he read
while writing his lectures – that Eliot is the same sort of romantic
mystic that he condemns:

> [*The Waste Land*] expresses a self-torturing and utter nihilism:
> there is nothing, nothing: nothing to say, nothing to do, nothing
> to believe, save to wait without belief for the miracle. . . . This
> is a voice from the Dark Night of the Soul of a St John of the
> Cross. . . . But the stupendous difference is that St John of the
> Cross was born a Catholic, who thought and felt instinctively
> in the categories of the Church. Mr Eliot was not; he was born
> into the same tormenting fluidity as the rest of us. . . . What
> can classicism mean for him? A spiritual technique he envies
> and cannot use; a certainty he longs for and cannot embrace –
> it could mean either of these things. But to envy classicism is
> not to be a classicist; it is to be, most unenviably, a romantic:
> a romantic who is conscious of sin in being what he is, and
> cannot take the plunge into the unknown; whose being knows
> that there is but one way, but whose mind, fascinated by ancient
> certitude, can discern only nothingness along the only way.[2]

Irritated by Murry's article, Eliot wrote the following paragraph to
deal with it:

> I think that if Mr Middleton Murry would study carefully the
> works of St John of the Cross, he would see that the parallel he
> draws between St John and myself is quite illusory; for what St
> John means by the 'dark night' and what Mr Murry means by
> my 'dark night' are entirely different things. (*Varieties*, 104)

Crossed out in the Houghton copy of the lectures, this digression
may not have been included in the lecture that Eliot actually
delivered. Coming as it does, however, immediately after his
distinction between the 'classical' mysticism of Aristotle and
Dante and the 'romantic' mysticism of the Spanish mystics St
Theresa and St John of the Cross, the digression confirms that The
Clark Lectures are energized by Murry's charge that Eliot is 'an

unregenerate and incomplete romantic'. Even his redeployment in these lectures of the terms romantic and classical suggests that Eliot understands The Clark Lectures to be an opportunity to defy Murry's demand for 'a public recantation of his "classicism"'.[3]

Significantly, however, Eliot does not address the interesting interpretation of *The Waste Land* that Murry offers in his analysis of Eliot's mysticism: '"The Waste Land" . . . is a station on the mystic path.'[4] By cutting the digression about Murry's observation from the lecture that he delivered, Eliot would have avoided the issue completely. Yet even in the paragraph that he wrote, he largely avoids the issue. He compares the apple of St John of the Cross's dark night and the orange of *Murry's understanding* of Eliot's dark night. He implies that Murry's understanding of the latter is inadequate, but coyly sidesteps the question whether for all his misunderstanding Murry might nonetheless be correct in his assertion that *The Waste Land* represents a stage of mystical experience. Although in a later essay like 'Cyril Tourneur' (1930), Eliot would apparently concede the truth of Murry's observation – 'the loathing and horror of life itself. . . . the hatred of life is an important phase – even, if you like, a mystical experience – in life itself' (SE, 190) – he is unwilling or unable to do so in The Clark Lectures. There is for Eliot too much involved in Murry's equation between *The Waste Land* and romantic mysticism for a single paragraph to answer.

One might also suspect that Eliot was tempted to eliminate this paragraph because it is superfluous. Its purpose – to respond to Murry's request that Eliot clarify the nature of his own mystical experience – is the business of all eight lectures, not just a single paragraph. We must not be misled by Eliot's suggestions that the discussion of mysticism in The Clark Lectures is merely a concession to the requirements of a thorough discussion of metaphysical poetry. Ostensibly, we come upon the subject of mysticism only indirectly: a discussion of metaphysical poetry apparently requires a discussion of the history of love, and a discussion of the history of love apparently requires a discussion of the history of mysticism. Even so indirect an involvement of mysticism in the story that Eliot would tell makes him unhappy:

> [A certain type of metaphysical poetry] elevates sense for
> a moment to regions ordinarily attainable only by abstract

thought, or on the other hand clothes the abstract, for a moment, with all the painful delight of flesh. To call it mystical is facile, and I hasten to discountenance the use of this word; for there are many kinds [and] qualities of mysticism, and I wish to emphasize the intellectual quality of this operation of poetry. With the more intellectual forms of mysticism, the *beatitudo*, or the experience of Theresa or John of the Cross, it may come in contact, as we shall see; but as this is a specific variation, and the generic character is not mystical at all, I prefer to keep the word mysticism out of the way. (*Varieties*, 55)

At least so he protests.

Yet far from keeping 'the word mysticism out of the way', Eliot keeps it front and centre. He anticipates and conducts discussions of mysticism throughout the lectures with relish:

I shall have occasion later, in connection with Crashaw, to refer to the Spanish Mystics. And in my lecture of next week I shall call your attention to a mysticism of the twelfth century which is different from that of the Spaniards and different from that of the Germans, and which is in the direct classical, Aristotelian tradition, and which is the mysticism of Dante. There are several mysticisms. But it may be as well to make clear that to me the Spanish mystics of the sixteenth century – St Theresa, St John of the Cross, Luis of Granada, . . . and St Ignatius, are as much psychologists as Descartes, and Donne, and as much romanticists as Rousseau. (*Varieties*, 84)

In fact, so important is the subject of mysticism in The Clark Lectures that one can perceive a logic at work in them opposite to the one that Eliot advertises. Given the stimulus provided by Murry – Eliot not only wrote the lectures in response to Murry's article but also had Murry to thank for the invitation to deliver them in the first place ('it was due to [Murry's] exertions, in the face of staunch opposition to an American, that Eliot was offered the next series of Clark lectures') – Eliot makes mysticism in general and his own mysticism in particular one of his more urgent concerns.[5] Since Eliot's mysticism depends upon the experience of the void in the middle of human relations, his mystical experiences can only be understood against the background of a history of love. From this point of view, the discussion of the metaphysical poets – not the discussion of mysticism – might seem the concession to the requirements of thorough discussion. Not surprisingly, then, the metaphysical poets are quickly turned into a symbol of the debilitated spirituality of the modern world – representatives of a romantic mystical sensibility by which Eliot can bring into relief the twelfth-century classical mystical sensibility that he envies.

Of course Eliot's quarrel with romantic mysticism in The Clark Lectures is not just a personal grouse against romantic tempera-ments. He criticizes romantic mysticism for its *complication* of a reality that he had realized ten years before must be true *simply*. He argues in his dissertation that 'For a metaphysics to be accepted, good-will is essential. Two men must *intend* the same object, and *both* men must admit that the object intended is the same' (KE, 168).[6] Europe once comprised a community of good-will sufficient for a shared metaphysics. Since the fragmentation of this medieval community, good-will in metaphysics has become less common and less concentrated. In The Clark Lectures, Eliot traces the collapse of a shared reality through attention to the fate of a once metaphysical Good and Evil:

> For several generations, we have been told by philosophers and half-philosophers, that if you cease to believe in good and evil, they do not exist. Good and Evil are concepts which have had their birth and development, . . . and concepts which have or have had at best economic, genetic, or hygienic justifications. We have not been so often told, what is equally true, that if we *do* believe in Good and Evil then they *do* exist. One generation doubted, one disbelieved, and the present generation has forgotten, that Good and Evil can be real. (*Varieties*, 207)

Eliot's point is not that we can choose whichever reality we might prefer. He had mocked sloppy pragmatists for just such language in his early philosophical essays and reviews. As Michaels observes, 'the point of insisting on the practical as well as the conventional is to deny that we can *choose* our account of the real. Our sense of the real is not necessary (i.e. imposed on us by a preexisting reality) but it is not freely chosen either.'[7] Eliot's point is that philosophers and half-philosophers now disagree about the object intended. For some, metaphysical Good and Evil have become natural Good and Bad; for others, they have become Right and Wrong; still others find in them a material history – whether economic, genetic or hygienic.

Agreement or disagreement depends upon whether we find ourselves within or without the same metaphysical system:

> To the builder of the [metaphysical] system, the identity binding together the appearance and the reality is evident; to anyone outside of the system it is not evident. To the builder the process is the process of reality, for thought and reality are one; to a critic, the process is perhaps only the process of the builder's thought. From the critic's standpoint the metaphysician's world may be real only as the child's bogey is real. The one thinks of reality in terms of his system; the other thinks of the system in terms of the indefinite social reality. (KE, 167)

On the one hand, the 'indefinite social reality' holds no purchase over the metaphysical system: 'a metaphysical doctrine pretends to be "*true*" simply, and none of our pragmatic tests will apply.' On the other hand, the 'truth' of a metaphysics holds no purchase over social reality: 'it makes no difference whether a thing really is green or blue, so long as everyone behaves towards it on the belief that it is green or blue.' In arguing that Good and Evil can be real regardless of the economic, genetic and hygienic arguments of philosophers and half-philosophers, Eliot makes the same point that he makes in his dissertation: 'A metaphysic may be accepted or rejected without our assuming that from the practical point of view it is either true or false' (KE, 169).

Eliot characterizes the difference between the thirteenth and the twentieth centuries as 'The difference between what I call *ontologism* and *psychologism*' (*Varieties*, 82–3). He returns in 1926 to his 1916 quarrel with psychology in *Knowledge and Experience*. On the one hand is the person whose metaphysical system constitutes reality, 'for thought and reality are one.' On the other is the person who no longer sees by means of the metaphysical system but rather comes to see the system itself as an object. Of the latter, at one extreme is the critic who displaces reality from metaphysics to an indefinite social reality, such that the metaphysical system no longer constitutes 'the process of reality' but 'only the process of the builder's thought'. The metaphysician's world becomes an internal mental event that 'may be real only as the child's bogey is real' (KE, 167). At another extreme is what Eliot calls the psychologist, one who displaces reality from the world to the internal mental event. In his dissertation, Eliot devotes a chapter to debunking the relatively new science of psychology. As Michaels observes, for Eliot 'The central unexamined assumption of contemporary psychology . . . is that a "mental content" is a simple "presentation" of an "external" reality, and that such presentations can themselves be treated as an independent class of objects.'⁸ Eliot argues that 'no distinct province of mental objects exists as the field of psychology' (KE, 84). Although he acknowledges the usefulness of studies of multiple personality, of the brain's reaction times, of localized functions in the brain, and so on, he insists that:

> we are not to say that there is a mental content which is mental. There is, in this sense, nothing mental, and there is certainly no such thing as consciousness if consciousness is to be an object or something independent of the objects which it has. (KE, 83)

Perception – and indeed consciousness itself – cannot be distinguished from its objects; perception consists in reference to objects. To imagine the act of perception to involve the intervention between a subject and an object of a mental presentation of the object is for Eliot a nonsense: 'Any attempt to separate percept from object merely doubles the object.' The nonsense arises because of a 'confusion . . . between reference and existence' (KE, 64, 63).

Eliot's implicit target in this attack on psychology is Descartes, yet it is only in The Clark Lectures that he can bring himself to speak of Descartes' role in the ruin of epistemology. According to Eliot, by stating that 'what we know is not the world of objects, but our own ideas of these objects', Descartes is responsible for 'a self-consciousness that had not been conspicuous in the world before'. Descartes' mind/body problem is imaginary: 'Instead of ideas as meanings, as references to an outside world, you have suddenly a new world coming into existence, inside your own mind and therefore by the usual implication inside your own head.' Eliot's analysis here – ideas are references to objects; treating them as objects creates an illusory 'reality' – is the same as that in his dissertation. His rhetoric, however, is less restrained. Citing Descartes' inability in his Sixth Meditation to deduce by argument the existence of body, Eliot can express only contempt: 'This extraordinarily crude and stupid . . . reasoning is the sort of thing which gave rise to the whole of the pseudo-science of epistemology which has haunted the nightmares of the last three hundred years' (*Varieties*, 80–1).

Descartes' retreat into the head – the tendency to regard thinking and feeling as themselves further objects of thinking and feeling – is an instance of what Eliot calls psychologism or romanticism. This phenomenon is anticipated in sixteenth-century mysticism, arising through the influence of St Theresa and her fellow Spanish mystics: 'There are several mysticisms. But it may be as well to make clear that to me the Spanish mystics of the sixteenth century – St Theresa, St John of the Cross . . . and St Ignatius, are as much psychologists as Descartes, and . . . as much romanticists as Rousseau' (*Varieties*, 84). According to Eliot, such mystics have contaminated their mystical experiences by allowing their own emotions to intervene as a 'presentation' between themselves and the divine object. Just as Descartes makes his own experience an object of further experience, so the Spanish mystics make their experience of ecstasy an object of further religious experience. Eliot finds in such mystics' experiences the same doubling of the object that he finds both in the philosophy of Descartes and in contemporary psychology. Taking a moment in his dissertation to explain why *attention* to the content of an experience is less reliable evidence of reality than the simple experience of that content – even though 'there is properly no such thing as internal perception' – Eliot also explains his grievance against romantic mysticism:

> To make an object of the content is to attend to something quite as uncertain in evidence as any other object. . . . There will be . . . evidence for object and evidence for content, but not necessarily stronger for one than the other, and in most cases, I am inclined to believe, stronger for object than for content. (KE, 98–9)

In short, romantic mystics have as little evidence of reality in their inner experiences as Descartes in his.

In The Clark Lectures, Eliot treats Donne as the seventeenth-century poetic equivalent of Descartes and St Theresa. Like them, Donne demonstrates the tendency to regard his experience as something to be experienced. The question we must always

ask about Donne, Eliot suggests, is whether he 'is attending
to the *meaning* of an idea or to its *existence* (the latter being
the *Pensée* of Descartes)' (*Varieties*, 156). Again we hear the
echo of the dissertation's language, 'The confusion of course is
between reference and existence: the idea is conceived to have
an existence apart from its object' (KE, 63). According to Eliot,
Donne is more often than not attending to the existence of an
idea, just as St Theresa is more often than not attending to the
existence of her *feeling* of ecstasy as opposed to the *meaning* of this
ecstasy. Donne is 'a voluptuary of thought'; St Theresa is one of the
'voluptuaries of religion' (*Varieties*, 158). The consequence of this
emotional psychologism for the Spanish mystics was auto-hypnosis
or habitual ecstasy: one mystic 'became so habitually ecstatic that
he was obliged to pray that he might receive the divine influx less
frequently' (*Varieties*, 157). Eliot regards this type of mysticism as a
'spiritual hashish, a drugging of the emotions' (*Varieties*, 106).[9] In
Donne, Descartes and St Theresa alike, Eliot finds consciousness
contaminated by illusory experience: poet, philosopher and mystic
have treated their own experience as a further object of experience
– the 'inner perception', 'percept' and 'presentation' that become
the 'Inner Light' that Eliot disdains.

Similarly, Eliot's celebration of classical mysticism in The Clark
Lectures is not just a celebration of his own temperament. His
definition of classical mysticism is a function of his dissertation's
definition of metaphysics as a faith-state. In the final chapter of the
dissertation, Eliot emphasizes that 'metaphysics depends upon our
ability and good-will to grasp appearance and reality as one' (KE,
161). In 'a metaphysical theory there is an attempt to bind together
all points of view in one' (KE, 163). This binding together of two
worlds or two types of object – such as appearance and reality, the
mental and the physical, subjectivity and objectivity, and so on – is
a matter of faith: 'the assertion that . . . two worlds are the same is
an act of faith, only to be contrasted with another act of faith to
the effect that the two are not the same'; 'two types [of object] can
only be held together by an act of faith'; 'every transformation of
type involves . . . a transmigration from one world to another, and
such a pilgrimage involves an act of faith' (KE, 160, 162, 163). Eliot
distances himself from Bradley's Absolute in precisely these terms
in an article published in October of 1916:

Bradley's universe, actual only in finite centres, is only by an act
of faith unified. Upon inspection, it falls away into the isolated
finite experiences out of which it is put together. . . . The
Absolute responds only to an imaginary demand of thought,
and satisfies only an imaginary demand of feeling. Pretending
to be something which makes finite centres cohere, it turns out
to be merely the assertion that they do. And this assertion is only
true so far as we here and now find it to be so.[10]

Without this faith, we are not susceptible to the claims of a
metaphysical system: 'the truth has to be *my* truth before it can be
true at all'; 'The question can always be asked of the closest-woven
theory: is this the reality of *my* world of appearance? and if I do not
recognize this identity, then it is not' (KE, 169, 168).

Classical mysticism turns out to be a faith-state grounded in an
extreme version of the recognition of this identity. For the builder
of any metaphysical system, 'thought and reality are one.' The truth
is indeed his or her truth, and the system's reality is indeed his or
her world of appearance. In The Clark Lectures, Eliot locates this
kind of metaphysician's experience in Dante's experience. Dante
experiences reality immediately. His thoughts and emotions are
one with reality; they are not objects themselves: 'In Dante . . . you
get a system of thought and feeling; every part of the system felt and
thought in its place, and the whole system felt and thought.' Eliot
emphasizes that 'you cannot say that it is primarily "intellectual"
or primarily "emotional", for the thought and the emotion are
reverse sides of the same thing' (*Varieties*, 183). There is none of
the habitual ecstasy, auto-hypnosis, spiritual hashish or drugging
of the emotions that Eliot associates with romantic mysticism.
Classical mysticism 'is wholly impersonal – as impersonal as a
handbook of hygiene – and contains no biographical element
whatever; nothing that could be called emotional or sensational'
(*Varieties*, 102). Dante's 'system' is for him the process of reality. His
experience and his coherent and comprehensive system of belief
are so much one that immediate experience passes into belief. But
for modern minds such as Donne's, 'The immediate experience
passes into thought; and this thought, far from attaining *belief*, is
immediately the object of another feeling' (*Varieties*, 133). Donne
lives in a world of mental chaos dependent upon his experience
of his own experience. Dante lives in a world of mental order

dependent upon his experience of his system of belief. As in the dissertation, the difference is between inhabiting a system (like Dante) and residing in its ruins (like Donne).

In the dissertation's terms, classical mysticism involves so thoroughly inhabiting a system as to become one with it – and thereby one with reality. Reality is for Eliot a point of view. As Micheals explains,

> points of view . . . are ways of looking at things . . . [that] Eliot thinks are primarily social and for which the individual self serves only as a location. The real is thus dependent not on individual autonomous selves . . . but on the already public character of the individual self. . . . A point of view is a situation, an intersection of habits or beliefs whose existence is social . . . a function of what Eliot calls a 'community of meaning' ([KE] 161), a community which he conceives not as a collection of individuals but as a point of view, a context. Prior to context there is no world; prior to context there is no self; context describes the intermingling of world and self from the beginning.[11]

In short, we are born into a point of view: world and self are a function of it – our reality. The experience of finding Good and Evil to be real is a consequence of finding ourselves in a reality that has always already been constructed – and not according to our will or desire: 'we have the right to say that the world is a construction. Not to say that it is *my* construction, for in that way "I" am as much "my" construction as the world is; but to use the word as best we can without implying any active agent' (KE, 166). Even the hypothetical master-builder of a metaphysical system is not an agent of the construction that is reality; he or she is as much a construction as the world. Yet to the master-builder is accorded an exalted consciousness of reality: 'To the builder of the system, . . . the process is the process of reality, for thought and reality are one' (KE, 167). It is this intellectual aspiration towards oneness with reality that the dissertation's metaphysician bequeathes to the classical mystic in The Clark Lectures.

Like the dissertation's metaphysics, classical mysticism consists in the oneness of thought and reality. According to Eliot, it 'is a type of religious mysticism which found expression in the twelfth century, and which is taken up into the system of Aquinas. Its origin is in the *Metaphysics* of Aristotle 1072b and elsewhere, and in the *Nichomachaean Ethics'* (*Varieties*, 99). The passage in Aristotle's *Metaphysics* to which Eliot draws attention focuses on the oneness of thought and its objects:

> thinking in itself is concerned with that which is in itself best, and thinking in the highest sense with that which is in the highest sense best. And thought thinks itself through participation in the object of thought; for it becomes an object of thought by the act of apprehension and thinking, so that thought and object of thought are the same.[12]

'Thinking in the highest sense' connects the human being with God. In the *Nichomachean Ethics*, Aristotle discusses contemplation ('thinking in the highest sense') as the highest virtue, 'since not only is reason the best thing in us, but the objects of reason are the best of knowable objects.'[13] As in the *Metaphysics*, the thing known through contemplation is that which is divine:

> it is not in so far as he is man that he will live so [that is, live a life of contemplation], but in so far as something divine is present in him. . . . The activity of God, which surpasses all others in blessedness, must be contemplative; and of human activities, therefore, that which is most akin to this must be most of the nature of happiness.[14]

According to Eliot, this description of an implicit participation in the divine through contemplation founds the mysticism of Aquinas and the Middle Ages in general: 'For the twelfth century, the divine vision or enjoyment of God could only be attained by a process in which the analytic intellect took part; it was through and by and beyond discursive thought that man could arrive at beatitude' (*Varieties*, 99). In the end, by his elision of thought and reality in the classical mysticism defined in The Clark Lectures, Eliot effectively converts his dissertation's metaphysical faith-state into the contemplative state of the classical mystic.

Parallel to this intellectual discussion of mysticism, however, is an equally interesting subtext in which Eliot reviews his own apparently mystical expriences. As we have seen, however much he might prefer mystical terms to account for his experience of the terrible and unknown something beyond the void that he perceives in the middle of all human relations, Eliot dimly perceives enough of the yet-to-be-named mother-complex behind his own experiences for him to be concerned about the extent to which his miraculous perception of something beyond the 'indestructible barriers between one person and another' is merely a psychopathological function of an incapacity for what he will later call the 'wonderful' and the 'life-giving' in human relations.[15] So difficult was the question that Murry put before Eliot that the latter could do no more in The Clark Lectures than construct the framework within which an answer might be articulated. The self-analysis initiated in them thus does not end with them. In fact, important essays that follow these lectures, 'Dante' (1929), 'Baudelaire' (1930) and the review of *Son Of Woman* (1931), need to be read in conjunction with them, for these texts combine to define Eliot's mystical genealogical project. They mark Dante's sensibility as Eliot's goal, Baudelaire's latently Dantean sensibility as the one modern sensibility that Eliot would accept as representing his own, and Lawrence's romantic sensibility as the one that Eliot must acknowledge as once having been his own – and as perhaps remaining his own despite his Baudelairean aspirations in 'the direction of beatitude' (SE, 428).

Eliot's preoccupation with his mystical genealogy leads him to attempt to trace a personal connection to Dante – a 'true mystic' (SW, 170). In a preface to the typescript of The Clark Lectures, he indicates that he is not confident of the scholarship upon which they rest – focusing in particular upon his treatment of Dante as inadequate: 'the whole of my case turns upon my interpretation of the Vita Nuova, which is only hinted at in Lecture III, and my interpretation of the childhood of Dante' (*Varieties*, 41). Accepting that he must justify these interpretations with more research and fuller arguments, he indirectly draws attention to the fact that the interpretation of the *Vita Nuova* and Dante's childhood experience that he offers in The Clark Lectures is grounded upon something other than research – and that is Eliot's intuitive sympathy with Dante:

> The *Vita Nuova* is to my thinking actual experiences reshaped into a particular form. This is indemonstrable. It is a kind of experience possible to a particular mental type, which persons of this type will always recognise. The emotions and sentiments, for instance, which Dante records as experienced at the age of

nine, are not at all incredible; they are possible at an even earlier age, though I do not assert that a young person of nine would be able to formulate them consciously in those words. (*Varieties*, 97–8)

When Eliot rewrites this part of Lecture III for his 1929 essay on Dante, he slightly obscures his personal identification with Dante by aligning himself less openly with Dante's experience:

> the type of sexual experience which Dante describes as occurring to him at the age of nine years is by no means impossible or unique. My only doubt (in which I found myself confirmed by a distinguished psychologist) is whether it could have taken place so *late* in life as the age of nine years. The psychologist agreed with me that it is more likely to occur at about five or six years of age. (SE, 273)

Although Eliot hides behind the opinion of modern psychologists in the later passage, in each case his interpretation rests on special knowledge – the knowledge that comes of being of the same mental type as Dante and of having the same kind of experience as Dante (perhaps even earlier than Dante did).

Dante is so important a part of the story of love and mysticism in The Clark Lectures that the *Vita Nuova* provides the first epigraph: 'Ladies, the end of my love was once the salutation of this lady whom you appear to mean; and in that dwelt my beatitude, which was the end of all my desires.'[16] The next is from what Eliot calls a 'Popular Song': 'I want someone to treat me rough. / Give me a cabman' (*Variety*, 40). Smith finds here 'represented in epitome the whole dilemma of spirit and flesh for one entertaining the ideal of their fusion and finding them, in reality, at odds'.[17] The quotation from Dante represents beatitude; the quotation from a 'Popular Song' represents animal passion; Smith implies that Eliot's theme is that the twain shall never meet. Yet in the lectures there is no such dilemma as Smith outlines, for Eliot finds that *in reality* (as opposed to the illusory modern 'reality') there is no disjunction between flesh and spirit in sexual activity. At issue here is the nature of reality, and as Manganiello points out, Eliot sides with Dante on this issue.[18] For Eliot's Dante, 'There is no imagined struggle of soul and body, only the struggle toward perfection' (*Varieties*, 114).

In opposition to the debasement of love represented in the popular modern song, Eliot would turn attention with the quotation from the *Vita Nuova* to the Golden Age of love in Dante's time. In the thirteenth century, Dante's Florentine school of love displaces the Provençal tradition of courtly love. Eliot quotes Remy de Gourmont at length on this subject:

> nothing could separate them [the Provençal knight and married lady] except, for a moment, death. It was a case of faithfulness in adultery.
>
> The Provençal lady is not at all deified. One does not fear her; one desires her . . .
>
> The new Florentine school . . . would profoundly modify the conception of love and, as a consequence, morality. The poet's love becomes pure, almost impersonal, its object no longer a woman, but beauty – femininity personified in an ideal creature. No idea of marriage or possession haunts them. . . . Love has all the characteristics of a cult. . . .
>
> It is a date in the evolution of human sentiments; it is a step in the direction of truth and an immense social advance. (*Varieties*, 94, my translation)

For Eliot, anything but the Florentine school's attitude toward love is nonsensical and unreal: 'whether you seek the Absolute in marriage, adultery or debauchery, it is all one – you are seeking it in the wrong place' (*Varieties*, 115).

Not only in The Clark Lectures, but also in 'Dante' (1929) and 'Baudelaire' (1930), Eliot emphasizes the necessary centrality of the distinction between Dante's love and modern love in any attempt to explain the twentieth century. In 'Baudelaire', he asserts that the experience of love requires 'the adjustment of the natural to the spiritual' – a process of adjustment that involves two stages, the adjustment 'of the bestial to the human and the human to the supernatural' (SE, 428). In the former, he argues that one can be more than a beast and yet still not fully human by completing only the first stage of the process of adjustment – a stunting of development illustrated by recent history: 'A great deal of sentiment has been spilt, especially in the eighteenth and nineteenth centuries, upon idealizing the reciprocal feelings of man and woman towards each other' (SE, 274). The result of this partial adjustment can be seen in romantic poetry, the 'sadness' of which 'is due to the exploitation of the fact that no human relations are adequate to human desires, but also to the disbelief in any further object for human desires than that which, being human, fails to satisfy them' ('Baudelaire', SE, 428). This is also Donne's predicament:

> What is there for Donne? This union in ecstasy ['between two souls'] is complete, is final; and two human beings, needing nothing beyond each other, rest on their emotion of enjoyment. But emotion cannot rest; desire must expand, or it will shrink. Donne, the modern man, is imprisoned in the embrace of his own feelings. There is little suggestion of adoration, of worship. (*Varieties*, 114)

According to Eliot, 'the love of man and woman (or for that matter of man and man) is only explained and made reasonable by the higher love, or else is simply the coupling of animals' ('Dante' (1929), SE, 274). He makes the same argument in 'Baudelaire' (1930):

> what distinguishes the relations of man and woman from the copulation of beasts is the knowledge of Good and Evil. . . . [T]he sexual act as evil is more dignified, less boring, than as the natural, 'life-giving', cheery automatism of the modern world. . . . So far as we are human, what we do must be either evil or good; so far as we do evil or good, we are human. (SE, 429)

Eliot's interest is not necessarily to revile the sexual act as evil (however much his puritan New England heritage might have predisposed him toward such a judgement), but rather to remind the modern world of Dante's effortless awareness of the spiritual dimension of sexual activity.

Dante was not distracted by the idealization of 'the reciprocal feelings of man and woman towards each other' that plagues the modern world. According to Eliot, the idealization of human relations that has occurred in Europe since Dante's time is what 'various realists have been irritated to denounce' ('Dante' (1929), SE, 274). Eliot is certainly one of these irritated denouncers: 'As if human love could possibly be an end in itself!'[19] His denunciation, furthermore, depends upon his Dantean realism. The idealization of human relations is betrayed in practice by a tendency to find the end of human love in a union of bodies and/or souls. It thus depends upon a dichotomy between body and soul that Eliot rejects. A phenomenon unknown to Dante, the struggle between body and soul is for Eliot not real, but merely 'imagined' (*Varieties*, 114). Eliot, the sad inhabitant of the dissociated modern world, would have us accept Dante as an example of the long-lost unified sensibility – a sensibility just sufficiently remembered in Eliot's own for Eliot to claim descent from Dante.

Yet complementing this identification with Dante, with Dante's experience of love and with Dante's 'reality' is an acknowledgement that Eliot once 'imagined' himself, his own experience of love and his own reality otherwise. He includes in his spiritual family tree ancestors antithetical to Dante – black sheep who played a large part in propagating the dichotomy between body and soul. Thus his initially puzzling introduction of puritanism into his account of Donne as a representative of the spiritual debilitation since Dante's time. In The Clark Lectures, we find not only that 'The separation of soul and body . . . is a modern conception', but also that 'The apparent "glorification of the body" appreciated by many admirers of Donne is really a puritanical attitude' (*Varieties*, 114). This observation draws attention to itself both for its perverseness and for its gratuitousness. The claim is perverse in that puritans – whether the historically specific Puritans of England and New England or merely the prudish in general who have ever since been known as puritans – have never been thought of as glorifying the body or celebrating sexual activity. That Eliot asserts that the glorification of the body is 'really' a puritanical attitude acknowledges that his claim goes against the grain. His reversal of perspective is worthy of Foucault's *History of Sexuality*.[20] Left largely unexplained, it is no less remarkable for its apparent gratuitousness. Having expanded the concept of puritanism such that it comes to include its seeming opposite, Eliot does nothing further with it. He seems interested not so much to explain puritanism as to associate Donne with it. That done, Eliot and his New England family become part of the story that Donne represents, and so – from Eliot's point of view – enough said.

As in the case of Dante, in short, so in the case of Donne, Eliot's analysis answers less to the standards of scholarship than to the interests of spiritual autobiography. Like his explanation of Dante's experience of human relations, his explanation of Donne's is a function of his intuition of a sympathy between himself and Donne. However oppositely, they are both puritans. Eliot's puritanism, of course, was of the sort that did not glorify the body or celebrate human sexual activity. His father, for instance, held that sex was 'nastiness'.[21] Eliot suppressed 'Ode' in part out of fear of his mother's puritanical attitudes about these matters, implying that she and other Americans would find him 'merely disgusting'.[22] He chafed at what on another occasion he called 'the typical American attitude in such matters', the attitude of Amy Lowell, 'who is always decrying abstract Puritanism, but who when faced with some particular work of art offensive to Puritan taste curls up like a hedgehog.'[23] Although by Eliot's own representation of him Donne seems as far from the puritan hedgehog as possible, Eliot's point in The Clark Lectures is that Donne's poetry is puritanical in accepting and reinforcing 'a distinction, a disjunction, between soul and body' (Varieties, 112). This disjunction is the diseased root alike of Donne's 'glorification of the body' and New England puritanism's condemnation of it.

The blackness of these sheep – whether as Donne's puritanism or the Eliot family's – consists in their being mistaken about final causes. Just as in the matter of love Donne's lovers rest in the emotion of enjoyment, so in moral matters Eliot's parents rested in the satisfaction of judging right from wrong. It is but a short step from Eliot's observation about the inadequacy of the illusory finality of Donne's puritanism in The Clark Lectures to his observation in 'Baudelaire' that Dante's knowledge of 'moral Good and Evil' must be distinguished from 'Puritan Right and Wrong' because the latter is based upon a conception of the Good that is 'imperfect, vague' (SE, 429). And it is but another short step from the latter to his observation years later that his parents never spoke of good and evil but only of what was 'done' and 'not done'.[24] In each case, what Eliot and other 'realists . . . denounce' is the substitution of original causes (formal, material and efficient) for Aristotle's final cause: 'The attitude of Dante to the fundamental experience of the Vita Nuova can only be understood by accustoming ourselves to find meaning in final causes rather than in origins. . . . The final cause is the attraction towards God' ('Dante' (1929), SE, 274). As Eliot implies in 'Baudelaire', those who replace Good and Evil with 'natural Good and Bad or Puritan Right and Wrong' are as mistaken as those who replace the love of God with the natural sexual activity of beasts or the emotion of enjoyment (SE, 429). In each case, their occlusion of the final cause leaves them searching for the perfect and final in that which is imperfect and not final.

The Clark Lectures thus define through Dante and Donne the complicated opposition of spiritual, intellectual and emotional ideals and actualities by which Eliot achieves his religious self-awareness of 1925 and 1926. He invokes this opposition between Dante and Donne, for instance, to explain his personal experience of the failure of love – his discussion of the differences between Dante's experience of love and Donne's experience of love referring indirectly to his own:

> the three attitudes toward love – of the provençal, of the Italian, of the English seventeenth century – represent differences in the spirit too wide for judgement, they belong to those differences which are reincarnated in different human beings every day, placing insuperable barriers between some of every handful of us. (*Varieties*, 95)

The temptation to assume that Eliot explains to himself here the failure of his own marriage is irresistible: his love is 'Italian'; Vivien's is 'English seventeenth century'. Dante and Donne do not mix.

In tracing through The Clark Lectures the development of the religious self-awareness in question, however, more important than this biographical speculation is the intertextual echo of Eliot's 1919 review, 'Beyle and Balzac'. The reference to the 'insuperable barriers between some of every handful of us' recalls the 'indestructible barriers between one human being and another' mentioned in the 1919 review as the foundation of 'a "mysticism" not to be extracted from Balzac, or even from Miss Underhill'. The echo suggests that within Eliot's discussion of love in The Clark Lectures lies a concern about the proper interpretation of the experience of the failure of human relations. In 1919, the 'indestructible barriers' are absolute; in 1926, the 'insuperable barriers' are historical rather than absolute – they are contingent upon sensibility. This intertextual revision is emblematic of Eliot's response to Murry's charge that Eliot is an example of the romantic

mystics that he disdains: what was once accepted as an intimation of
the absolute must now be considered as perhaps merely an illusory
experience contingent upon a historically specific — and suspect
— spiritual temperament. Eliot's task is to determine whether his
sense of the indestructible and insuperable barriers between people
is a function of his perception of the final cause of love or merely
a function of mistaking his emotion of enjoyment (in this case
the enjoyment of loathing and horror) for something complete
and final.

Eliot would prefer to understand his mystical experience of the
failure of human relations as potentially Dantesque. In the effort to
do so, he fixes upon the example of Charles Baudelaire — his model
of a person who comes to recognize modern spiritual debilitation
and, consequently, the need both for a love based on more than the
emotion of enjoyment and a morality based on more than 'natural
Good and Bad or Puritan Right and Wrong'.

The first hint of this argument occurs in the last of The Clark
Lectures. Eliot introduces Baudelaire in the form of his surrogate,
Jules Laforgue. In the latter,

> there is a continuous war between the feelings implied by his
> ideas, and the ideas implied by his feelings. . . . What he
> wants, you see, is either a *Vita Nuova* to justify, dignify and
> integrate his sentiments toward the *jeune fille* in a system of
> the universe, or else some system of thought which shall keep
> a place [for and] even enhance these feelings and at the same
> time enable him to *feel* as intensely the abstract world. (*Varieties*,
> 215–16)

Laforgue is caught between the natural and the supernatural
(represented in Eliot's symbolism, respectively, by women and
the Absolute): 'On the one hand he was fascinated by Miss
Leah Lee, the English governess, and on the other hand by
the Kantian pseudo-Buddhism of Schopenhauer and Hartmann'
(*Varieties*, 216). The story of Laforgue, however, is really the story
of Baudelaire:

> I am aware that I have left a gap; I should have proved that
> Baudelaire was occupied with the problem of Good and Evil,
> instead of merely assuming that he was . . . and I should have

shown that the problem of Laforgue, instead of being, as it appears, more comprehensive than Baudelaire's, was a smaller and less mature version of it. But these gaps I must for the present leave you to fill in. (*Varieties*, 220)

Like Laforgue, Baudelaire needs a Dantean system for thought and feeling and a *Vita Nuova* by which to accommodate his experience of human relations.

Eliot fills in the gap between Laforgue and Baudelaire with his 1930 essay, 'Baudelaire'. With Baudelaire, 'The romantic idea of Love is never quite exorcized, but never quite surrendered to. . . . [T]here is all the romantic idea, but something more: the reaching out towards something which cannot be had *in*, but which may be had partly *through*, personal relations' (SE, 428–9). Eliot's language here and in The Clark Lectures recalls his observation in 1919 about 'the awful separation between potential passion and any actualization possible in life'. The context for Eliot's remarks then about 'the indestructible barriers between one human being and another' was Balzac's 'Adieu':

the General, at a fashionable dinner-table, is asked by a lady why . . . he does not marry. 'All the world smiles upon you.' '*Oui, mais c'est un sourire qui me tue*' [Yes, but it is a smile that kills me]. A facile escape for the General, still more facile for his creator. But the patient analysis of human motives and emotions, and human misconceptions about motives and emotions, is the work of the greatest novelists.

Eliot celebrates 'The exposure, the dissociation of human feeling'. Human feeling is no ground for the Absolute:

Beyle and Flaubert strip the world. . . . The surface of existence coagulates into lumps which look like important simple feelings, which are identified by names as feelings, which the patient analyst disintegrates into more complex and trifling, but ultimately, if he goes far enough, into various canalizations of something again simple, terrible and unknown.[25]

The arrival of Beyle and Flaubert at 'something . . . simple, terrible and unknown' after the disintegration of feeling prefigures in Eliot's writing about human relations Baudelaire's intuition of 'something more' beyond 'the romantic idea of Love'. The theme in 1919 and the theme in 1930 are the same: the availability through analysis of human relations of something beyond.

Unable to harmonize his experience with his ideal needs, Baudelaire is in the position of Beyle and Flaubert. Just as the latter are aware of 'the awful separation between potential passion and any actualization possible in life' and of 'the indestructible barriers between one human being and another', so Baudelaire knows that 'no relations are adequate to human desires' and that 'the purely natural and the purely human' are unsatisfactory (SE, 428, 423). Furthermore, in each case, human feeling is found inadequate as a ground of the Absolute. Beyle and Flaubert strip away the surface of simple feelings about such a thing as marriage until something 'simple, terrible and unknown' is exposed beyond misconceptions about human motives and emotions. Baudelaire reaches 'out towards something which cannot be had *in* . . . human relations'. One presumes that Eliot's observation in 1919 about the struggle of Beyle and Flaubert to cope with these truths applies equally to Baudelaire: 'This is a "mysticism" not to be extracted from Balzac, or even from Miss Underhill.'

Like Baudelaire, Beyle, and Flaubert, Eliot finds a death in the smiles of others – what he calls 'the void . . . in the middle of all human happiness and all human relations'. His essay 'Baudelaire' speaks of this experience in terms that make it clear that the experience is Eliot's own. For Baudelaire, as for Eliot, 'there is . . . a gap between human love and divine love' (SE, 429). This is for Eliot the void 'which there is only one thing to fill'.[26] From the fact that Baudelaire's 'human love is definite and positive' and his 'divine love vague and· uncertain' comes 'his insistence on the evil of love' and 'his constant vituperations of the female' (SE, 429). Apparently the fact that he knows himself stranded across a gap from divine love (he has 'a dim recognition of the direction of beatitude'), and the fact that his one definite and positive experience of love – human love – is inadequate to his desires, combine to create resentment of human love in general and the particular woman who is its object (SE, 428). The story is the same as that told in Eliot's poetry – particularly in *The Waste Land*. Whether as a sea or as a silence, the same gap between lovers is apparent, and the misogyny matches Baudelaire's. Combining his own theory of the impersonality of poetry with Gourmont's theory of the impersonality of thirteenth-century love, Eliot explains the 'vituperations of the female' that appear in Baudelaire's work (and, of course, in his own):

> there is no need to pry for psychopathological causes, which would be irrelevant at best; for his attitude towards women is consistent with the point of view which he had reached. . . . He has arrived at the perception that a woman must be to some extent a symbol; he did not arrive at the point of harmonizing his experience with his ideal needs. (SE, 429–30)

Not perceived from the point of view of the final cause of love, Baudelaire's feelings for women are misperceived by Baudelaire as disjunct from divine love. As for the early Eliot, so for Baudelaire: woman is symbolically the body side of puritanism's body/soul dichotomy.

The misogyny is apparently nothing personal. According to Eliot, had Baudelaire 'been a woman he would, no doubt, have held the same views about men' – a point that Eliot makes by his own shift of perspective in Part III of *The Waste Land* (where we view the void at the centre of human relations ostensibly from a woman's point of view) (SE, 428–30). Rather, the misogyny in question – Eliot's as much as Baudelaire's – is the equal and opposite of Dante's love: 'The complement, and the correction to the *Journaux Intimes*, so far as they deal with the relations of man and woman, is the *Vita Nuova*, and the *Divine Comedy*' (SE, 430). Baudelaire's misogyny is to Dante's love as genuine blasphemy is to belief: the latter is 'a way of affirming belief'; the former is a way of affirming love (SE, 421). Once Baudelaire's idiosyncratic experience of human relations is explained away, so is Eliot's: 'I cannot assert it too strongly – Baudelaire's view of life, such as it is, is objectively apprehensible, that is to say, his idiosyncrasies can partly explain his view of life, but they cannot explain it away' (SE, 430). There is in the misogyny of Baudelaire and Eliot something more than is dreamt of in psychopathology: 'the reaching out towards something which cannot be had *in*, but which may be partly had *through*, personal relations' (SE, 428). And so, just as in the interests of his identification with Donne Eliot expands the concept of puritanism so as to make of Donne a perverse puritan who glorifies the body, so he expands the concept of the Dantean so as to make of Baudelaire a perverse Dante who hates his Beatrice – for once Baudelaire becomes Dantean, so does Eliot.

Yet that Eliot still feels Murry's challenge about the nature of his mysticism – despite having aligned himself with Dante and Baudelaire – is indicated by his review of Murry's book, *Son of Woman*. Eliot's review subtly undermines his construction of a Dantean Baudelaire by aligning the latter with Lawrence – if there ever was one, surely the twentieth-century's version of the perversely puritan Donne. In effect, although Eliot would claim for himself the same 'true form of *acedia*' that he locates in Baudelaire's struggle towards the spiritual life, he betrays a suspicion that he can explain away his reactions to marriage, women and sexual activity – and so explain his mystical perception of the void – by psychopathological means (SE, 423).

Lawrence is a descendant of Donne. According to Eliot, an

> illustration of Lawrence's ignorance, and a fault which corrupts his whole philosophy of human relations . . . is his hopeless attempt to find some mode in which two persons – of the opposite sex, and then as a venture of despair, of the same sex – may be spiritually united.[27]

Like Donne, Lawrence is one of those who seeks through human relations to become spiritually united with another soul. The phrase here that rejects as hopeless the attempt to achieve this union by either heterosexual *or* homosexual love is significant. It is an intertextual acknowledgement that Lawrence is the bogey behind Eliot's parenthetical argument in 'Dante' (1929) that 'the love of man and woman (or for that matter of man and man) is only explained and made reasonable by the higher love, or else is simply the coupling of animals' (SE, 274).

Yet that Baudelaire should be regarded as different from Lawrence on this score is by no means clear, for Eliot's portraits of these two figures are more like than unlike. Eliot argues that 'the whole history of Lawrence's life and of Lawrence's writing . . . is the history of his craving for greater intimacy than is possible between human beings, a craving irritated to the point of frenzy by his unusual incapacity for being intimate at all.'[28] Baudelaire had a similar incapacity; he 'was thoroughly perverse and insufferable: a man with a talent for ingratitude and unsociability, intolerably irritable, and with a mulish determination . . . if he had friends, to alienate them' (SE, 422). Lawrence's story 'is an appalling narrative of spiritual pride, nourished by ignorance, and possibly also by consciousness of great powers and humble birth.'[29] Baudelaire 'had the pride of the man who feels in himself great weakness and great strength' (SE, 422).

In the case of Baudelaire's behaviour – just as, initially, in the case of his own – Eliot abjures a psychopathological explanation: 'His *ennui* [boredom] may of course be explained, as everything can be explained in psychological or pathological terms; but it is also, from the opposite point of view, a true form of *acedia*, arising from the unsuccessful struggle towards the spiritual life' (SE, 423). In the case of Lawrence, however, a psychopathological explanation of his behaviour is preferred: he has an 'emotional disease'. Furthermore, Lawrence has

> a fluctuating ability of diagnosis, without the further and total ability of prescription and regime. That, in my view, is only to be found – and only in our time with great difficulty if at all – in Christian discipline and asceticism. To this Lawrence could not and would not come; hence his relapse into pride and hatred.[30]

Eliot would have it that whereas Baudelaire dwells in a moral universe bounded by 'Heaven and Hell' (SE, 423), Lawrence and 'his two principal disciples, Mr Murry himself and Mr Aldous Huxley', dwell in 'limbo' because they 'try to believe in a spectral abstraction called Life'.[31]

Yet the language by which Eliot explains Lawrence – he is a 'demon' whom Murry would exorcise; he wilfully 'would not come' to Christianity; he fell into 'pride and hatred' – casts him in the role of Satan. Eliot's language, in short, makes Lawrence something of a Baudelaire, whose Satanism attracted Eliot's attention:

> When Baudelaire's Satanism is dissociated from its less creditable paraphernalia, it amounts to a dim intuition of a part, but a very important part, of Christianity. Satanism itself, so far as not merely affectation, was an attempt to get into Christianity by the back door. Genuine blasphemy, genuine in spirit and not merely verbal, is the product of partial belief, and it is as impossible to the complete atheist as to the perfect Christian. It is a way of affirming belief. (SE, 421)

Eliot does not imply that Lawrence is a Satanist, but his language implies that Lawrence's frenzy on behalf of Life is the equivalent of Baudelaire's *ennui* or acedia: each is the product of partial belief.

Since Lawrence's blood mysticism is of the sort that Eliot condemns in The Clark Lectures as romantic, the pressure to deny similarity between Lawrence and Baudelaire (and thereby between Lawrence and Eliot) is great. It is not as surprising as it might otherwise be, therefore, to find that in Eliot's review of Murry's *Son of Woman*, Lawrence is damned for the very thing that earns Baudelaire praise. In the end, however, the systematic intertextual similarity between the account of Baudelaire and the account of Lawrence works to undercut the distinction that Eliot would draw between these figures. This resistance to the argument that Eliot would apparently *like* to make – that Baudelaire is spiritually healthy and Lawrence spiritually sick – is a function of his insight in The Clark Lectures into the similarity between puritanical contempt for the body and puritanical glorification of the body. For all his attempts to distinguish Baudelaire from Lawrence, Eliot senses the extent to which – however oppositely – they are distracted equally by the body.

Inevitably, Eliot's interpretation of his own spiritual life is involved in this interpretation of the merits and demerits of Baudelaire and Lawrence. However much Eliot would align himself with Baudelaire and therefore against Lawrence, analysis of his writing about these matters allows one to see Baudelaire – and therefore Eliot himself – as not only different from Lawrence but also similar to him. Midway through the review, for instance, Eliot quotes a long passage from *Lady Chatterly's Lover* that Murry himself quotes (in the passage below, the word that Eliot changed and the phrase and the sentence that he omitted in copying Murry's text are in brackets):

> I held forth with rapture to her, positively with rapture. I simply went up in smoke. And she adored me. The serpent in the grass was sex. She somehow didn't have any; at least, not where it's supposed to be. I got thinner and thinner [crazier]. Then I said we'd got to be lovers. I talked her into it [, as usual]. So she let me. I was excited, and she never wanted it. [She just didn't want it.] She adored me, she loved me to talk to her and kiss

her: in that way she had a passion for me. But the other she just didn't want. And there are lots of women like her. And it was just the other that I *did* want. So there we split. I was cruel and left her.[32]

Accepting Murry's assurance that Mellors is Lawrence and that this 'is the most veracious account of Lawrence's early sex life that he has given', Eliot expresses 'shock' at 'Such complacent egotism': 'The girl was obviously in love with him, in the way appropriate to her youth and inexperience; and it was not good enough for Lawrence.'[33] Lawrence is 'a man who is totally incapable of intimacy'; his is 'a very sick soul'.[34] Nowhere else does Eliot's criticism of Lawrence become so harshly *ad hominem* as in this review in general, and after this passage in particular. My suspicion is that Eliot recognizes in Lawrence's behaviour the pattern of his own behaviour in his relationship with Vivien.

There is reason to suspect that Eliot's own marriage had been interpreted to him in similar terms. As early as 1915 Bertrand Russell apparently analysed Eliot's relationship with Vivien in Lawrentian terms. That he shared with the Eliots his analysis of the Lawrentian psychology implied by their behaviour is suggested by letters to Russell written by Eliot in 1925: 'I want words from you which only you can give. But if you have now ceased to care at all about either of us, . . . I will tell you now that everything has turned out as you predicted 10 years ago. You are a great psychologist.'[35] Written in the midst of marital crisis, Eliot's letter suggests why Eliot acknowledged to Russell in a letter two years before that Vivien regarded Russell as 'one of the very few persons who might possibly see anything' in *The Waste Land*.[36] The Eliots' relationship is depicted in the poem, and Russell is an expert on the relationship. Russell's pairing of these letters in his autobiography – the one about the marriage, the other about the poem – implies that such was his understanding of the connection between *The Waste Land* and the crises in the Eliots' marriage.

At the very point that Russell became involved in the relationship between Tom and Vivien Eliot, he was an admirer of Lawrence's psychology:

We both imagined that there was something important to be said about the reform of human relations, and we did not at first realise that we took diametrically opposite views as to the kind of reform that was needed. . . . I was already accustomed to being accused of undue slavery to reason, and I thought perhaps that he could give me a vivifying dose of unreason. I did in fact acquire a certain stimulus from him.[37]

In July of 1915, one of Russell's letters to Ottoline Morrell has only two subjects: Lawrence in the first paragraph, the Eliots in the second. First Russell observes that Lawrence's 'psychology of people is amazingly good up to a point'. Then follows his analysis of the Eliots:

> She is light, a little vulgar, adventurous, full of life. . . . He is exquisite and listless; she says she married him to stimulate him, but finds she can't do it. Obviously he married in order to be stimulated. . . . He is the Miss Sands type of American.

We find in letters like this the very terms of Russell's analysis of his own relationship with Lawrence in his autobiography: Lawrence and Vivien are vivifying; they represent unreason, life, stimulus. Russell characterized Vivien later the same year as likely to end 'as a criminal or a saint' – a dichotomy suggested to him by his conversations with Lawrence. His description of her as a potential 'criminal' echoes Lawrence's description of himself in contemporaneous letters to Russell as an 'outlaw'; his description of her as a potential 'saint' reflects Lawrence's sense of himself as a visionary preacher (in trying to save Russell from 'reason', Lawrence explained that he '*must* preach', to which Russell responded by challenging Lawrence to try 'preaching' in Trafalgar Square).[38] Vivien is thus constructed by Russell as being for Eliot the potentially stimulating embodiment of life and unreason that Lawrence is for Russell. Similarly, Vivien's role as Lawrence-surrogate is paralleled by Eliot's role as Russell-surrogate. In characterizing him as 'the Miss Sands type of American', Russell redeploys his description of Eliot in an earlier letter as one 'who is civilized . . . but has no vigour or life – or enthusiasm'.[39] Like Russell, the too-rational Eliot needs stimulation by unreason.

By the end of 1916, Vivien seems to have become a Lawrence-surrogate not for Eliot but for Russell himself. The latter wrote of his relationship with Vivien Eliot in such terms to Ottoline Morrell as his affair with the latter was ending:

I shall soon have come to the end of the readjustment with Mrs E. [Mrs T.S. Eliot]. . . . I have been realising various things during this time. It is odd how one finds out what one really wants, and how very selfish it always is. What I want permanently – not consciously, but deep down – is stimulus. . . . I get a stimulus most from the instinctive feeling of success. Failure makes me collapse. . . . The real trouble between you and me has always been that you gave me a sense of failure. . . . I had a sense of success with Mrs E. because I achieved what I meant to achieve (which was not so very difficult). . . . Instinctively, I turn to things in which success is possible, just for the stimulus.[40]

Russell's language again betrays influence by Lawrence's theories of blood-consciousness and again reveals the Lawrentian role as 'stimulus' (now for himself) that he has constructed for Vivien Eliot.

Finally, as Ackroyd notes, 'Russell characterized Vivien as possessing mental passion but not physical passion . . . she wished for male devotion but did not particularly enjoy any physical expression of it.'[41] The situation that Russell describes is very similar to that described in the passage from *Lady Chatterly's Lover* that Eliot quotes. The problem is sex: the woman does not want it and the man does. Eliot, in fact, wished to get rid of his virginity and confessed to sometimes thinking it advisable 'to do so before marriage' – a goal apparently not realized before his marriage six months after expressing this wish.[42] If, as I suspect, Russell's 1915 psychological analysis of the Eliots (an analysis to which Eliot alludes in his letter to Russell ten years later) included the sort of analysis to which Ackroyd refers above, Eliot's sensitivity to Lawrence's passage is understandable. The passage hits too close to home, threatening like so many others to reveal similarity where Eliot tries so hard to establish difference.

Furthermore, Eliot could not have missed the personal relevance of the Lawrence/Mellor's defence of a man's right and responsibility to abandon the kind of woman under consideration. On the one hand, one of Eliot's 1925 letters to Russell mentions the possibility of some sort of separation from Vivien:

I don't know to what extent the changes which have taken place, since we were in touch with you, would seem to you material. What you suggest seems to me of course what should have been done years ago. Since then her health is a thousand times worse. Her only alternative would be to live quite alone – if she could. And the fact that living with me has done her so much damage does not help me to come to any decision.[43]

Without Russell's letter, Eliot's letter remains cryptic, but it nonetheless hints that Russell had advised Eliot to consider some form of separation – both in 1925 and 1915. On the other hand, Eliot's spiritual adviser, Father Underhill, had advised him to separate from Vivien – only a few months before he wrote his review of Murry's book.[44]

Eliot's attack upon the Lawrence of *Lady Chatterly's Lover* is thus another attempt in this review to present as difference what is at the same time similarity. It is in this light that one must consider his disdain for Lawrence's complaints about 'the sad burden of the unsatisfactoriness of human relations':

> What a pity that he did not understand the simple truth that of any two human beings each has privacies which the other cannot penetrate, and boundaries which the other must not transgress, and that yet human intimacy can be wonderful and life-giving: a truth well known to Christian thought, though we do not need to be Christians to understand it. And that the love of two human beings is only made perfect in the love of God. These are very old and simple truths indeed.[45]

Eliot's criticism is unclear: 'Lawrence, as I believe Murry says, remembered the second injunction of the Summary of the Law and hoped to practise it without recognizing the first.' The ambiguity is double. What are the two injunctions in question? And do the adjectives 'first' and 'second' refer to the order in which the injunctions occur in Eliot's writing or to the order in which they are hierarchically ranked in the moral universe?

Is injunction number one that we should not penetrate privacies and transgress boundaries, and is injunction number two that human intimacy should be life-giving? If so, Eliot's complaint is that Lawrence is after the life-giving quality without practising respect for privacies and boundaries. This reading would make sense of Eliot's complaints earlier in the review about Lawrence's egotism and his lack of respect for the other person: 'Even in his travels to more primitive lands, he could never take the crude peoples simply for what they are; he must needs always be expecting something of them that they could not give, something peculiarly medicinal for himself.'[46]

Is the first injunction – first in moral importance, although rhetorically presented second – that love between human beings can only be made perfect in the love of God? The second injunction would then be the double admonition to respect privacies and boundaries in a nonetheless life-giving way. If so, Eliot's complaint is that Lawrence is aware only of human love and not divine love. Such a reading would account for his derisive snort: 'As if human love could possibly be an end in itself!' It would also reveal Eliot's complaint to be the same as Murry's:

> It is not physical tenderness to each other that men and women need to be taught as the one thing needful. What they need to learn is something to avail them when physical tenderness is torn away, and happy love is a faint and far-off dream. . . . The truth is simple. 'He that loseth his life, the same shall save it.' The one truth that Lawrence never learned.[47]

The second reading is thus just as plausible as the first.

And yet there is another reading – apparently neither plausible nor even possible. Could one not read the *first* injunction as a double admonition to respect privacies and boundaries in a nonetheless life-giving way? The second injunction would then become the admonition to perfect human love in God's love. Such a reading would seem nonsensical, given both that Eliot allows that Lawrence practises the second injunction – on the reading now under consideration, the injunction to perfect human love in God's love – and that it is precisely Lawrence's failure to recognize God's love that Eliot criticizes. Even this reading, however, makes sense once we recall the extent to which Lawrence functions for Eliot as an image of himself.

Eliot's uncharacteristically imprecise prose here suggests that something more than meets the eye is afoot. The attempt to focus attention on just two injunctions is undermined by the reference to three truths. There is 'the simple truth' about privacies and boundaries; there is the truth about life-giving intimacy, 'a truth well known to Christian thought'; and there is the truth about human love made perfect in God's – 'These are very old and simple truths indeed.' These three truths just do not fit comfortably into the two injunctions. Eliot seems most concerned about Lawrence's neglect of two truths – his refusal to respect the privacy of others and his refusal to recognize God – but he has condensed what amounts to two complaints into a sentence that pretends to speak of one.

Fortunately, Eliot's concluding metaphor unfolds his concerns in a way that allows us to appreciate the three elements in the story: 'It is the old story that you cannot get a quart out of a pint pot; and the astonishing fact you cannot even get a pint out of it unless you fill it.' The quart represents human love perfected: two people, neither of them penetrating privacies or transgressing boundaries, both of them involved in life-giving intimacy whose final cause is the love of God. The two pints that make up the quart consist of a pint of divine love and a pint of human love. The first stage of the metaphor therefore repeats Eliot's complaint that Lawrence does not recognize God's love; he has no divine pint. Yet the metaphor is developed further to suggest that even Lawrence's pint of human love is not full. Here is Eliot's complaint that Lawrence cannot get beyond 'his craving for greater intimacy than is possible between human beings'.[48]

Lawrence is down a pint of divine love and half a pint of human love. Murry – whom Eliot accuses of trying 'to believe in a spectral abstraction called Life' – is down a pint of divine love. Eliot is the other figure to be factored into this metaphor: he is worried that he himself is down half a pint of human love. The values in opposition in the review are those in opposition at the beginning of 'A Game of Chess'. Behind the person who would penetrate the privacies and transgress the barriers of others is the woman in Part II of *The Waste Land* – Vivien Eliot, the Lawrence figure in Russell's psychology. The man across the sea of silence from her who cannot find that which is 'wonderful and lifegiving' in their relationship is Eliot himself. The similarity between his own behaviour with Vivien and Lawrence's and Mellors's behaviour with their first loves – however unwilling Eliot is to recognize the similarity – makes Lawrence to a certain extent an Eliot-surrogate. Appreciating the aspect of identity that underlies the awareness of difference that motivates Eliot's writing about Lawrence here, one can begin to make sense of the apparently nonsensical option in the readings of the sentence about injunctions. The 'Lawrence' who respects the second injunction (on this reading, the injunction rhetorically introduced second, the injunction that entails making human love perfect in the love of God), but who does not respect the first injunction (the injunction that entails a wonderful and life-giving intimacy respectful of privacies and boundaries), is Eliot himself. His brimful pint of divine love notwithstanding, he has not topped up his half pint of nonpenetrating, nontransgressive human love with wonderful and life-giving intimacy. The incapacity for intimacy against which Eliot rails in this review is as much his own as Lawrence's – a fact that the imprecisions in his writing both conceal and reveal.

The Clark Lectures thus initiate a confidential investigation into the nature of Eliot's own mystical experiences. Try as he will, he cannot escape the suspicion that for all his classical impulses there remains always in his mystical moments an element of romanticism. He castigates Donne, Richard Crashaw and St Theresa for resting in their emotion of enjoyment. Such a mental habit qualifies them for psychopathological analysis:

> [Richard Crashaw] lost his mother, and even his step-mother, very early; it is possible that unsatisfied filial cravings are partly responsible for his adoration of St Theresa. (Incidentally, it is possible that St Theresa herself suffered from somewhat the same trouble; we remark that in her vision of paradise, the first persons she identified were her father and mother.) (*Varieties*, 163)

Eliot would not do this to a Dante – or even a Baudelaire – and so he would not do this to himself. Yet although it takes a long time – he has to travel from 'Ode' to 'Coriolan' – Eliot slowly begins to realize that the very same analysis might be applicable to the broken Coriolanean mystic within him: 'Mother / May we not be some time, almost now, together' (CPP, 130).

8

Risking Enchantment in Four Quartets

The Clark Lectures inaugerate for Eliot both a reassessment of his mysticism and a reassessment of his poetic. The effort in these lectures to distinguish between romantic and classical mysticisms, for instance, is certainly rooted in Eliot's reflections on the proper course for modern poetry. He wants to show how Dante's system of thought and feeling produces 'a simple, direct and even austere manner of speech', whereas experiencing thought (rather than believing through it), as in 'Donne and in *some of our contemporaries*', produces 'an affected, tortuous, and often over-elaborate and ingenious manner of speech' (*Varieties*, 120, emphasis mine).

Eliot's remarks here are related to his concluding words in his earliest essay on Dante (1920):

> When most of our modern poets confine themselves to what they had perceived, they produce for us, usually, only odds and ends of still life and stage properties; but that does not imply so much that the method of Dante is obsolete, as that our vision is perhaps comparatively restricted. (SW, 171)

Modern poets are contrasted with Dante. The latter's philosophy was 'something *perceived*' – not something studied, but 'the articulate formulation' of a 'vision of life' 'so nearly complete . . . that the significance of any single passage . . . is incomplete unless we ourselves apprehend the whole' (SW, 170–1). The difference between the perception of modern poets and the perception of Dante is not clear: it may be that their ability to perceive is not as good as Dante's ability to perceive, or it may be that the world that they perceive is not as whole as the world that Dante perceives. Eliot's observation that modern 'vision is perhaps comparatively restricted' does not resolve the ambiguity, for 'vision' refers both to the act of seeing and the thing seen. On the one hand, like Donne (who experienced the fragments of a metaphysical system that was for Dante a whole), modern poets perhaps experience the odds and ends of a truth in which they no longer participate. On the other hand, also like Donne, they perhaps become lost in inner perception – substituting for a vision of life a vision of their inner life, an illusory 'reality' whose illusoriness is hinted at by Eliot's characterization of the thing that modern poets perceive as an abstraction from reality, merely a 'still life' or collection of 'stage properties'.

The question that Eliot indirectly takes up in his discussion of modern poetry in The Clark Lectures is whether *The Waste Land* is romantic or classical in its mysticism. The problem is to determine whether *The Waste Land* is 'only odds and ends of still life and stage properties' (the result of Eliot's 'comparatively restricted' vision as modern) or whether the poem of fragments is, like *The Divine Comedy*, a nearly complete vision and articulate formulation of the life made by the modern mind, an almost immediate acceptance of the philosophical idea within the modern world. *The Waste Land* might constitute through its 'odds and ends' a *seeing* comparable in its articulate vision of disorder to Dante's vision of order, or it might constitute only the 'odds and ends' of the dark night of the soul of a romantic sensibility, as Murry suggests.

Eliot's various comments about the springs of the poem in his own emotional life hint that he came to see it as a romantic, psychological document. Although the *Times Literary Supplement* described *The Waste Land* as the 'poet's vision of modern life', although Gilbert Seldes assured readers that Eliot had expressed 'something of supreme relevance to our present life', and although Conrad Aiken argued that the poem gives 'an impression of an intensely modern, intensely literary consciousness which perceives itself to be not a unit but a chance correlation or conglomerate of mutually discolorative fragments', Eliot rejected these opportunities to understand his poem as a Dantean example of the modern world *perceived*.[1] These reviews of 1922–3 are in his mind in 1931: 'When I wrote a poem called *The Waste Land* some of the more approving critics said I had expressed "the disillusionment of a generation", which is nonsense' (SE, 368). He not only disclaimed any such intention, but also accounted for the poem in terms of implicitly non-intellectual activities:

Various critics have done me the honour to interpret the poem in terms of criticism of the contemporary world, have considered it, indeed, as an important bit of social criticism. To me it was only the relief of a personal and wholly insignificant grouse against life; it is just a piece of rhythmical grumbling.[2]

Interviewed in his seventies, Eliot made the same point: 'In *The Waste Land* I wasn't even bothering whether I understood what I was saying.'[3]

Eliot defines the perspective from which he finds *The Waste Land* wanting in his analysis of Richard Crashaw in The Clark Lectures. He notes that one finds in a romantic mystical poet like Crashaw that emotions occur in a sequence instead of in a structure. The poetry of emotions in sequence is psychological, for the poet tends 'to follow up one impression by another, rather than to build one into another' (*Varieties*, 170). In short, the poet betrays the psychologism by which the experience that is a feeling or thought becomes an experience *of* that feeling or thought. Whereas Dante's image is interested in the idea to be conveyed, for instance, Donne's image may be interested in a variety of things (ingenuity, difficulty, forced resemblances). Dante's 'image always makes this idea or feeling more intelligible. In Donne, the interest is dispersed' (*Varieties*, 120). Dante is Eliot's preferred model: a poet's immediate experience ought to be like the classical mystic's experience – passing not into thoughts and feelings that merely constitute further experience, but into 'divine contemplation', which he defines as 'the development and subsumption of emotion and feeling through intellect into the vision of God' (*Varieties*, 103–4). The poet's emotion in structure is akin to the classical mystic's 'development and subsumption of emotion' in contemplation.

From this perspective, much of *The Waste Land* might seem romantic or psychological – a sequence of emotions, a retreat into the head. Celebrating in 1926 the intellectual structure of experience in Richard of St Victor's classical mysticism, Eliot was bound to be concerned by the apparent exclusion of the analytic intellect from the poem's sequence of images. As David Perkins observes, 'In the style of *The Waste Land*, one could not meditate, reason, argue, opine, generalize, judge, or conclude.'[4] It was precisely the possibility of a more intellectual poetry that Eliot sought in 1926. Complementing the celebration of the role of the intellect in classical mysticism in The Clark Lectures is Eliot's celebration of classicism and reason in his launching of *The New Criterion* at the same time:

I believe that the modern tendency is toward something which, for want of a better name, we may call classicism. . . . [T]here is a tendency – discernible even in art – toward a higher and clearer conception of Reason, and a more severe and serene control of the emotions by Reason.

He points to H.G. Wells, G.B. Shaw and Bertrand Russell as instances of those who 'exhibit intelligence at the mercy of emotion'.[5] Yet Eliot does not pretend to have turned the trick himself whereby emotion is subsumed through intellect into the vision of God. Rather, however different in his tendency from Wells, Shaw and Russell, he implies that he is a victim of the same disorder as they:

The artist in the modern world . . . is heavily hampered in ways that the public does not understand. He finds himself, if he is a man of intellect, unable to realise his art to his own satisfaction, and he may be driven to examining the elements in the situation – political, social, philosophical or religious – which frustrate his labour.[6]

These comments – bracketing the discussion of poetry in The Clark Lectures – imply that Eliot's greatest public success to date, *The Waste Land*, is from the perspective of 1926 evidence of the man of intellect's art unrealised, the man of intellect's labour frustrated.

Reading Eliot's analysis of Richard of St Victor's style against this background brings into relief in The Clark Lectures his attempt to link his pre-1926 poetic to his subsequent poetic. On the one hand, Eliot constructs a criticism of Richard's Latin that makes the virtues of Richard's prose a prefiguration of Eliot's own pre-1926 virtues as a modern poet. Richard's work is 'written in a clear, simple and economical style'. In fact,

every phrase makes what went before it a little more intelligible; there is not a word wasted. Furthermore Richard is very sparing of tropes and figures. . . . It is prose which seems to me to satisfy the primary demands of writing, that is, to write what you think in the words in which you think it, adding no embellishment; to avoid metaphors and figures of speech, and to keep your emotion out of it. (*Varieties*, 102–3)

That there should be 'not a word wasted' recalls Pound's determination as Imagist 'To use absolutely no word that does not
contribute to the presentation'.[7] Similarly, avoidance of 'embellishment' and 'metaphors and figures of speech' recalls the spareness
of language that Pound, the Imagists and early modernists in general
recommended. Such efficiency and such spareness in the economy
of words are characteristic of Eliot's various styles from 'Prufrock'
to *The Waste Land*. The need to 'keep your emotion out of it' also
recalls, of course, Eliot's advice to this effect in 'Tradition and the
Individual Talent'.

    On the other hand, Eliot's analysis of Richard's virtues as a writer
of prose can be seen in restrospect to prefigure his new style as poet.
The repetition and monotony praised in Richard, for instance,
become principles of composition in *Ash-Wednesday*: 'Because I
do not hope to turn again / Because I do not hope / Because
I do not hope to turn' (CPP, 89). Moreover, as in Richard's
prose, so in Eliot's poetry of the 1930s and 1940s 'every phrase
makes what went before it a little more intelligible'. Thus the
repetition in *Ash-Wednesday* is not so much simple repetition as
subtle amplification and refinement of meaning. Similarly, just as
Richard writes what he thinks in the words in which he thinks it,
so does the new Eliot – especially in *Burnt Norton*:

> Time present and time past
> Are both perhaps present in time future
> And time future contained in time past.
> If all time is eternally present
> All time is unredeemable. (CPP, 171)

The result is relatively dry, philosophical verse. Celebrated by
some, condemned by others, the poem's discursive dimension is
consistent with Eliot's development as classical mystic; it is as clear
a demonstration as possible of this former philosopher's allegiance
both to what he thinks and to the words in which he thinks it.

    Saying what one thinks in the words in which one thinks it,
Richard's habit in *prose*, is judged by Eliot 'to satisfy one of
the primary demands of *writing*' – a term that includes poetry:
Richard's prose seems 'an admirable influence for the formation
of style either in prose or verse' (*Varieties*, 106). The exercise
of defining a classical mystical style by reference to Richard of
St Victor thus plays an important part in taking Eliot from one

stage of his writing to the next – from his relatively Imagistic, stream-of-consciousness style in 'Prufrock', 'Preludes', 'Rhapsody', 'Gerontion' and *The Waste Land* (the latter too close for comfort in its non-discursive juxtaposition of images and emotions to the 'spiritual hashish' and 'drugging of the emotions' that he had identified in romantic mystics and romantic poets alike) to the relatively discursive style of his meditative poetry in the 1930s and 1940s – poetry that has become 'intellectual preparation for spiritual contemplation'.

The result of Eliot's long contemplation in his poetry and prose of the epistemological claims of mysticism is signalled in a little-known interview from 1948. Prompted by the interviewer's observations about the inhibition of mysticism by intellect in Valéry's creative process, Eliot talked about mysticism in general:

> Eliot then said what seemed to me the centre and luminous point of the entire interview:
> 'But intellect pushed to its depths leads to mysticism.'
> 'Do you not believe', I asked him . . . , 'that intellect and mysticism are two faculties opposed in human nature?' A sign of denial was his only response, and this affirmation: 'All human faculties pushed to their limits end in mysticism.'[8]

Eliot keeps faith with the classical mysticism of Aristotle, Aquinas and Dante. The assertion that 'intellect . . . leads to mysticism' is part of the definition in The Clark Lectures of classical mysticism – its method and goal 'the divine contemplation, and the development and subsumption of emotion and feeling through intellect into the vision of God' (*Varieties*, 103–4). That the lectures delivered two decades before have not been forgotten is also suggested by the claim that 'All human faculties . . . end in mysticism', which echoes the claim in The Clark Lectures that mysticism is inescapable: 'I wish to linger a little over this twelfth-century mysticism, not because we are interested in mysticism, but because we cannot get away from it. There is always some type of mysticism about' (*Varieties*, 100). Yet in these 1948 comments there is no hint of the distinction in The Clark Lectures between romantic and classical mysticisms. In fact, assuming an opposition between intellect and mysticism, the interviewer gives Eliot an opportunity to point out her failure to distinguish between classical and romantic mysticisms, yet Eliot instead makes a more sweeping assertion to the effect that mysticism is the ground of all human knowledge and experience. This is an aspect of his thinking about mysticism hinted at in his ambiguous reference to mysticism and metaphysics in 'Tradition and the Individual Talent' but not fully realized until *Four Quartets*.

The mysticism in *Four Quartets* was evident to readers from the moment of publication. In the 1940s, Helen Gardner pointed to passages from *The Cloud of Unknowing*, Dame Julian of Norwich, Walter Hilton and St John of the Cross. Critics like Gardner, celebrating *Four Quartets* as 'Eliot's masterpiece' and finding themselves largely in sympathy with his Christian turn of 1927, accept the allusions to Christian mystics as clues to Eliot's spiritual state during the process of composition.[9] Sister Corona Sharp and Paul Murray represent the culmination of this trend. Sharp documents the references to Christian mystics (especially St John of the Cross) and thereby explains the integrity and coherence of Eliot's spiritual quest: in 'Little Gidding' the 'mystical journey ends . . . in "complete simplicity" or total self-giving. Having passed through the fires of purgation, the soul is ready to go forth from this life.'[10] In his far more comprehensive study, Murray reaches a similar conclusion. He finds in 'complex metaphors, in patterns of thought, and even in the overall intellectual framework of the poem' many 'themes and symbols from a variety of Christian and non-Christian mystical sources'. By means of them Eliot offers 'an authentic expression of a state of soul that one can only call mystical'.[11] Others have preferred to explore the influence of Eastern mysticism upon the poem. Sri, finding that 'the Indian face of Eliot has not been quite captured', suggests that Eliot is 'a *kavi*, a poet who attempts to see deep into the design of the universe'.[12] Depending upon our perspective, then, our interpretation of the moments traditionally marked 'mystical' in *Four Quartets* – the moment in the garden when the lotus rises, the moment 'Quick now, here, now, always', the moment of 'Midwinter spring' when 'The soul's sap quivers' – will vary (CPP, 176, 191). For some, the mystical moment represents Eliot's location of the point of contact between the individual Christian soul and Christ; for others, it represents the point of contact between samsara and nirvana.

Kearns regards the references to Eastern mysticism in an otherwise Christian poem as serving a more secular epistemology.

Arguing that Eliot defines the reading process as involving cease-less surrender to a new point of view and then renunciation of it, she finds that in *Four Quartets* the

> Indic tradition, among many other points of view, is essential to this renunciation, for only through its counterpoint can Eliot enact the destabilization of an old perspective and the movement to a new one, which is all we know, at least in this life, of transcendence.[13]

This secular sense of transcendence as an entirely human experi-ence of changes in point of view is found in the dissertation: 'the life of a soul . . . consist[s] in . . . passing, when possible, from two or more discordant viewpoints to a higher which shall somehow include and transmute them' (KE, 147). Kearns describes the dissertation as 'in part a refutation of mystical philosophy' because it limits transcendence to the experience of movement from one 'point of view' to another as opposed to the mystic's claim to have experienced the Absolute.[14] Yet the dissertation is also in part a justification of mystical experience, for Eliot's conclusions about metaphysics prove to be a reworking of James's conclusions about mysticism in *The Varieties of Religious Experience*. Addressing the question of whether mysticism furnishes any 'warrant for the truth' of its claims, James makes three points. First, 'Mystical states, when well developed, usually are, and have the right to be, absolutely authoritative over the individuals to whom they come.'[15] Such a mystic is Eliot's metaphysician, for whom 'thought and reality are one' in a well-built system; he 'thinks of reality in terms of his system' (KE, 167–8). Second, James suggests that 'No authority emanates from them which should make it a duty for those who stand outside of them to accept their revelations uncritically'.[16] Similarly, Eliot acknowledges that 'For a metaphysics to be accepted, good-will is essential.' If one does not recognize the truth and the reality of the metaphysical system as one's own, then its claims have no authority over one: 'From the critic's standpoint the metaphysician's world may be real only as the child's bogey is real' (KE, 168, 167). Third, James finds that mystical states

> break down the authority of the non-mystical or rationalistic consciousness, based upon the understanding and the senses alone. They show it to be only one kind of consciousness. They

open out the possibility of other orders of truth, in which, so far as anything in us vitally responds to them, we may freely continue to have faith.[17]

For Eliot, metaphysics opens out the possibility of other orders of truth: 'a metaphysical doctrine pretends to be *"true"* simply, and none of our pragmatic tests will apply.' Like the mystical state, the metaphysical faith-state is vital: 'our theories make all the difference in the world, because the truth has to be *my* truth before it can be true at all' (KE, 169). Eliot's metaphysician is James's mystic: 'The mystic is . . . *invulnerable*, and must be left, whether we relish it or not, in undisturbed enjoyment of his creed. Faith, says Tolstoy, is that by which men live. And faith-state and mystic state are practically convertible terms.'[18]

The dissertation's ambiguously mystical and mundane experience of transcendence is precisely the perspective that Eliot reinvigorates in *Four Quartets* in order to explain the mystical foundation of human knowledge and experience.

'Burnt Norton' demonstrates more than the practical impact upon the form of Eliot's poetry that comes of the *poetic* reorientation begun in The Clark Lectures; it also demonstrates the practical impact upon his poetry's content that comes of the *mystical* reorientation begun in them. In fact, however much of 'Burnt Norton' derives from lines unused in *Murder in the Cathedral*, a considerable motivation for the writing of the poem is Eliot's desire to rewrite *The Waste Land* so as to reconsider its grumbling romantic grouse against life from the point of view of an aspiring classical mystic.

'Burnt Norton''s intertextual nod in the direction of *The Waste Land* is pronounced. Its five-part structure, for instance, seems to have its source in the five-part structure of the earlier poem. Pound's pruning of Part IV of *The Waste Land* until it became a relatively brief and lyrical section is apparently the reason that the fourth section of 'Burnt Norton' – and each of the subsequent poems in *Four Quartets* – is equally brief and lyrical. 'Burnt Norton''s thrush – however different as a species from the North American thrush in *The Waste Land* – is like the thrush in the earlier poem in its deceptive ways: the one deceives about water, the other about gardens. Furthermore, 'Burnt Norton''s reference to the 'heart of light' in the rose garden reproduces this phrase from *The Waste Land*, where it refers to a very similar experience in a very similar garden.

Gordon links the two poems in terms of Eliot's biography. She suggests that 'Burnt Norton' documents a mystical moment inspired by the poet's 'deeply emotional encounter with a first love'. The silent person addressed in *Burnt Norton* is Emily Hale – the girl in *The Waste Land*'s hyacinth garden, and before that the girl in 'La Figlia Che Piange' where, 'in 1912, Eliot had rehearsed an autumn departure from the garden of young love'. A meeting with Emily Hale in the garden of Burnt Norton in the autumn of 1934 'presented the temptation to replay that scene, that past, those other selves that might have been.' In fact, Eliot replays in 'Burnt Norton' the *replay* in *The Waste Land* of the original garden scene from 1912:

> He feels the same indescribable ecstasy recalled in *The Waste Land* where, leaving a garden, rapt by the 'hyacinth girl' whose arms were full of flowers, a man stares suddenly 'into the heart of light, the silence', only to collapse, in bitter frustration, into the sterility of present life, with its abortive sexual relationships in a polluted London. So, too, at Burnt Norton, the moment passes: a cloud shuts off the sun, the pool is dry once more, and Eliot is left to lament 'the waste sad time / Stretching before and after'.

Although Gordon contrasts *The Waste Land* with 'Burnt Norton' by claiming that the former is confined to an awareness only of the mysticism of 'the way up' by the light of grace whereas the latter is aware of both the 'way up' and the mystical 'way down' to sublime insight through a remaking of the sinful self, a more important difference between the poems consists in the contemplative mode present in the later poem but absent in the earlier one.[19]

Analysis of the first section of 'Burnt Norton' reveals that Eliot models the poem's classical mysticism upon Evelyn Underhill's definition of contemplation in *Mysticism*. Although, as we have seen, Eliot studied Underhill's famous book at Harvard almost as soon as it came out (1911), and although a passage in Eliot's Clark Lectures suggests that he kept the book at hand when researching these lectures in 1925 and 1926, Underhill exercised her greatest influence over Eliot in the 1930s. They met for the first time in London in 1930. In the decade that followed, Eliot regularly solicited reviews from Underhill for *The Criterion*. As editor of the *Spectator*, Underhill solicted 'Studies in Sanctity' from Eliot in 1932. They socialized throughout the 1930s.[20] She was greatly impressed by *The Rock* in 1934; Eliot visted in 1935.[21] When she died in 1941, Eliot drafted a letter to supplement an obituary notice of her in a journal or newspaper – a letter that hints at her role in Eliot's spiritual life:

> I should like to supplement your admirable notice of the late E.U. (Mrs S.M.) with a word about the side of her activity which is not preserved in her published work or known to most of her readers. She concerned herself as much with the practice as with the theory of the devotional life.

Eliot's comments imply that however theoretical his original interest in Underhill's work, her role in his spiritual life was in the end quite a practical one: 'She gave . . . herself to many, in retreats which she conducted and in the intercourse of daily life – she was always at the disposal of all who called upon her'; 'she helped to support the spiritual life of many more than she could in her humility have been aware of aiding.' This support and aid seems to have consisted in reinforcing Eliot's own sense of the importance of contemplation: 'her studies of the great mystics had the inspiration not primarily of the scholar or the champion of forgotten genius, but of a consciousness of the grievous need of the contemplative element in the modern world.'[22]

   'Burnt Norton' concentrates on what Underhill calls 'Recollection', the first stage of mystical contemplation. According to Underhill, all recollection begins as meditation 'upon some one aspect of Reality. . . . Christian contemplatives set before their minds one of the names of God, a fragment of Scripture, an incident of the life of Christ' (*Mysticism*, 375). Despite the biographical inspiration to which Gordon traces the poem, 'Burnt Norton' presents itself as a contemplation of God's name as '*logos*', 'light', 'Word' and 'Love'. The contemplation focuses first upon the meaning of the word *logos* for the pre-Christian Heraclitus, signalling the contemplation of God as *logos* that is to follow, then discovers God as the 'heart of light', and finally contemplates God as 'The Word in the desert' and as 'Love . . . itself unmoving, / Only the cause and end of movement' – the Unmoved Mover in which Aristotle's contemplation becomes complete (CPP, 172, 175).

Eliot depends upon this stage of contemplation in 'Burnt Norton' to avoid *The Waste Land*'s psychologism. Murry's charge that *The Waste Land* was the work of a romantic mystic, the absence of the discursive intellect in *The Waste Land*, and Eliot's awareness of his similarities with the psychopathological Lawrence combined to make Eliot suspect that his famous poem was modern less in its 1920s style than in its epistemological retreat into the head through a perversely Donne-like enjoyment of negative emotion. Confronted again by the mystical experience of the indestructible barriers between one person and another, Eliot's speaker embarks on an ambitious attempt to develop the emotions in this situation and subsume them through intellect into a vision of God. Attention to *logoi*, logic and accurate language in the face of intense emotion is Eliot's self-defined Aristotelian alternative to the romantic mystic's drugging of the emotions.

The process of Recollection entails an experience of reverie consequent upon the intitial contemplation of an aspect of 'Reality':

> The self, concentrated upon . . . image or idea, . . . falls gradually and insensibly into the condition of reverie. . . . It is a kind of half-way house between the perception of Appearance and the perception of Reality. . . . Consciousness seems like a blank field, save for the 'one point' in its centre, the subject of the meditation. Towards this focus the introversive self seems to press inwards from every side; still faintly conscious of the buzz of the external world outside its ramparts, but refusing to respond to its appeals. Presently the subject of meditation begins to take on a new significance; to glow with life and light. . . . Through it hints are coming to him of mightier, nameless things. . . . [He] apprehends to some extent – though how, he knows not – the veritable presence of God. (*Mysticism*, 376)

After the first ten lines of 'Burnt Norton', the speaker falls into the sort of reverie described here and receives a vision that turns Burnt Norton – both as property and as poem – into a 'half-way house' between appearance and reality. It is as though 'Burnt Norton' were modelled on this very passage: the 'one point' is the 'still point'; the glowing 'with life and light' is both the glittering 'out of heart of light' and the 'white light still and moving'; the buzz of the external world is still present in the speaker's awareness of the travellers on the London tube; and hints of mightier, nameless things are present in the implications of a presence 'Quick now, here, now, always' that cannot be named or placed (CPP, 173, 172, 173, 176).

The stages in the development of this visionary experience are obscure, but one can nonetheless discern in the first section of the poem a pattern in which meditation upon intellectual concerns culminates in an experience of mystical knowledge that answers the concerns in question. As the poem begins, the speaker is meditating upon a problem that his contemplation of *logoi* has turned up: perhaps 'all time is eternally present' (CPP, 171). This tentative hypothesis about the nature of time seems to pose a threat, for the speaker has arrived at a determinism in which past, present and future are part of a continuum of cause and effect that precludes the possibility that any event could have been or could be other than it was, is and will be: every moment is present in every other moment. The speaker therefore begins his meditation by considering the possibility that redeeming the past is impossible and that all speculation about 'what might have been' is pointless. Yet he proceeds to just such speculation – 'What if we had gone down the passage and through the door into the rose-garden?' – and so through his resistance to the hypothesis reveals a problem. As the dissertation puts it, the reality implied in such a metaphysics is not the speaker's, its truth not his.

The source of the problem is suggested in the language of the hypothesis itself: 'If all time is eternally present / All time is unredeemable' (CPP, 171). The word 'unredeemable' suggests that one of the speaker's major concerns is Original Sin. The reference later to 'our first world' and the ghostly people within it (identifiable as, among others, Adam and Eve) reinforces this suggestion. And so, percolating within the logical analysis of time is the unsettling recognition that according to the logic that the speaker constructs, Original Sin remains an eternal fact: sin, error, evil is present in every moment of human time (post-apple) – always has been present and always will be. The speaker has rediscovered the insight of Eliot's New England Puritan ancestors that the human heart is full of evil: 'there is not one empty corner in it; it is brimful; and there is no Sin but what is there.'[23]

As is to be expected in recollection, meditation upon ideas and images is supplemented by mystical vision – in this case, a vision that resolves the problem. Symbolically representing the speaker's concern about redemption, Adam and Eve approach so as to explain the significance of events in the Garden of Eden ('our first world'). They are 'guests' – and ghosts 'invisible, / Moving without pressure over the dead leaves' – visiting from the beginning of human time. They are 'accepted and accepting'; the two couples virtually dance together: 'So we moved, and they, in a formal pattern' (CPP, 171–2). Original Sin is thus marked as part of the past from which the ghosts arrive and as part of the present moment in which they are welcomed into the garden. All time is eternally present.

Images of dance and reflection acknowledge the continuity between the poet, on the one hand, and Adam and Eve (and Original Sin), on the other, but events near the pool also suggest a new possibility. The effect of the preposition that locates the ghostly couple 'behind' the poet and his companion after he looks into the pool is to situate the couples physically (in the spatial terms of the rose-garden vision) in a way in which they were not situated before the vision. The ghostly couple is no longer equal with the poet and his companion – no longer dancing across from them and no longer looking down into the drained pool with them. *Before* the poet, now, is the pool as still point; *behind* him is the ghostly couple. The poet and his companion are now the fulcrum across which the ghostly couple and the still point balance. During the mystical experience, then, the relationship between the couples changes, and so does the speaker's knowledge of matters spiritual. Reinterpreting the spatial relationships in terms of the temporal and spiritual relationships that they figure, we can say that the ghostly couple seems to be consigned to a time outside the present moment of vision, a time that is now 'behind' the poet and his companion. The preposition, then, is theologically significant in this enquiry into the relationship between time and redemption. The poet thereby places Original Sin at a distance from the present moment, a distance that the poem's opening analysis cannot conceive. The phrase 'they were behind us' in effect reproduces Christ's retort when 'The Word in the desert / [Was] most attacked by voices of temptation' – 'Get thee behind me, Satan' (CPP, 172, 175).[24]

This answer to the problem of Original Sin is confirmed in the experience of the light revealed in the garden. Meditation on the word *logos* has led to the uncovering of another of God's names: light. It is Christ as the 'Light' described in the first chapter of the Gospel of St John that Eliot introduces as the 'heart of light'.[25] The engagement with the *logos* in 'Burnt Norton' has thus moved from a logic bound within human concepts to its supplement, divine revelation. Significantly, then, the last lines of the first section virtually repeat the opening lines: 'Time past and time future / What might have been and what has been / Point to one end, which is always present' (CPP, 172). Yet although the words are the same, the understanding of the Word has changed dramatically: since Christ is eternally present, all time *is* redeemable.

The 'heart of light' that had been obscured by emotion in *The Waste Land* is thus the subject of contemplation in 'Burnt Norton'. The earlier sequence of emotion *enjoyed* thereby becomes a structure of emotion *understood*. Yet despite Eliot's determination to employ the contemplative techniques of the classical mystic in this 'Burnt Norton' replay of *The Waste Land*, and despite his apparent success in this instance, his conclusion in *Four Quartets* as a whole – a conclusion hinted at in 'Burnt Norton', the first poem of the sequence – is that there is no such proof against romantic mysticism as he seeks.

Tempering Eliot's classical mysticism in *Burnt Norton* is a scepticism as much a part of his nature as his mystical impulse. This scepticism derives from this awareness of the ineradicable human element in our knowledge and experience. Despite 'Burnt Norton''s attempt to develop knowledge and experience by means of classical mysticism into a vision of God where the Heraclitean fire and the sempiternal rose are one, the poem also makes a point about the necessary duplicity and destructibility of human experience – an argument that one can trace back to the dissertation and contemporary essays on philosophy and anthropology. The reading of the first section of this poem highlights the route that the speaker seems to follow from intellectual preparation to an actual vision of God: the classical mystic's recollective exercise has apparently led to a moment of divine illumination. Yet such a reading is by no means exhaustive. Accompanying the speaker's ostensibly confident interpretation of his experience as an instance of genuine communion with the divine is a pattern of image and idea complicating such an interpretation by the suggestion that the speaker is not the best judge of whence his inspiration comes. The 'reality' of which 'human kind / Cannot bear very much' may be the fact that a good deal of the Other that we perceive in such moments is in fact us – as in the worst of romantic mysticisms (CPP, 172).

Contemporaneous with 'Burnt Norton' and providing a gloss for its scepticism is Eliot's explanation in *After Strange Gods* (1934) of the perils in any mystical experience:

> Of divine illumination, it may be said that probably every man knows when he has it, but that any man is likely to think that he has it when he has it not; and even when he has had it, the daily man that he is may draw the wrong conclusions from the enlightenment which the momentary man has received: no one, in short, can be the sole judge of whence his inspiration comes.[26]

Such a passage implies questions to be asked of the experience represented in 'Burnt Norton': Was the experience of the momentary man genuine? Is the interpretation of the daily man accurate? *After Strange Gods* links the speaker in 'Burnt Norton' to the 'palpitating Narcissi' identified in 'The Function of Criticism' – mystical devotees of the 'inner voice', that which (like Narcissus) 'breathes the eternal message of vanity, fear, and lust' (SE, 27). By the time of *After Strange Gods*, Eliot's figure for the 'inner voice' of the romantic mystic's narcissism is 'Inner Light' – 'the most untrustworthy and deceitful guide that ever offered itself to wandering humanity.'[27] Against this background, the vision of reality that the speaker experiences in Burnt Norton's rose-garden is doubly undercut. First, there is the image of the speaker as the romantic, Narcissus-like figure who happens 'To look down into the drained pool' – a posture that would yield him an image of himself should the pool be filled (CPP, 172). Second, when the pool is filled, sure enough what fills it is an ambiguous *light* – according to the Eliot of *After Strange Gods*, a light as likely to be the 'Inner Light' of 'palpitating Narcissi' as the light of divine illumination.

Insofar as his epistemological and metaphysical concerns endure from the dissertation days to the 1930s, Eliot is bound to ask these questions about the role of the self in mystical recollection. Underhill herself draws attention to the presence of the self in this stage of mysticism: 'the self still feels very clearly the edge of its own personality: its separateness from the Somewhat Other' (*Mysticism*, 376). The Eliot of 1916 would not have been surprised by the presence of the self here. He argued then that what is known is never simply the Other, but always the Other and the self: 'we have not one science, but a whole universe of sciences, corresponding to the self as found expressed in the structure of social civilization, in its works of science, in the laws of thought, in image or in sensation' (KE, 74). The self is always a part of knowledge and experience: 'wherever there is the *Ich* [I], there is a continuity between the *Ich* and its object; not only in the case of perception, but in every case of knowledge' (KE, 74). Because of the presence of the self, the Eliot of the 1930s (as much as the Eliot of 1916) would have to regard recollection – so important a part of his programme of classical mysticism – as inevitably psychological or romantic. Aware of the same problem, Underhill argues that in the ecstatic state that is the 'apotheosis of contemplation' the mystic's 'unified state of consciousness does not merely pore upon something already possessed. When it only does this, it is diseased. . . . Its goal is something beyond itself' (*Mysticism*, 437). Infected by self, mystics perceive not the divine, but merely their own perception of the divine. Eliot's image of his speaker in the position of Narcissus reminds us ever so subtly that the question remains open whether the speaker here attends to divine light or merely to his own perception of divine light.

Uncertainty about the nature of the object observed by the speaker is also raised by the ambiguity of the bird's speech: 'Go, go, go, said the bird: human kind / Cannot bear very much reality' (CPP, 172). It is not clear whether the reality that cannot be borne is represented by 'the heart of light' or the 'cloud' (CPP, 172). The poem sustains either reading. This ambiguity reintroduces Eliot's conclusion in his dissertation: 'For a metaphysics to be accepted, good-will is essential. Two men must *intend* the same object, and *both* men must admit that the object intended is the same' (KE, 168). The ambiguous mystical moment of 'Burnt Norton' reveals that the 'good-will' essential to metaphysics is not present even within Eliot's single speaker. The nature of reality remains a mystery as the daily man draws his uncertain conclusions about the experience of the momentary man. The speaker is thus revealed as trapped in the romantic world – Eliot, like Wordsworth, struggling with the awareness that what eye and ear perceive they also 'half create'.[28]

One can trace the tension between scepticism and belief in the interpretation of mystical moments in *Four Quartets* back to Eliot's pre-dissertation analysis of the philosophies of Henri Bergson and William James. On the one hand is Bergson, high priest of the Life Force. On the other is James, judging the worth of ideas by their practical consequences or 'cash value'. As Eliot knew them, they both offered themselves as honest brokers between the ideal and the real, hoping (in Bergson's terms) to solve a good number of metaphysical disputes 'by merely getting rid of the clumsy symbols round which we are fighting' (TFW, xix). Eliot allowed neither claim, however, treating James as representative of the subject side of philosophy and treating Bergson as representative of the object side. His response to their limitations was to embark on his search for a viable mysticism – a search that we have followed into the 1930s, a search that culminates in the mysticism of the middle way in *Four Quartets*.

As we have seen, living in a world overwhelmed by science and materialism, Eliot was attracted to Bergsonian mysticism by the promise of union with the Life Force – something that he later dismissed as a 'promise of immortality' with a 'somewhat meretricious captivation'.[29] Bergsonism's desire to achieve union with the movement of the vital impulse earned it the label 'mystical' from both its admirers and detractors. Russell attacked it 'with all imaginable ferocity'.[30] Eliot dismissed it as 'a weakling mysticism'. It is somewhat surprising, then, to find that this is the mysticism that Paul Douglass finds in *Four Quartets*.[31] Certainly the opening lines of 'Burnt Norton' are highly charged with Bergsonian echoes:

Time present and time past
Are both perhaps present in time future
And time future contained in time past.
If all time is eternally present
All time is unredeemable.
What might have been is an abstraction

Remaining a perpetual possibility
Only in a world of speculation. (CPP, 171)

On the one hand, talk of redeeming time reveals the Anglo-
Catholic's concern about Original Sin, and talk of the apparent
impossibility that things 'might have been' otherwise reveals the
regret of the husband recently separated from Vivien Eliot at his
having impulsively forsaken Emily Hale twenty years before. On
the other hand, however, the lines acknowledge a philosophical
concern about determinism and so imply a concern about the
relationship between time and free will – the very question raised
in these very terms in Bergson's first work, known in English as
Time and Free Will (1889).

Douglass argues that largely through the influence of Bergson's
mystical philosophy *Four Quartets* finally sorts out the relationship
between Being and Becoming, 'the crucial issue of Eliot's career as
poet'. The point of the first quartet is to make the mystic way more
fully real to its readers: '"Burnt Norton" enacts, insofar as it can, a
process of awakening to the meaning of an intuitive experience.'
The syllogistic reasoning at the beginning of 'Burnt Norton' is
therefore abandoned: according to Bergson and Eliot, reality
cannot be thought; it must be intuited.[32] Thus Eliot's observation
that 'To be conscious is not to be in time' echoes Bergson's claim
that 'We do not *think* real time. But we *live* it' (CPP, 173; CE,
46). Douglass documents many such Bergsonian elements in *Four
Quartets*, concluding that because of Bergson the 'world we see
at "Little Gidding"'s conclusion is a transfigured one in which
history may be defined not as a nightmare, a chaos, but rather as
an unending process of self-discovery, full of suffering, certainly,
but also full of growth and divine love.' Bergson's emphasis on
life as creation helps to make sense of the familiar compound voice
(known as one's own and yet belonging to another) in 'Little
Gidding': the point is to emphasize the '*dédoublement* [splitting] . . .
at the heart of the intuition, the revelation. The words themselves
have engendered the world in which they are heard. . . . There
is a sense in which the moment *creates itself*.' Unconsciously, here,
and consciously, in talk of the interpenetration of beginnings and
endings, the poet is reconciling himself 'to a world in which the
only finality is continuous Becoming'. Douglass finds, in the end,
that 'The poet takes his place with those who accept, not deny life,

knowing that every vital action is a leap to a fall but nevertheless part of the creative impulse of the universe.'[33] The Eliot that Douglass discovers in *Four Quartets* is thus theologically something of a modernist – like Rashdall, Temple and Major, defining reality as an unending process, an evolution of the human in the direction of the divine.

Douglass's conclusions about Bergson's role in *Four Quartets* are diametrically opposed by Murray's:

> The poem represents . . . [a] conscious and purposeful rejection by the poet of the mystical attitude of Henri Bergson. The experience of vision within *Four Quartets* is not attained by a deliberate stripping of the mind of its rational modes of thinking in order thereby to enter naked into the flow of immediate experience. On the contrary, ecstatic or visionary experience is almost always preceded by, and is even seen in some way to be dependent on, a process of disciplined philosophical reflection and meditation.[34]

Such is the classical mysticism that Eliot celebrates at the time of The Clark Lectures. With regard to *Four Quartets*, however, it is possible to argue both that Murray is right to discover in it a classical mystic and that Douglass is right to discover in it a romantic mystic.

Bergson is present in the poem, but *Four Quartets* rehearses his arguments only ventriloquially within its rehearsal of the dissertation's arguments against him. In one of the few references to Bergsonism in his dissertation, Eliot notes that 'An *élan vital* or "flux"' is no less an abstraction from immediate experience than any other object, 'for it is only in departing from immediate experience that we are aware of such a process' (KE, 19). In his earlier essay on Bergson, after accusing the latter of contradictorily locating reality on some occasions in consciousness and on others in matter, he asks: 'Where . . . is the reality – in the consciousness, or in that which is perceived? Where is the one reality to subsume both of these, and can we or can we not know it?' (Paper, 18–19). These are the metaphysical and epistemological questions that animate the dissertation. They reappear in *Four Quartets* by means of one of 'Burnt Norton''s Heraclitean fragments: 'The way up is the way down.' Perhaps inspired by Underhill's observation that Bergsonism goes back to Heraclitus and his concept of

"'Logos" or Energizing Fire', Eliot describes the Bergson of
Creative Evolution as one for whom 'Reality, though apparently
one at bottom . . . , divides itself into a Cartesian dichotomy –
the way up, consciousness, and the way down, matter' (*Mysticism*,
33; Paper, 13–14). Thus, although Eliot's early interest in Bergson
is insinuated intertextually into *Four Quartets* from the very beginning, Bergson is remembered as representative of a metaphysical
problem – not its solution.

Bergson is just one figure in a complicated philosophical
dynamic in *Four Quartets*. Eliot was from the beginning unhappy
with Bergson's notion of the vital impulse – the celebration of
'the creative impulse of the universe' that Douglass attributes to
Four Quartets. He initially regarded Bergson as an idealist (he was
interested in his early paper 'to show certain inconsistencies –
idealism vs. realism – in B[ergson]'s position . . . based on the
conviction that the idealistic is . . . the more fundamental'), but
he came to regard him as representing the object side of experience
(Paper, 11). In short, Bergson represents for Eliot but one half of
the metaphysical impulse. The philosophy that comes to represent
the other half of this impulse – the subject side explanation of
experience – is a version of James's pragmatism. The latter prevents
the dissertation's arrival at Bradley's Absolute, and it complicates
Four Quartets' drive towards a mystical 'still point', for there is a part
of Eliot that accepts James's claim that truth is always in process,
ever a function of human need. Bergson certainly impressed Eliot
initially with his talk of creative evolution, but James's claim that
the human being is the truly creative agent in the world was one
that Eliot struggled with much longer.

We recall that according to James, 'The truth of an idea is not
a stagnant property inherent in it. Truth *happens* to an idea. It
becomes true, is *made* true by events.' He offered pragmatism not
as a philosophy about truth or reality but as a 'method of settling
metaphysical disputes that otherwise might be interminable':

Is the world one or many? – fated or free? – material or
spiritual? . . . The pragmatic method in such cases is to try
to interpret each notion by tracing its respective practical
consequences. What difference would it practically make to
anyone if this notion rather than that notion were true.
If no practical difference whatever can be traced, then the

alternatives mean practically the same thing, and all dispute is idle.

In the end, James describes absolute truth as merely the 'ideal vanishing-point towards which we imagine that all our temporary truths will some day converge', and so he advises that we 'live to-day by what truth we can get to-day, and be ready to-morrow to call it falsehood.'[35]

Since Peirce and James first articulated their versions of the philosophy, pragmatism has come to rival deconstruction as the champion of anti-platonism. The pragmatist, Richard Rorty observes, is one who 'sees the Platonic tradition as having outlived its usefulness'. In the platonic tradition, to know the Good is to do the good, to know the Truth is to speak the truth. According to the pragmatist, however, thinking about Truth will not help us to say something true; thinking about Goodness will not help us to act well. Truth and Goodness have no essence. They are concepts relative to time and place. In short, there is no ultimate platonic text behind the world; the world is an infinite series of texts. The pragmatist finds that 'there is nothing deep down inside us except what we have put there ourselves, no criterion that we have not created in the course of creating a practice'. The result of a rigorous pragmatism is a 'post-Philosophical culture' – 'one in which men and women [feel] themselves alone, merely finite, with no links to something Beyond'.[36]

The Eliot of *Four Quartets* is no pragmatist in Rorty's sense of the term; after all, he believes in God. He is what Rorty would call an intuitive realist, one who thinks that 'deep down beneath all the texts, there is something which is not just one more text but that to which various texts are trying to be "adequate"'.[37] Eliot speaks in these very terms at the time of his conversion:

> I should say that it was at any rate essential for Religion that we should have the conception of an immutable object or Reality the knowledge of which shall be the final object of the will; and there can be no permanent reality if there is no permanent truth. I am of course quite ready to admit that human apprehension of truth varies, changes and perhaps develops, but that is a property of human imperfection rather than of truth.[38]

Eliot acknowledged in 1914, however, that 'Pragmatism has perhaps seized the right view of the relation of philosophy [to] human
life; philosophy *is* to fit a need' (Relation, 21). Along these lines,
he argues in the dissertation that the world is a practical construct.
Recognizing this fact will put an end to metaphysical disputes:

> The process of development of a real world . . . works in two
> directions; we have not first a real world to which we add our
> imaginings, nor have we a real world out of which we select *our*
> 'real' world, but the real and the unreal develop side by side. If
> we think of the world not as ready made . . . but as constructed,
> or constructing itself, . . . at every moment, and never more than
> an approximate construction, a construction essentially practical
> in its nature: then the difficulties of real and unreal disappear.
> (KE, 136)

Talk of satisfying needs, of construction and of practicality, on the
one hand, and the desire to get beyond metaphysical squabbles, on
the other, echo James. Indeed, the dissertation's concluding chapter
accepts the pragmatic criterion for truth: a theory must be 'capable
of making an actual practical difference'; 'all that we care about is
how [a truth] works' (KE, 161, 169).

That Eliot retained this 1916 pragmatic cast of mind alongside his
Anglo-Catholicism is confirmed by his post-conversion poetry. In
Ash-Wednesday, for instance, the language of pragmatism endures:

> Because I know that time is always time
> And place is always and only place
> And what is actual is actual only for one time
> And only for one place
> I rejoice that things are as they are and
> I renounce the blessèd face
> And renounce the voice
> Because I cannot hope to turn again
> Consequently I rejoice, having to construct something
> Upon which to rejoice. (CPP, 89)

The poet's recognition of his situation as a function of a certain
time and place is generally pragmatic: he accepts that 'what is
actual is actual only for one time / And only for one place'.
But to accept the loss of what seems to have been present once
(a sustaining vision of a blessed face and voice), and to begin

from this post-vision time and place to 'construct' the object of belief – that is, 'something / Upon which to rejoice' – is to use the very terms of his dissertation's pragmatism. Renouncing the blessed face and voice, and rejoicing that things are as they are, is like the renunciation of 'immediate experience' and the cordial acceptance of the consequences of this renunciation that we see in his dissertation: 'if anyone assert that immediate experience, at either the beginning or end of our journey, is annihilation and utter night, I cordially agree' (KE, 31). In *Ash-Wednesday*, part of Eliot's struggle is to make room in his poem not just for the dogmatic Truth of Christianity, but also for the small 't' truth of pragmatism. Within these lines, therefore, one can hear the murmur of his pragmatism: 'the line between the experienced, or the given, and the constructed can nowhere be clearly drawn' (KE, 18).

The same determination to accept time and place – to accept not only one's own philosophical situation in particular, but also the situation of human beings in general (situation between the extremes of 'unbeing and being' (CPP, 175) within a world of constant becoming) – is evident in 'East Coker' (1940). The discovery that language is unable to express a presence or essence – that every attempt to use words 'Is a wholly new start, and a different kind of failure', a 'raid on the inarticulate / With shabby equipment always deteriorating' – aligns this moment in *Four Quartets* with the dissertation's insistence on the remoteness of the Absolute from any verbal formula that tries to embody it (CPP, 182). The emphasis upon the present moment (the 'now'), even though it seem 'unpropitious', and the emphasis on 'only the trying', are all pragmatic, recalling *Ash-Wednesday*'s celebration of the need to construct something upon which to rejoice (CPP, 182). Yet most pragmatic of all is the conclusion that 'The rest is not our business' (CPP, 182). This is the properly pragmatic conviction of the dissertation that metaphysics as the science of ultimate questions is none of our business: 'The Absolute . . . is neither real nor unreal nor imaginary' (KE, 169). There is trying and testing, but the rest is not our business because we cannot judge a metaphysics: 'what we actually know of a judgement is not its truth but its utility (and truth never *is* utility)' (KE, 167). In the end, then, we find in both the dissertation and *Four Quartets* the pragmatic insistence that truths be tested and verified instead of referred to an inaccessible ideal standard.

For an understanding of Bergsonism's and pragmatism's bearing on interpretation of *Four Quartets*, just as important as an appreciation of the individual impact of these philosophies upon Eliot is an appreciation of their impact as a tandem. Bergsonism and pragmatism are the backbone of Eliot's scepticism because they divide the metaphysical spectrum between them. Eliot argued in 1914 that Bergsonians and pragmatists agree insofar as both regard history as a 'process in which human purposes are illusory'. The problem with Bergson and James is 'their confusion . . . of human and cosmic activity'. Bergson makes everything cosmic, makes everything part of the Life Force. 'Bergson denies human values', Eliot complains; for him, 'history is a vitalistic process in which human purposes do not exist' (Relation, 21, 20, 20–1). The problem with pragmatism is the opposite:

> for pragmatism man is the measure of all things. . . . You choose a point of view because you like it. You form certain plans because they express your character. Certain things are true because they are what you need; others, because they are what you want. (Relation, 20–1)

Eliot's description of pragmatism is a caricature: he implies that we approach reality with a shopping list of things we need, whereas the pragmatic claim that reality is convention means only that reality is contingent, and not that it is the result of a decision. As Eliot himself notes in his dissertation, 'we have not . . . a real world out of which we select *our* "real" world' (KE, 136). That Eliot resorts to caricature, however, reveals the design of the rhetoric: there must be straw figures of the subject and object sides of experience for the mediating rhetoric of Eliot's philosophical prose to function.

Eliot prepares the space for his own philosophy – Michaels calls it 'the story of the middle' – by criticizing Bergsonism and pragmatism as extremes inadequate to the experience of human being that he locates between these extremes.[39] For Bergson, he complains, 'purposes and intentions are replaced by pure feeling'. We are supposed to 'have been living among shadows'. Eliot protests: 'It is not so. . . . Our world of social values is at least as real as his' (Relation, 20). Yet the pragmatist's insight that philosophy is a human instrument designed to fit a need does not strike Eliot 'as a great emancipation', but rather as 'a tedious truism'. Pragmatism does not release us from our need to pretend that philosophical theories are final: 'What pretension to finality does Plato make for his theory . . . that any man who uses his mind to theorise must not make?' (Relation, 7). 'It may be true', he concedes, 'that man does not live by bread alone, but by making fictions and swallowing them alive & whole. This seems to reduce the high cost of living by eliminating living' (Relation, 15).

Here is part of the argument and imagery of *Four Quartets*. First there is the argument by Bergsonian, Christian and Indian mystics alike that the moment of illumination reveals (as in Plato's metaphor of the cave) the distinction between reality and its mere shadow. The sunlight fills the empty pool; presence is overcome by absence; meaning seems to be revealed. Then there is Eliot's reservation about the platonic language of light and shadow. Is the light (presumably the Light of the Gospel of John that becomes the Word by the end of this poem) real, marking all else as merely shadow? Or is shadow real (the darkness that comes with the cloud), marking the momentary light as merely an illusion? It is not clear which of these phenomena the bird is calling 'reality'. The ambiguity is no accident; it comes from Eliot's disenchantment with the 'meretricious captivation' of the sort of 'promise of immortality' that he had encountered in Bergsonism. As Eliot acknowledged in 'The *Pensées* of Pascal' (1931), the test of the mystical moment is always pragmatic: not 'even the higher form of religious inspiration suffice[s] for the religious life; even the most exalted mystic must return to the world, and use his reason to employ the results of his experience in daily life.' Such moments 'can be judged only by their fruits' (SE, 405).

And yet pragmatism is no simple alternative to the conviction of certainty experienced in the mystical moment – Christian, Buddhist, Bergsonian or otherwise. One therefore also finds in 'Burnt Norton' the twenty-year fear of pragmatism's replacement of the spiritual part of our diet by fiction. The mysterious, lyrical fourth section of the poem focuses upon this fruitless option. The puzzling rhetorical questions serve to mock the pragmatic proposition that reality is a function of human need and that 'man is the measure of all things'. The passing away of the sun (as in the first section of the poem, symbolically the reality outside the human being) exposes the ludicrousness of the suggestion that we could replace such an Absolute: 'Will the sunflower turn to us, will the clematis / Stray down, bend to us; tendril and spray / Clutch and cling?' (CPP, 174). How can the world's being depend on human being? This section of the poem ironically reverses the bird's claim that human kind cannot bear very much reality: it is no longer *to bear* reality in the sense of 'to endure' reality; it is *to bear* reality in the sense of 'to sustain, support, create' reality. Eliot anticipates this argument in 'Frances Herbert Bradley' (1927): 'the great weakness of Pragmatism is that it ends by being of no *use* to anybody' (SE, 454).

The problem that Eliot identifies in 1914 as shared by Bergson and James is the problem that he himself faces in *Four Quartets*: Bergson and James lack 'a clear conception of what the word *human* implies' (Relation, 19). It is this definition of human being that Eliot continues to pursue in *Four Quartets*. He implies that we all know intuitively and that we all know equally well what human being is: 'The question can always be asked of the closest-woven theory: is this the reality of *my* world of appearance? and if I do not recognize the identity, then it is not' (KE, 168). Bergson and James are inadequate to this intuitive knowledge: 'they give us two forms of escape from reality as we know it in ordinary experience, a reality in which we find a constant friction between the mechanical and the volitional. One exalts mechanism, the other impulse. It amounts to the same thing' (Relation, 22). Bergson claims that we do not live fully until we become one with the Life Force (a claim with a 'meretricious captivation' for Eliot). Pragmatism's sleight of hand is similar: 'if *all* meaning is human meaning, then there is no meaning'. In Bergsonism's mechanism and in pragmatism's apparent voluntarism, Eliot recognizes – respectively – the twin spectres of complete determination and complete freedom: 'Complete freedom or complete determination, for a human being, is unthinkable' (Relation, 19). Eliot means *literally* 'unthinkable'.

To think that we are either completely free or completely determined is to contradict our experience of human being. By means of the spectres of complete determination and complete freedom, Eliot depicts the metaphysical extremes implicit in object–side and subject–side points of view. Pragmatism measures human experience from the subject side, postulating the object; the Bergsonism of *Creative Evolution* measures experience from the object side, postulating the subject. Eliot finds in the latter the suggestion that we are nothing and in the former the suggestion that we are everything. Thus the syllogistic reasoning at the beginning of 'Burnt Norton' wrestles with the spectre of complete determination and the fourth section of the poem wrestles with the spectre of complete freedom – Eliot knowing each of these conceptions of human being to be inadequate, for he had demonstrated in his dissertation that these metaphysical extremes of subject-side and object-side points of view are literally unthinkable because the points of view of subject and object inevitably imply one another.

It is the contemplation of this dichotomy with which the dissertation begins and it is the inevitable failure of philosophers to get beyond it that Eliot goes on to explain. He introduces this distinction between subject and object as the root of traditional philosophical debate between the positions of idealism, on the one hand, and realism or materialism, on the other. Our metaphysics is a function of these two points of view. For the idealist, the objective or material world is reducible to a subject's consciousness – whether the solipsistic individual's or God's. For the realist, the ideal world – whether it be regarded as a phenomenon or epiphenomenon – is reducible to the interaction of objects:

> We have no right, except in the most provisional way, to speak of *my* experience, since the I is a construction out of experience, an abstraction from it; and the *thats*, the browns and hards and flats, are equally ideal constructions from experience. . . . Everything, from one point of view, is subjective; and everything, from another point of view, is objective; and there is no *absolute* point of view from which a decision may be pronounced. (KE, 19–22)

The subject/object dichotomy is itself, for human beings, an absolute – a precondition of human knowledge and experience. Davidson observes that Eliot's argument anticipates Heidegger's: we are determined by the world and we determine the world simultaneously – as in the hermeneutic circle that we find in 'Tradition and the Individual Talent'.[40] Shusterman discovers Gadamer in the same text: 'The formative presence of the past in the present underlies the importance of what Eliot calls "the historical sense" (a clear prefiguration of Gadamer's "effective historical consciousness").'[41] For Eliot, human being participates always in a dialectic of interpretive transcendence:

the life of a soul does not consist in the contemplation of one consistent world but in the painful task of unifying (to a greater or less extent) jarring and incompatible ones, and passing, when possible, from two or more discordant viewpoints to a higher which shall somehow include and transmute them. (KE, 147–8).

The process produces the sort of moving horizon that Gadamer defines in *Truth and Method*: 'The historical movement of human life consists in the fact that it is never utterly bound to any one standpoint, and hence can never have a truly closed horizon. The horizon, rather, is something into which we move and that moves with us.'[42] Eliot concludes his dissertation with a similar observation. A metaphysics is not so much true or false as practically useful, and so metaphysics is an open-ended process of understanding: 'The point is that the world of practical verification has no definite frontiers, and that it is the business of philosophy to keep the frontiers open' (KE, 169). In the light of Shusterman's identification of this hermeneutic aspect of Eliot's thought in his prose of the 1930s and 1940s, it is not surprising to find Eliot making a point in 'Little Gidding' similar to that made in the dissertation:

> what you thought you came for
> Is only a shell, a husk of meaning
> From which the purpose breaks only when it is fulfilled
> If at all. Either you had no purpose
> Or the purpose is beyond the end you figured
> And is altered in fulfilment. (CPP, 192)[43]

Our purposes arise from and react with the time and place into which we are thrown to produce our world, just as the individual talent reacts with tradition to produce the literary world.

Bradley's attempt to resolve the contradiction between subject-side and object-side points of view within a realm of immediate experience ('an all-inclusive experience outside of which nothing shall fall') and Bergson's attempt to resolve it within a realm of undifferentiated 'feeling' are for Eliot nonsensical (KE, 31). Immediate experience or feeling (Eliot treats them as much the same thing) is beyond human knowledge and experience: 'if anyone assert that immediate experience, at either the beginning or end of our journey, is annihilation and utter night, I cordially agree'; 'feeling, in which the two [points of view] are one, has no history; it is, as such, outside of time altogether, inasmuch as there is no further point of view from which it can be inspected' (KE, 31, 22). 'Burnt Norton' warns of this threat to human being beyond the mortal beginning and end that bracket human knowledge and experience:

> the enchainment of past and future
> Woven in the weakness of the changing body,
> Protects mankind from heaven and damnation
> Which flesh cannot endure. (CPP, 173)

As human beings, we are 'Caught in the form of limitation / Between unbeing and being' (CPP, 175). As in the dissertation, so in 'Burnt Norton': there is no point of view from which our experience can be inspected other than the *human* point of view.

The poet of *Four Quartets* is suspended between the object-side and subject-side points of view, between suggestions that human being is a function of outer determination by object and a projection of need from within the subject. The poet apparently longs for the release from this suspension between contradictory metaphysics, longs for 'The inner freedom from the practical desire, / The release from action and suffering, release from the inner / And the outer compulsion' (CPP, 173). Reference to the inner and outer compulsion recalls the respectively pragmatic and Bergsonian explanations of reality as determined from within by the subject and from without by the object. But Eliot recognizes immediately that there is nothing but annihilation and utter night beyond the extremes that bracket human being. According to Eliot, *human* being is a balance between 'the annihilation and utter night' that he cordially acknowledges in his dissertation and the 'heart of light' of which both *The Waste Land* and 'Burnt Norton' speak. We live in the 'partial ecstacy' and the 'partial horror' of a complication of object-side and subject-side points of view.

The state of 'feeling' or 'immediate experience' that is 'outside of time altogether' and that betokens 'annihilation and utter night' sounds like something that might be available to human experience through mysticism. Yet Eliot's point is not that annihilation and utter night are potential mystical experiences but rather that they are impossible experiences: 'no actual experience could be merely immediate, for if it were, we should certainly know nothing about it' (KE, 18). There would be no subject distinct from the immediate experience – in short, neither a knower nor a thing to be known. The experiences that we have as human beings, therefore, can always already be explained by a double narrative – one from the subject-side of experience and the other from the object-side of experience: 'we can only discuss experience from one side and then from the other, correcting these partial views' (KE, 19). Experience is never one, therefore, but always double and destructible.

From this point of view, Eliot might seem a sceptic: 'In the growth and construction of the world we live in, there is no one stage, and no one aspect, which you can take as the foundation' (KE, 151). The ideal is no more fundamental than the real, and vice versa. As Michaels observes, 'at least one form of the relativism (or scepticism) with which pragmatism is sometimes identified is clearly a possible consequence of this initial denial.'[44] According to Eliot himself, 'we find that we are certain of everything, – relatively, and of nothing, – positively, and that no knowledge will survive analysis. The virtue of metaphysical analysis is in showing the destructibility of everything' (KE, 157). As Michaels notes, however, Eliot goes on to insist that 'the fact that we can adduce no ultimate justification for such distinctions [between the real and the ideal] does not mean that they are in any sense "invalid"'. Reality is conventional, and yet no less absolute:

> To acknowledge the conventionality of our own account of the real is to acknowledge its contingency without undermining its validity, its power over us. . . . What Eliot means when he calls reality conventional is that the real is what we *believe*, and that we cannot anchor our beliefs in something more real than they are. And yet, while there is nothing more real than our beliefs, it is clearly impossible to regard them as just one set of conventions among others, since, if they really are our beliefs, we must believe them.[45]

It is this necessity of believing absolutely in the face of the equally compelling certainty that nothing can be known for certain that Eliot explores in *Four Quartets* and to which he alludes in his cryptic comments about mysticism in his 1948 interview.

Eliot's conclusion that we inevitably believe absolutely in a conventional reality is also a result of his analysis of the attempt by Bradley and the philosophers of the idealist tradition to overcome the subject/object dichotomy by postulating a state of 'immediate experience' or 'feeling' in which 'as yet neither any subject or object exists'.[46] From the idealist's point of view 'Experience . . . both begins and ends in something which is not conscious. . . . [T]he original unity – the "neutral entity" – though transcended, remains, and is never analysed away' (KE, 28–30). Eliot characterizes this original unity, however, as no more than a hypothesis. Immediate experience is merely a requirement of theory: 'there is indeed no such stage . . . at which experience is merely immediate. . . . We are forced, in building up our theory of knowledge, to postulate something given upon which knowledge is founded' (KE, 16–17).

This word 'forced' marks Eliot's awareness that the hypothesis of an original unity upon which knowledge is founded is not just an intellectual hypothesis. His accounts of our philosophizing give prominence to this word: 'in our theory of knowledge, when we leave the moment of immediate experience, we are forced to present our account either as a history of mind [subject] in its environment [object], or as a history of the world [object] as it appears to mind [subject]' (KE, 22). Similarly, 'We are forced to the assumption that truth is one, and to the assumption that reality is one' (KE, 168). The word 'forced' points to the fact that the assumption of oneness is not just a theoretical necessity, but also a practical necessity. It is a part of our behaviour – an element of our human being.

As he had discovered in his early essays on anthropology, particularly in 'The Interpretation of Primitive Ritual', all the difference in the world is made by whether we observe a belief from the outside or from the inside:

> if you take a purely external point of view [of religious behaviour], then it is not behaviour but mechanism, and social phenomena (and ultimately, I believe all phenomena) simply cease to exist when regarded steadfastly in this light. You *must* take into account the internal meaning: what is a religious phenomenon for example which has not a religious meaning for the participants?[47]

The view from the outside cannot comprehend the meaning in question, which is available only from inside. As Eliot argued in another paper at this time, 'If you did describe the thing as it really is, the whole truth about it, you would not be describing, you would be presenting; described and description would be *identical*.'[48] These insights and arguments inform Eliot's comparisons of the view from inside a metaphysics to the view from outside a metaphysics in the conclusion of his dissertation:

> To the builder [of the metaphysical system] the process is the process of reality, for thought and reality are one; to a critic, the process is perhaps only the process of the builder's thought. . . . The one thinks of reality in terms of his system; the other thinks of the system in terms of the indefinite social reality. (KE, 167–8)

Eliot recalls these conclusions ten years later in his introduction to his mother's long poem, *Savonarola* (1926):

> Some years ago, in a paper on *The Interpretation of Primitive Ritual*, I made an humble attempt to show that in many cases no interpretation of a rite could explain its origin. For the meaning of the series of acts is for performers themselves an interpretation; the same ritual remaining practically unchanged may assume different meanings for different generations of performers; and the rite may have originated before 'meaning' meant anything at all.[49]

Twenty years after this, and thirty years after the original essay, the early discussion of belief and behaviour returns in *Notes Towards the Definition of Culture* (1948), where Eliot recalls that 'what we believe is not merely what we formulate and subscribe to', for 'behaviour is also belief, and . . . even the most conscious and developed of us live also at the level at which belief and behaviour cannot be distinguished'.[50] From the standpoint of the believer (whether the believer in metaphysics or the believer in religious ritual), belief is unassailable because for such people description of reality and the reality described are identical: metaphysics and ritual are themselves meaning.

Eliot's conclusion is that we always already inhabit a belief system:

Facts are not merely found in the world and laid together like bricks, but every fact has in a sense its place prepared for it before it arrives, and without the implication of a system in which it belongs the fact is not a fact at all. . . . There is a sense, then, in which any science – natural or social – is *a priori*: in that it satisfies the needs of a particular point of view, a point of view which may be said to be more original than any of the facts that are referred to that science. (KE, 60)

So completely constitutive of awareness is this point of view that self-consciousness of it will always postdate the shift to a new belief system: 'To realize that a point of view is a point of view is already to have transcended it' (KE, 148). Every aspect of our knowledge and experience is a function of a point of view that precedes us.

A human being is thus born into a world already constructed in the direction of a certain understanding. Absolute truth is available nowhere, but through common 'understanding', people know how to use experience:

no judgement is true until you understand it; and you never wholly understand it, because 'understanding' experience means merely knowing how to use it; so that what we actually know of a judgement is not its truth but its utility (and truth never *is* utility). (KE, 167)

Human beings cannot judge a metaphysics, only utility. Our 'understanding' of experience is our reality. This 'utilitarian' understanding can be characterized as a contingent oneness or *logos*. We practise an assumption of oneness – whether or not we theorize such a oneness – because of the derivation of our utilitarian conventions from and because of their convergence upon the truth and reality that is constructed as our world. Eliot argues that 'whereas we may change our point of view, it is better not to say that the point of view has changed. For if there is a noticeable change, you have no identity of which to predicate the change' (KE, 148). Eliot recalls this conclusion about the practical necessity of a meta-point-of-view years later in *Notes Towards the Definition of Culture*:

It is against a background of Christianity that all our thought has significance. An individual European may not believe that Christian Faith is true, and yet what he says, and makes, and does, will all spring out of his heritage of Christian culture and depend upon that culture for its meaning. Only a Christian culture could have produced a Voltaire or a Nietzsche. I do not believe that the culture of Europe could survive the complete disappearance of the Christian Faith.[51]

With the *complete* disappearance of the Christian Faith, the cultural 'identity of which to predicate the change' would have disappeared.

Underlying change is a constant focus: 'Two points of view . . . can be said to differ only so far as they intend the same object' (KE, 149). Thus difference of opinion about metaphysics is not telling, for it is in practice or behaviour that one finds evidence of a common metaphysics or a common belief: 'it makes no difference whether a thing really is green or blue, so long as everyone behaves toward it on the belief that it is green or blue' (KE, 169). In practice, we are bound by an identity in what one might call a meta-point-of-view underlying the changes in point of view that we experience in living our lives – just as much, in fact, as we are bound in theory to posit a unity to serve as the ground of knowledge. Furthermore, the construction of our world not only begins with this meta-point-of-view but also moves towards it, 'passing, when possible, from two or more discordant viewpoints to a higher which shall somehow include and transmute them' (KE, 147–8). The last complete sentence in the dissertation confirms the direction in which our utilitarian standards move us: 'this emphasis upon practice – upon the relativity and the instrumentality of knowledge – is what impels us towards the Absolute' (KE, 169). The Absolute is both the hypothetical ground implicit in the common understanding of the instrumentality of knowledge *and* the hypothetical end towards which knowledge is instrumentally oriented. To experience such an Absolute would be annihilation and utter night, but the Absolute is nonetheless a hypothesis implied as much in the lived epistemological practice of human beings as in their epistemological theories.

The conclusion offered during the Castro interview now makes sense. Conceive of human faculties as converging in origin and end upon a conventional reality understood according to standards of utility and the conclusion follows that human knowledge and experience involve a knowing and experiencing of degrees of oneness. Pursue human faculties to their limits and you will find at one end the meta-point-of-view that informs them and at the other end the hypothetical oneness (the Absolute as meta-object of perception) that is the constant focus of their attention. In such a pursuit, you are bound to arrive at the hypothesis of an original unity and ultimate end that all epistemological practice locates at the beginning and end of the distinction between subject and object. In the terms of the 1948 interview: 'All human faculties pushed to their limits end in mysticism'.

The journey of *Four Quartets* is towards recovery of the dissertation's 'cordial' acceptance of a vision of human being, and therefore a vision of reality (they are the same thing for the dissertation Eliot), as this very suspension between the absolute and the relative. In both works, the main energy derives from the question of the relationship between belief and reality. Although a metaphysics always pretends to be true, for all people and for all time, Eliot argues that 'A metaphysic may be accepted or rejected without our assuming that from the practical point of view it is either true or false' (KE, 169). The 'shaky ground and vanishing goal' of Eliot's philosophy, Michaels concludes, is 'the suspension of what . . . we might call belief'.[52] The achievement of the dissertation is to redefine reality not as subject or object, but as belief. From this point of view, the achievement of *Four Quartets* is similar: the poet is determined to acknowledge both his experience of belief as absolutely powerful and valid ('The hint half guessed, the gift half understood, is Incarnation') and his experience of belief as local and practical (located in East Coker and Little Gidding, for instance, 'Where prayer has been valid') (CPP, 190, 192).

The poem is therefore a dynamic tension between the momentary mystical experience of belief as absolutely powerful and valid and the daily experience of belief as a series of propositions that (from the pragmatic point of view) do not absolutely work. In the mystical moments of *Four Quartets*, the poet offers for inspection the moment when absolute reality seems to be apprehended, the moment when not to believe is impossible. The part of Eliot that converted to Bergsonism in 1910 and to Anglo-Catholicism in 1927 wants to accept the mystical moment as illumination, as revelation of ultimate reality. It seems that the presumption of the poet describing the mystical moment is that description of that moment is equivalent to presentation of reality. But there is a part of Eliot that remains a pragmatist, that continues to be disturbed by his own pragmatic questions about what we identify as 'objective' truth: 'So long as our descriptions and explanations can vary so greatly and yet make so little practical difference, how can we say that our theories have that intended identical reference which is the objective criterion for truth and error?' (KE, 168–9).

Thus the fear of committing himself to a particular formula of words that would then be subject to pragmatic inspection: 'do not call' the moment fixity; we can only say '*there* we have been' and 'cannot say' where or for 'how long' (CPP, 173). On the one hand, the poet cannot specify time and place because the experience is ostensibly outside time and space; but on the other hand, he cannot specify time and place for fear of the sceptical reaction of the pragmatic dimension of his sensibility that regards all experience – indeed, regards reality itself – as a function of time and place. There is a part of Eliot in *Four Quartets* that still understands the mystical moment as the dissertation Eliot does – as the experience of the power of one's beliefs, as the experience of the epistemological and metaphysical practice of one's age, as an *illusory* (but nonetheless inevitable) experience of belief not as contingently but as absolutely valid. The attempt as poet to express this experience in propositional or descriptive form inevitably exposes the contingency of the belief, for the belief is always a formula expressed in words – words that 'Crack and sometimes break, under the burden', words that 'will not stay in place, / Will not stay still', words that are 'shabby equipment always deteriorating' (CPP, 175, 182).

In the dissertation, Eliot argues: 'Without words, no objects' (KE, 132). A similar suspicion can be seen in the fussing about words in *Four Quartets*, for if there are no words that will suffice in defining an object, 'how can we say that our theories have that intended identical reference which is the objective criterion for truth and error' (KE, 169)? Disrupting the Christian Eliot's conviction that variation in the 'human apprehension of truth' is 'a property of human imperfection rather than of truth', I suggest, is the nagging suspicion of the pragmatic Eliot that variation in the apprehension of truth is indeed a property of truth – the suspicion, that is, that 'Truth *happens* to an idea. It *becomes* true, is *made* true by events'.[53]

The very language of the affirmation that 'The hint half guessed, the gift half understood, is Incarnation' reminds us that there is another half of the hint and gift to be guessed and understood – reminds us (in the dissertation's terms) that the line between the gift and the construction placed upon it can nowhere be clearly drawn (CPP, 190). And so, at times in *Four Quartets*, opposing the conviction that life is or should be a progress vertically towards the Absolute is the suspicion that life is merely a lateral process, a drift from one contingent belief to another:

> There is no end, but addition: the trailing
> Consequence of further days and hours,
> While emotion takes to itself the emotionless
> Years of living among the breakage
> Of what was believed in as the most reliable –
> And therefore the fittest for renunciation. (CPP, 185)

This section of 'The Dry Salvages', having asked 'Where is there an end of' this process of 'addition', and having decided that 'There is no end', concludes as the dissertation does: 'We cannot think . . . / of a future that is not liable / Like the past, to have no destination' (CPP, 186). This complexly negative assertion seems to mean that we must accept the vision of life as a practice with no ultimate purpose. A similar point is made in 'Little Gidding': 'Either you had no purpose / Or the purpose is beyond the end you figured / And is altered in fulfilment' (CPP, 192). In both the dissertation and 'The Dry Salvages', Eliot observes that we create a practical fiction simply to cope with what the dissertation marks as 'annihilation and utter night' and what the poem marks as 'the final addition', the threat of 'Death': 'We have to think' of the fishermen 'as forever bailing, / Setting and hauling' – 'Not as making a trip that will be unpayable / For a haul that will not bear examination' (CPP, 186). This sense of there being no end to the process of belief and the sense also that the fiction of an end as valid and valuable purpose is necessary ironically prefaces the introduction of 'the one Annunciation' – a version of the 'one' in the dissertation in which we are forced to think that truth and reality culminate.

Four Quartets, like the dissertation, thus marks human being as suspension between the Absolute and the relative (between the object to which our knowledge strives to become adequate and the subject that tries to make the world adequate to its need). The poet is suspended between the hope that his belief is founded upon ultimate reality and the fear that his belief is a fiction. In the grip of belief – in the rose garden, sudden in a shaft of sunlight, in the 'distraction fit' – the absolute is undeniable: '*there* we have been', in its presence (CPP, 190, 173). The poem in part documents the experience of the mysticism of metaphysics, the experience that the dissertation describes as being 'forced to the assumption that truth is one, and to the assumption that reality is one' (KE, 168). The poem actually concludes on this note, seeking what the dissertation defined as no more than a convention – the 'complete simplicity' in which 'the fire and the rose are one' (CPP, 198). But the poem's assertion in its last section that 'We shall not cease from exploration' echoes the dissertation's conclusion 'that the world of practical verification has no definite frontiers, and that it is the business of philosophy to keep the frontiers open' (CPP, 197; KE, 169). As always, the irresistible impulse toward the Absolute is resisted by the suspicion that there is no such Absolute for the exploration to discover. In the interference of the poem's mystical and pragmatic moments with each other, Eliot approaches once more – this time in a different medium – the awareness of 1916 that 'the line between the experienced, or the given, and the constructed can nowhere be clearly drawn' (KE, 18). In the Gadamerian words of the poet in 'East Coker',

> There is, it seems to us,
> At best, only a limited value
> In the knowledge derived from experience.
> The knowledge imposes a pattern, and falsifies,
> For the pattern is new in every moment
> And every moment is a new and shocking
> Valuation of all we have been. (CPP, 179)

The key words in the dissertation's title – knowledge and experience – reappear here as though to recall the advice of 1916: 'think of the world not as ready made . . . but as constructed, or constructing itself, . . . at every moment, and never more than an approximate construction, a construction essentially practical in its nature' (KE, 136).

Despite the disagreement between the Christian Eliot and the pragmatic Eliot – the former convinced that there is an objective

Truth, the latter suspecting that there is only subjective truth –
the agreement of Eliot the word-bound mystic and Eliot the
world-bound pragmatist that the expression of an objective truth
is not possible in language ironically leads to the same conclusion:
we must construct something upon which to rejoice. In the end,
by following Eliot's opposition of Bergson and James through both
the dissertation's and *Four Quartets'* opposition of subject-side and
object-side points of view, and by following the opposition in *Four
Quartets* of mystical and pragmatic moments, we can see that *Four
Quartets* does not locate in what are traditionally identified as its
mystical moments the 'complete simplicity' of an experience of
reality-as-essence. Since metaphysics is none of our business, but
human being is, the poem also locates in such moments a very
human reality: the experience of tension between certainty and
scepticism. As early as 1914, Eliot had observed that 'all faith should
be seasoned with a skilful sauce of scepticism. And scepticism too
is a faith – a high and difficult one.'[54] In 'Francis Herbert Bradley'
(1927), he noted that scepticism is 'a useful equipment for religious
understanding' (SE, 450). In 'The *Pensées* of Pascal' (1931), the
assertion is the same: 'every man who thinks and lives by thought
must have his own scepticism, that which stops at the question,
that which ends in denial, or that which leads to faith and which
is somehow integrated into the faith which transcends it' (SE, 411).
The mystical experience of certainty – within which Eliot was once
concerned to discern a hierarchy in terms of a distinction between
classical and romantic mysticisms – thus comes to be seen as but
one *part* of human experience, a part of experience always to be
supplemented by scepticism (itself a high and difficult faith), for
even classical mystics, the most responsible of religious adventurers,
are romantics at heart – if they are human, and especially if they are
sons and lovers.

Appendix:
Dating 'The Love Song of Saint Sebastian'

The date of the composition of 'The Love Song of Saint Sebastian' is not known. Eliot sent a copy of it to Conrad Aiken as an enclosure in a letter of 25 July 1914.[1] On the basis of a letter six days earlier in which Eliot refers to having 'written some *stuff* – about 50 lines', and on the basis of his reference in the same letter to '*three great St Sebastians*' that he has recently seen, Gordon concludes that 'The Love Song of Saint Sebastian' represents the fifty lines that Eliot had recently composed after seeing the paintings and that the other lines of poetry beginning 'Oh little voices' represent 'the *thing*' that Eliot showed Aiken 'some time ago' (Eliot, *The Letters of T.S. Eliot*, **1**, 40–3).[2]

It is more likely, however, that 'The Love Song of Saint Sebastian' is 'the *thing*' that Eliot had already shown Aiken 'some time ago'. Eliot writes of the enclosures in his 25 July letter as follows: 'I enclose some *stuff* – the *thing* I showed you some time ago, and some of the themes for the "Descent from the Cross" or whatever I may call it.' The two letters suggest that when 'the *thing*' is subtracted from the packet that Eliot sent Aiken, what remains are the 'about 50 lines' recently composed. Subtracting 'The Love Song of Saint Sebastian' from 'Oh little voices' and 'Appearances appearances' leaves forty-nine lines in the Berg text of the poem (Berg Collection, New York Public Library), and forty-eight lines in the version published in *The Letters of T.S. Eliot*. 'The Love Song of Saint Sebastian' is only thirty-eight lines – too small to be a candidate on its own for the lines recently composed. The other combination of lines that approximates a total of 'about 50' ('The Love Song of Saint Sebastian' and 'Oh little voices' add up to fifty-one lines) is not consistent with Eliot's characterization of the enclosures as divided into 'the *thing*' and 'themes'. 'The Love Song of Saint Sebastian' is the only self-sufficient 'thing' among the enclosures; the other poetry sent to Aiken is divided into parts that Eliot calls an 'Introduction' ('Oh little voices') and a 'theme' ('Appearances appearances') (*The Letters of T.S. Eliot*, **1**, 44).

Furthermore, Eliot's letter pleads the case for using 'The Love Song of Saint Sebastian' as a title: 'The S. Sebastian title I feel almost sure of; I have studied S. Sebastians – why should anyone paint a beautiful youth and stick him full of pins (or arrows) unless he felt a little as the hero of my verse? . . . So I give this title *faute de mieux* [for lack of a better]' (*The Letters of T.S. Eliot*, **1**, 44). Eliot writes as though it were not *the poem* that was inspired by his acquaintance with the '*three* great St Sebastians', but rather his interpretation of the poem and his title for it – the title implicitly suggesting that the state of mind of his hero mirrors that of the painters of the St Sebastians.

It seems likely, then, that 'The Love Song of Saint Sebastian' was written 'some time ago' – perhaps as early as 1910 or 1911, when Aiken was shown 'The Love Song of J. Alfred Prufrock' (the poem recalled in the title that Eliot defends in his letter to Aiken).

Notes

Preface

1 Martin Seymour-Smith, *Funk & Wagnalls Guide to Modern Literature* (New York: Funk & Wagnalls, 1973), 253–4.

2 Caroline Spurgeon, *Mysticism in English Literature* (Cambridge: Cambridge University Press, 1913), 1.

3 Frank Lentricchia, *After the New Criticism* (Chicago: University of Chicago Press, 1980), 177.

4 John Guillory, 'The ideology of canon formation: T.S. Eliot and Cleanth Brooks', *Critical Inquiry*, **10** (1983), 173–98 (186, 185, 188, 194). For Brooks on poetry as 'the language of paradox', see Cleanth Brooks, *The Well Wrought Urn* (New York: Harcourt Brace, 1947), 3–21.

5 T.S. Eliot, *The Complete Poems and Plays of T.S. Eliot* (London: Faber and Faber, 1969), 173, hereafter cited parenthetically in the text as CPP.

6 Perry Meisel, *The Myth of the Modern: A Study in British Literature and Criticism after 1850* (New Haven: Yale University Press, 1987), 109.

7 T.S. Eliot, Letter to B. Dobrée (12 Nov. 1927), in Bonamy Dobrée, 'T.S. Eliot: A Personal Reminiscence', in *T.S. Eliot: The Man and His Work*, ed. Allen Tate (London: Chatto & Windus, 1967), 65–88 (75).

8 Kristian Smidt, *Poetry and Belief in the Work of T.S. Eliot* (Norway, 1949; repr. London: Routledge & Kegan Paul, 1961), 179.

9 Fayek M. Ishak, *The Mystical Philosophy of T.S. Eliot* (New Haven: College and University Press, 1970), 44.

10 See *The Protestant Mystics*, ed. Anne Fremantle, introd. W.H. Auden (Boston: Little, Brown, 1964).

11 Sister Corona Sharp, '"The unheard music": T.S. Eliot's *Four Quartets* and St John of the Cross', *University of Toronto Quarterly*, **51** (1982), 264–78 (276).

12 F.O. Matthiessen, *The Achievement of T.S. Eliot*, 3rd edn (New York: Oxford University Press, 1958), 9.

13 P.S. Sri, *T.S. Eliot, Vedanta and Buddhism* (Vancouver: University of British Columbia Press, 1985), 122. As Sri observes in the introduction to this study, the Indic threads in this coat are as

many-coloured and as widely distributed throughout Eliot's work as the Christian threads (see pp. 1–4).

14 Helen Gardner, *The Art of T.S. Eliot*, 3rd edn (London: Cresset Press, 1949; repr. London: Faber & Faber, 1968), 164, 170, 176, 184.

15 Staffan Bergsten, *Time and Eternity: A Study in the Structure and Symbolism of T.S. Eliot's Four Quartets* (Stockholm: Svenska Bokförlaget, 1960), 36–7.

16 R.L. Brett, 'Mysticism and Incarnation in *Four Quartets*', *English* **16**.93 (Autumn 1966), 94–9 (97).

17 Lyndall Gordon, *Eliot's Early Years* (Oxford: Oxford University Press, 1977), 1. Eloise Knapp Hay disagrees with Gordon's conclusions, seeing a recognizably Christian spiritual orientation 'only in the middle of [Eliot's] career'. See Hay, *T.S. Eliot's Negative Way* (Cambridge, Mass.: Harvard University Press, 1982), 2.

18 Harold Bloom, *The Breaking of the Vessels* (Chicago: University of Chicago Press, 1982), 17.

19 Bloom, 20, 18.

20 Meisel, 110, 113, 114, 118.

21 C.K. Stead, *Pound, Yeats, Eliot and the Modernist Movement* (New Brunswick, NJ: Rutgers University Press, 1986), 223–31.

22 Terry Eagleton, *Literary Theory: An Introduction* (Oxford: Blackwell, 1983), 39–40.

23 Luce Irigaray, *Speculum of the Other Woman*, trans. Gillian C. Gill (Ithaca, NY: Cornell University Press, 1985), 191.

24 Toril Moi, *Sexual/Textual Politics: Feminist Literary Theory* (London: Methuen, 1985), 137.

25 Irigaray, 192. For '*féminin*', Gill's word 'female' is amended to read 'feminine'.

26 Irigaray's interest is in mysticism that has avoided becoming 'theologized' – her term for mysticism that has been recuperated as what Moi calls 'another example of male specularization where the hom(m)osexual economy of God desiring his Son (and vice versa) becomes reflected in the nothingness (néant) in the mystic's heart' (Moi, 137).

27 Moi, 137.

28 T.S. Eliot, *For Lancelot Andrewes: Essays on Style and Order* (London: Faber & Gwyer, 1928), ix.

29 T.S. Eliot, *Knowledge and Experience in the Philosophy of F.H. Bradley* (London: Faber & Faber, 1964), hereafter cited parenthetically in the text as KE.

30 Cleo McNelly Kearns, *T.S. Eliot and Indic Tradition: A Study in Poetry and Belief* (Cambridge: Cambridge University Press, 1987),

130, 245.
31 Sanford Schwartz, *The Matrix of Modernism: Pound, Eliot, and Early Twentieth-Century Thought* (Princeton: Princeton University Press, 1985), p. 4.
32 Walter Benn Michaels, 'Philosophy in Kinkanja: Eliot's pragmatism', in *Glyph 8* (Baltimore: Johns Hopkins University Press, 1981), 170–202 (174).
33 Richard Shusterman, *T.S. Eliot and the Philosophy of Criticism* (London: Duckworth, 1988).
34 Harriet Davidson, *T.S. Eliot and Hermeneutics* (Baton Rouge: Louisiana State University Press, 1985), 71.
35 William V. Spanos, 'Repetition in *The Waste Land*: A Phenomenological De-Struction', *Boundary 2*, **3** (1979), 225–85 (229, 231).
36 Davidson, 23, 61, 55.
37 See Shusterman, chs 5, 7.
38 Davidson, 54.
39 Michael Beehler, *T.S. Eliot, Wallace Stevens, and the Discourses of Difference* (Baton Rouge: Louisiana State University Press, 1987), 22, 20, 19, 36.
40 James Longenbach, *Modernist Poetics of History: Pound, Eliot, and the Sense of the Past* (Princeton: Princeton University Press, 1987), 212, 215.
41 Longenbach, 210–18.
42 Gordon, *Eliot's Early Years*, 60–70.
43 Lyndall Gordon, *Eliot's New Life* (Oxford: Oxford University Press, 1988), chs 1–4.

Introduction

1 T.S. Eliot, 'Eeldrop and Appleplex, I', *Little Review*, **4.1** (May 1917), 7–10, (8), and T.S. Eliot, 'Eeldrop and Appleplex, II', *Little Review*, **4.5** (Sep 1917), 16–19, hereafter cited parenthetically in the text as 'E&A I' and 'E&A II', respectively.
2 Bertrand Russell, 'Mysticism and logic', in *Mysticism and Logic and Other Essays* (London: Longman, Green, 1925), 1–32 (1, 3, 3, 16) (first publ. *Hibbert Journal*, **12** (1914), 780–803).
3 Schwartz, 5.
4 See Leon Surette, *The Birth of Modernism: Ezra Pound, T.S. Eliot, W.B. Yeats and the Occult* (Kingston and Montreal: McGill-Queen's University Press, 1993).
5 Rupert Brooke, Letter to Ben Keeling, in Colin Wilson, *Poetry and Mysticism* (London: Hutchinson, 1970), 120.
6 Richard Aldington, *The Complete Poems of Richard Aldington* (London: Wingate, 1948), 15–16.

7 John Gould Fletcher, *Goblins and Pagodas* (Boston: Houghton Mifflin, 1916), xvi–ii.

8 T.E. Hulme, *Speculations: Essays on Humanism and the Philosophy of Art*, ed. Herbert Read (London: Kegan Paul, Trench, Trubner, 1924), 147.

9 T.E. Hulme, *Further Speculations*, ed. Sam Hynes (Minneapolis: University of Minnesota Press, 1955), 67.

10 *Speculations*, 127.

11 *Further Speculations*, 98.

12 Irving Babbitt, *The New Laokoön: An Essay on the Confusion of the Arts* (Boston: Houghton Mifflin, 1910), 67, 146.

13 George Santayana, *Interpretations of Poetry and Religion* (London: Black, 1900), 225–6.

14 T.S. Eliot, *Selected Essays*, 3rd enlarged edn (London: Faber and Faber, 1951), 17, hereafter cited parenthetically in the text as SE.

15 T.S. Eliot, *The Varieties of Metaphysical Poetry*, ed. Ronald Schuchard (London: Faber & Faber, 1993), 82, hereafter cited parenthetically in the text as *Varieties*; Hulme, *Further Speculations*, 67.

16 *Speculations*, 47.

17 Aristotle, *De Anima*, trans. R.D. Hicks (Cambridge: Cambridge University Press, 1907), 1.4.13–14.

18 T.S. Eliot, *The Sacred Wood: Essays on Poetry and Criticism*, 2nd edn (London: Methuen, 1928), 170, hereafter cited parenthetically in the text as SW.

1 The Meretricious Promise of Fantastic Views

1 Evelyn Underhill, *Mysticism: A Study in the Nature and Development of Man's Spiritual Consciousness*, 3rd edn, rev. (London: Methuen, 1912), x, hereafter cited parenthetically in the text as *Mysticism*.

2 Spurgeon, 1.

3 T.S. Eliot, 'Commentary', *Criterion*, **14** (1935), 260–4 (261).

4 T.S. Eliot, *After Strange Gods: A Primer of Modern Heresy* (New York: Harcourt Brace, 1934), 50.

5 Eliot, 'Commentary', *Criterion*, **14** (1935), 261.

6 Ibid.

7 See Peter Ackroyd, *T.S. Eliot* (London: Hamilton, 1984), 113.

8 Vivien Eliot, Letter to Ezra Pound (2 Nov 1922), in *The Letters of T.S. Eliot, Volume 1: 1898–1922*, ed. by Valerie Eliot (London: Faber & Faber, 1988), **1**, 588.

9 Janet Oppenheim, *The Other World: Spiritualism and Psychical Research in England, 1850–1914* (Cambridge: Cambridge University Press, 1985), 3.

10 See Oppenheim, 163–5.

11 See Oppenheim, 174–8.

12 T.S. Eliot, Letter to Eleanor Hinkley (23 March 1917), *The Letters of T.S. Eliot*, **1**, 169.

13 T.S. Eliot, Letter to Eleanor Hinkley (23 March 1917), *The Letters of T.S. Eliot*, **1**, 168.

14 Ackroyd, 113.

15 Leon Surette, '*The Waste Land* and Jessie Weston: a reassessment', *Twentieth-Century Literature*, **34** (1988), 223–44 (227).

16 T.S. Eliot, 'Notes on Philosophy', (bMs Am 1691 (129)) by permission of the Houghton Library, Harvard University, n.p., hereafter cited parenthetically in the text as 'Notes'. For a general list of the reading that Eliot did at this time, see Gordon, *Eliot's Early Years*, Appendix 1, 141–2.

17 T.S. Eliot, *The Waste Land: A Facsimile and Transcript of the Original Drafts*, ed. Valerie Eliot (London: Faber & Faber, 1971), 1; T.S. Eliot, '*Paris Review* interview', in *Writers at Work*, ed. Van Wyck Brooks, 2nd series (New York: Viking, 1963), 91–110 (105) (first pub. 'The art of poetry, I: T.S. Eliot', *Paris Review*, **21** (Spring/Summer 1959), 47–70).

18 Gordon, *Eliot's Early Years*, 15. Hay disagrees with Gordon's reading of 'Silence' (June 1910), finding no delight in a timeless moment, but rather 'terror in the face of such peace' (72). Hay suggests that Eliot's reading on the subject of mysticism 'was done chiefly for Josiah Royce's seminar on comparative methodology in the fall and winter of 1913–14' (74). Yet Eliot's research into mysticism and the occult does not appear in the papers that Eliot delivered in the course. Even if Royce's seminar were the stimulus for the initial research, Eliot's wide reading suggests that it was driven by other interests as well.

19 Bruce F. Campbell, *Ancient Wisdom Revived: A History of the Theosophical Movement* (Berkeley: University of California Press, 1980), 19.

20 Oppenheim, 120. James quotes from the publication in question in his first note on 502 (William James, *The Varieties of Religious Experience: A Study in Human Nature* (New York: Modern Library, 1936)). That Eliot paid attention to James's notes is suggested by his own notes, where he reminds himself of a 'Capital note on 392 Anesthetic Revelation of a woman' (Notes). In the edition to which I refer, the note that interested Eliot occurs on pp. 383–4.

21 James, *The Varieties of Religious Experience*, 514.

22 T.S. Eliot, Letter to J.H. Woods (6 May 1915), *The Letters of T.S. Eliot*, **1**, 98.

23 Oppenheim, 265.

24 T.S. Eliot, 'Report on the ethics of Kant's critique of practical

reason' (25 May 1913), Hayward Bequest, King's College Library, Cambridge, 6.

25 William McDougall, 'In memory of William James', *Proceedings of the Society for Psychical Research*, **25** (March 1911), 12–23 (23), in Oppenheim, 264.

26 T.S. Eliot, 'William James on immortality', *New Statesman*, **9** (1917), 547.

27 Eliot, 'Commentary', *Criterion*, **14** (1935), 262.

28 See Grover Smith, *T.S. Eliot's Poetry and Plays: A Study in Sources and Meaning* (Chicago: University of Chicago Press, 1956), 49.

29 It is just possible that Eliot knew little of Blavatsky and that the connection between Blavatsky and trance comes second-hand from Yeats, who would undoubtedly have spoken of her in his conversations with Eliot several years before. Eliot's train of thought on these matters is suggestive. He remarks that trance is associated with 'mediums, theosophy, crystal-gazing' and 'occultism . . . and hermetic writings' (*The Use of Poetry and the Use of Criticism* (London: Faber & Faber, 1933), 140; *After Strange Gods*, 48). Trance and theosophy (with its hermetic writings) are always linked in his writing. Yet apart from 'A Cooking Egg', Eliot almost invariably associates trance with Yeats instead of with Madame Blavatsky. He observes that Yeats 'was very much fascinated by self-induced trance states'. He notes that in 'Who Goes with Fergus', 'There is a deliberate evocation of trance' (*The Use of Poetry*, 140; *After Strange Gods*, 49). Eliot's connection of Madame Blavatsky and trance, therefore, may derive from information provided by Yeats or may be a generalization from his awareness of the importance of trance to a theosophist like Yeats.

30 Smith, 49.

31 Helena Petrovna Blavatsky, *The Secret Doctrine: The Synthesis of Science, Religion, and Philosophy*, 3 vols (Adyar, India: Theosophical Publishing House, 1978), 515.

32 Eliot, 'Commentary', *Criterion*, **14** (1935), 261–2.

33 Campbell, 61.

34 T.S. Eliot, 'A Sermon Preached at Magdalene College Chapel by T.S. Eliot, O.M.' (Cambridge: Cambridge University Press, 1948), 5.

35 T.S. Eliot, 'A prediction in regard to three English authors: writers who, though masters of thought, are likewise masters of art', *Vanity Fair*, **21** (Feb 1924), 29, 98 (29).

36 See Philip Le Brun, 'T.S. Eliot and Henri Bergson', *Review of English Studies*, n.s. **18** (1967), 149–61, 274–86; Piers Gray, *T.S. Eliot's Intellectual and Poetic Development 1909–1922* (Brighton: Harvester,

1982); and Paul Douglass, *Bergson, Eliot, and American Literature* (Lexington: University Press of Kentucky, 1986).

37 Le Brun, 285.

38 Eliot, 'A prediction', 29.

39 Henri Bergson, *Time and Free Will*, trans. F.L. Pogson (London: MacMillan, 1910), 70, hereafter cited parenthetically in the text as TFW.

40 T.S. Eliot, 'A paper on Bergson', (bMs Am 1691 (132)) by permission of the Houghton Library, Harvard University, hereafter cited parenthetically in the text as 'Paper'. Lyndall Gordon argues that the handwriting style and the paper used in this essay date from 1913 or 1914 (*Eliot's Early Years*, 41). Douglass summarizes 'A paper on Bergson' (59–61).

41 On Jacques Derrida's concept of supplement, see Barbara Johnson, translator's introduction, *Dissemination*, by Jacques Derrida (Chicago: University of Chicago Press, 1981), x-xiii.

42 Henri Bergson, *Creative Evolution*, trans. A. Mitchell (London: Macmillan, 1911), 263, hereafter cited parenthetically in the text as CE.

43 Eliot, 'A prediction', 29.

44 Douglass, 59.

45 Douglass, 61.

46 See my discussion of Bergsonian interpretations of this poem in Donald J. Childs, 'T.S. Eliot's rhapsody of matter and memory', *American Literature*, **63** (1991), 474–88.

47 See Roland Barthes, *S/Z*, trans. Richard Miller (London: Cape, 1975).

48 Henri Bergson, *An Introduction to Metaphysics*, trans. T.E. Hulme (London: Macmillan, 1913), 7.

49 Ibid.

50 T.S. Eliot, 'Shakespeare and Montaigne', *TLS*, **1249** (1925), 895.

2 Philosophy Perceived

1 Gordon provides a selected bibliography of Eliot's reading in *Eliot's Early Years*, Appendix 1, 141–2.

2 Gordon, *Eliot's Early Years*, 58.

3 Gordon, *Eliot's Early Years*, 60; Hay, 74, 98.

4 See Harry T. Costello, *Josiah Royce's Seminar, 1913–14: as recorded in the notebooks of Harry T. Costello*, ed. by G. Smith (New Brunswick, NJ: Rutgers University Press, 1963). See also Piers Gray's account of the same period.

5 In general, Underhill admired Bergson, but her admiration was not uncritical. She thoroughly revised *Mysticism* in 1930, relegating

Bergson to a much less important role than the one that he had in the earlier editions.

6 Gordon, *Eliot's Early Years*, 40.
7 Ackroyd, 50.
8 Eagleton, 39–40.
9 Davidson, 81.
10 T.S. Eliot, 'Leibniz's monads and Bradley's finite centres', in KE, 198–207 (202) (first publ. in *Monist*, **26** (1916), 566–76).
11 Michaels, 196.
12 Diversion and note are equal in length to the third part of the essay (each is about 2000 words long).
13 I.A. Richards, *Science and Poetry* (New York: Norton, 1926), 76.
14 Eliot refers readers to p. 271 of *Practical Criticism*. He appears to have in mind Chapter 7, 'Doctrine in Poetry'. See I.A. Richards, *Practical Criticism: A Study of Literary Judgement* (London: Routledge & Kegan Paul, 1929).
15 Davidson, 74.
16 Anticipating the more comprehensive term that he will use to replace 'tradition' in *After Strange Gods* (1934), and confirming the intertextual revision of 'Tradition and the Individual Talent' under way in 'Dante' (1929), Eliot introduces the word 'Orthodoxy' as the practical, conventional truth that resolves contradictions.
17 Dante Alighieri, *The Paradiso of Dante Alighieri* (London: J.M. Dent, 1910), canto xxxiii, ll. 139–41.
18 *The Paradiso*, canto iii, l. 85. See Matthew Arnold, 'The Study of Poetry', in Matthew Arnold, *Essays on English Literature*, ed. F.W. Bateson (London: University of London Press, 1965), 117.
19 *The Paradiso*, canto xxx, ll. 95–6.
20 *The Paradiso*, canto xxxiii, ll. 137–8.

3 Modernism and Pragmatism

1 T.S. Eliot, Letter to Bertrand Russell (11 Oct 1915), *The Letters of T.S. Eliot*, **1**, 119.
2 T.S. Eliot, Letter to his mother (6 Sep 1916), *The Letters of T.S. Eliot*, **1**, 149.
3 T.S. Eliot, Letter to his mother (18 Nov 1915), *The Letters of T.S. Eliot*, **1**, 120.
4 Sri Ananda Acharya, *Brahmadarsanam, or Intuition of the Absolute, Being an Introduction to the Study of Hindu Philosophy* (London: Macmillan, 1917); Eliot, *After Strange Gods*, 43.
5 Clement C.J. Webb, *Group Theories of Religion and the Religion of the Individual* (London: Allen & Unwin, 1916); Wilhelm Wundt, *Elements of Folk Psychology: Outline of a Psychological History of the*

Development of Mankind, trans. E.L. Schaub (London: Allen & Unwin, 1916); Emile Boutroux, *Philosophy and War*, trans. Fred Rothwell (London: Constable, 1916). For a list of Eliot's reviews for *IJE*, see Donald Gallup, *T.S. Eliot: A Bibliography* (London: Faber & Faber, 1969).

6   T.S. Eliot, 'Popular theologians: Mr Wells, Mr Belloc and Mr Murry', *Criterion*, **5** (1927), 253–9 (258).

7   George Tyrrel, *Christianity at the Cross-Roads* (London: Longmans, 1909), 5, in Gabriel Daly, *Transcendence and Immanence: A Study in Catholic Modernism and Integralism* (Oxford: Clarendon Press, 1980), 4.

8   William James, *Pragmatism* (Cambridge, Mass: Harvard University Press, 1975), 97.

9   Edouard Le Roy, 'Aujourd'hui introuvable', *Revue de Metaphysique et de Morale* (1907) (repr. in *Le Problème de Dieu* (Paris: [n. pub] 1930); in Daly, 112–13.

10 Alfred Loisy, *Autour d'un Petit Livre* (Paris: Picard et fils, 1903), 191, in Daly, 67 (translation mine).

11 T.S. Eliot, 'Commentary', *Criterion*, **13** (1934), 451–4 (452).

12 Ibid.

13 T.S. Eliot, 'Commentary', *Criterion*, **8** (1928), 185–90 (188).

14 Alan M.G. Stephenson, *The Rise and Decline of English Modernism* (London: SPCK, 1984), 10.

15 T.S. Eliot, Review of *Conscience and Christ: Six Lectures on Christian Ethics*, by Hastings Rashdall, *IJE*, **27** (1916), 111–12 (111).

16 Hastings Rashdall, *Conscience and Christ: Six Lectures on Christian Ethics* (London: Duckworth, 1916), 5, 30 (emphasis added).

17 Eliot, Review of *Conscience and Christ*, 111–12.

18 Rashdall, 201.

19 Eliot, Review of *Conscience and Christ*, 112.

20 Rashdall, 283, 284.

21 Eliot, Review of *Conscience and Christ*, 112.

22 T.S. Eliot, 'The relation between politics and metaphysics', (bMs Am 1691 (25)) by permission of the Houghton Library, Harvard University, 11–12, hereafter cited parenthetically in the text as 'Relation'.

23 Eliot, Review of *Conscience and Christ*, 112.

24 Rashdall, 277 (emphasis added), 284–5 (emphasis added).

25 Eliot, Review of *Conscience and Christ*, 112.

26 James, *Pragmatism*, 106.

27 Webb, 43, 173, 203–4.

28 Webb, 22, 62.

29 T.S. Eliot, Review of *Group Theories of Religion and the Religion of*

the Individual, by Clement C.J. Webb, *IJE,* **27** (1916), 115–17 (117, 116–17) (first publ. in *New Statesman,* **8** (1916), 405–6).

30 T.S. Eliot, Review of *Group Theories of Religion,* 117.

31 Webb, 203–4.

32 Emile Durkheim, *The Elementary Forms of Religious Life,* trans. Joseph Ward Swain (London: Allen & Unwin, 1968), 422.

33 T.S. Eliot, 'An emotional unity', *Dial* **84** (1928), 109–12 (112).

34 T.S. Eliot, Review of *The Ultimate Belief,* by A. Clutton-Brock, *IJE,* **27** (1916), 127.

35 Ibid.

36 T.S. Eliot, Review of *La Guerra Eterna e Il dramma del Esistenza,* by Antonio Aliotta, *IJE,* **28** (1918), 444–5 (445).

37 Eliot, Review of *The Ultimate Belief,* 127.

38 T.S. Eliot, Review of *Mens Creatrix,* by William Temple, *IJE,* **27** (1917), 542–3 (543, 542).

39 Eliot, Review of *Mens Creatrix,* 542, 542–3.

40 T.S. Eliot, Review of *A Manual of Modern Scholastic Philosophy,* by Cardinal Mercier and others, *IJE,* **28** (1917), 137–8 (137, 138).

41 T.S. Eliot, 'A contemporary Thomist', *New Statesman,* **10** (1917), 312.

42 Daly, 45.

43 Eliot, 'A contemporary Thomist', 312.

44 Ibid.

45 T.S. Eliot, 'Commentary', *Criterion,* **12** (1932), 73–9 (77).

46 Stephenson, 10.

47 Henry D. Major, *A Modern View of the Incarnation* (Knaresborough: Parrs, 1915), 22, in Stephenson, 92.

48 *Pascendi Dominici Gregis: Encyclical of Pope Pius X on the Doctrines of the Modernists, Sept. 8, 1907,* in *The Papal Encyclicals 1903–1939,* ed. Claudia Carlen Ihm, 5 vols (Raleigh: McGrath, 1981), **3**, 71–98 (76) (first publ. in English in *Tablet* **110** (28 Sep 1907), 501–15).

49 W.R. Inge, *Christian Mysticism* (London: Methuen, 1899), 392.

50 *Pascendi,* 89, 76.

51 See *Mysticism,* 115.

52 *Pascendi,* 89.

53 See *Mysticism,* 128

54 Daly, 127.

55 T.S. Eliot, 'Beyle and Balzac', *Athenaeum,* **4642** (1919), 392–3 (393).

56 T.S. Eliot, Review of *Elements of Folk Psychology: Outlines of a Psychological History of the Development of Mankind,* by Wilhelm Wundt, *IJE,* **27** (1917), 252–4 (253–4).

57 Eliot, 'Beyle and Balzac', 392.

58 T.S. Eliot, 'The new Elizabethans and the old', *Athenaeum*, **4640** (1919), 134–5 (135).

59 Ibid.

60 T.S. Eliot, 'London letter', *Dial* **71** (1921), 452–5 (455).

61 T.S. Eliot, 'The Silurist', *Dial* **83** (1927), 259–63.

62 T.S. Eliot, 'The mysticism of Blake', *Nation and Athenaeum*, **41** (1927), 779. See Wordsworth's headnote to 'Ode: Intimations of Immortality', from notes by Wordsworth, compiled in 1843 by Isabella Fenwick.

63 T.S. Eliot, 'Mr Chesterton (and Stevenson)', *Nation and Athenaeum*, **42** (1927), 516.

64 Matthew 18.3.

65 T.S. Eliot, Review of *Theism and Humanism*, by A.J. Balfour, *IJE*, **26** (1916), 284–9 (285, 286, 287).

66 Eliot, Review of *Theism and Humanism*, 285.

67 Eliot, 'Popular theologians', 254, 255.

68 See Daly, especially Chapter 6.

69 Eliot, 'An emotional unity', 111.

70 T.S. Eliot, 'Commentary', *Criterion*, **8** (1928), 185–90 (188).

71 Eliot, 'An emotional unity', 109, 112.

72 See Stephenson's index, bibliography, and Appendix C.

73 Eliot, Review of *Group Theories of Religion*, 117.

74 Ernest Shanzer, 'Mr Eliot's Sunday Morning Service', in *T.S. Eliot: 'Prufrock', 'Gerontion', 'Ash Wednesday' and Other Shorter Poems*, ed. B.C. Southam (London: Macmillan, 1978), 186–91 (186–7) (first publ. in *Essays in Criticism*, **5** (1955), 153–8).

75 Shanzer, 187, 191, 188.

76 Shanzer, 190; David Ward, 'Mr Eliot's Sunday Morning Service', in *T.S. Eliot: 'Prufrock', 'Gerontion', 'Ash Wednesday' and Other Shorter Poems*, 191–5 (192) (first publ. in *Between Two Worlds: A Reading of T.S. Eliot's Poetry and Plays* (London and Boston: Routledge & Kegan Paul, 1973), 31–5).

77 Ward, 193–4.

78 Shanzer, 187.

79 B.C. Southam, *A Student's Guide to The Selected Poems of T.S. Eliot*, 6th edn (London: Faber & Faber, 1994), 116–17.

80 Daly, 96–7.

81 Lucien Laberthonnière, *Pages Choisis du P. Laberthonnière* (Paris: J. Vrin, 1930), 26 (translation mine).

82 In a 1927 review, Eliot refers knowingly to Laberthonnière (among other Catholic modernists) to prove that the author of the book that he is reviewing is indeed a modernist and pragmatist: 'Professor Gardner avows himself a pragmatist; he is not only a disciple of

James, but has some sympathy with MM. Blondel, Laberthonnière and Le Roy in France'. See Eliot, 'Popular Theologians', 258.

83 Jean Verdenal, Letter to T.S. Eliot (July 1911), in *The Letters of T.S. Eliot*, **1**, 22–4.

84 T.S. Eliot, 'Commentary', *Criterion*, **13** (1934), 451–4 (452).

85 Laberthonnière, 146–7 (translation mine).

4 Mystical Personae

1 See the Appendix regarding the date of composition.

2 T.S. Eliot, 'Appearances appearances', in T.S. Eliot, Letter to Conrad Aiken (25 July 1914), *The Letters of T.S. Eliot*, **1**, 45–6.

3 T.S. Eliot, Letter to Conrad Aiken, **1**, 44.

4 F.H. Bradley, *Appearance and Reality: A Metaphysical Essay*, 9th impression authorized and corrected (Oxford: Clarendon Press, 1930), 120, 460.

5 Eliot, 'Appearances appearances', 45.

6 Ibid.

7 Bradley, 6, 249.

8 T.S. Eliot, 'The Love Song of Saint Sebastian', in T.S. Eliot, Letter to Conrad Aiken, **1**, 46–7. Further citations from the poem refer to this text.

9 Solomon 1.13.

10 James Doleman, 'Song of Songs', *A Dictionary of Biblical Tradition in English Literature*, ed. by David Lyle Jeffrey (Grand Rapids, Mich: Eerdmans, 1992), 728.

11 Eliot, Letter to Conrad Aiken, **1**, 44.

12 Hay, 80.

13 Eliot, Letter to Conrad Aiken, **1**, 44.

14 Ovid, *Metamorphoses*, trans. Frank J. Miller (Cambridge, Mass: Harvard University Press, 1916), 155.

15 Gordon, *Eliot's Early Years*, 92.

16 T.S. Eliot, Letter to J.H. Woods (28 Jan 1915), *The Letters of T.S. Eliot*, **1**, 84.

17 Gordon, *Eliot's Early Years*, 58, 142.

18 Further citations from the poem refer to this text.

19 Gordon, *Eliot's Early Years*, 101.

20 See Southam 70, 75.

21 Eliot, Review of *Group Theories of Religion and the Religion of the Individual*, 117.

22 T.S. Eliot, Review of *Religion and Philosophy*, by R.G. Collingwood, *IJE*, **27** (1917), 543.

23 Lancelot Andrewes, *Seventeen Sermons on the Nativity* (London: Griffith, Farran, Okeden and Welsh, 1887), 200–1.

240 *T.S. Eliot: Mystic, Son and Lover*

24 Andrewes, 197.
25 Ibid.
26 Smith, 60.
27 Andrewes, 197.
28 Andrewes, 196.
29 Andrewes, 203, 204, 203.
30 Saint Augustine, *The Enchiridion of Augustine*, trans. James F. Shaw (London: Religious Tracts Society, 1887), Ch. 30.
31 Andrewes, 200, 259.
32 Andrewes, 102, 114.
33 Hebrews 2.3–4. Further quotations from Hebrews are cited parenthetically in the text.
34 Smith, 64.
35 Eliot, Letter to Conrad Aiken, **1**, 44.
36 Eliot, Review of *Conscience and Christ*, 112.
37 George Williamson, *A Reader's Guide to T.S. Eliot* (London: Thames & Hudson, 1955), 110–11.
38 Smith, 64.
39 This version of 'Gerontion' is contained in 'Poems 1909–1920' included in 'Complete Poems of T.S. Eliot', a holograph manuscript signed but undated, with the author's corrections, in the Berg Collection of the New York Public Library, 7.
40 Smith, 63–4.
41 Eliot, 'Beyle and Balzac', 393.
42 The retreat from sex in 'Gerontion' is the conclusion of the alternating fascination with sexuality and withdrawal from it that operates in 'The Love Song of J. Alfred Prufrock', 'The Love Song of Saint Sebastian', 'The Death of Saint Narcissus', 'Hysteria', and 'Ode'. Many of these poems seem autobiographical, 'Hysteria' and 'Ode' apparently deriving from Eliot's sexual experiences with Vivien. One could interpret 'Gerontion' in the same way – Gerontion's withdrawal from his partner mirroring Eliot's own distate for the sexual aspect of his relationship with Vivien and the reference to passion become 'adulterated' recalling Vivien's flirtation (if not affair) with Bertrand Russell. (These matters are discussed further in ensuing chapters.)
43 Eliot, 'Beyle and Balzac', 393.
44 J.H. Newman, *Apologia Pro Vita Sua*, ed. M.J. Svaglic (Oxford: Clarendon Press, 1967), 111.
45 Eliot, 'Beyle and Balzac', 393.
46 T.S. Eliot, 'A sceptical patrician', *Athenaeum*, **4647** (1919), 361–2 (362).
47 From this point of view, 'The Love Song of J. Alfred Prufrock' can

be seen as an early attempt to articulate the same experience: there
is both the awful separation between Prufrock's passionate dream
world and his trivial tea party and the indestructible barrier between
Prufrock and the person to whom he would speak.

48 Eliot, 'A sceptical patrician', 361–2.
49 Eliot, 'A sceptical patrician', 362.

5 The Waste Land's Mystical Void

1   T.S. Eliot, Letter to Ezra Pound (24? Jan 1922), *The Letters of T.S. Eliot*, **1**, 504.
2   Ezra Pound, Letter to T.S. Eliot (27? Jan 1922), *The Letters of T.S. Eliot*, **1**, 505.
3   Gordon, *Eliot's New Life*, 14, 16.
4   Eliot, 'Beyle and Balzac', 393.
5   Further citations of this poem refer to this text. As here, line numbers in parenthesis follow each quotation.
6   T.S. Eliot, *The Waste Land: A Facsimile*, 79.
7   Dominic Manganiello, *T.S. Eliot and Dante* (London: Macmillan, 1989), 54.
8   Calvin Bedient, *He Do the Police in Different Voices: The Waste Land and Its Protagonist* (Chicago: University of Chicago Press, 1986), 48.
9   Dante Alighieri, *The Vision; or Hell, Purgatory, & Paradise of Dante Alighieri*, trans. Henry Francis Cary (New York: Hurst, 1844), *Inferno*, canto 34, ll. 22–5.
10 T.S. Eliot, 'Silence', in 'Complete Poems of T.S. Eliot', a holograph manuscript signed but undated, with the author's corrections, in the Berg Collection of the New York Public Library, 9.
11 Hay, 72.
12 T.S. Eliot, Letter to P.E. More, in Paul Murray, *T.S. Eliot and Mysticism: The Secret History of Four Quartets* (New York: St Martin's Press, 1991), 99.
13 Eliot, 'Beyle and Balzac', 393.
14 Eliot, Letter to P.E. More.
15 Eliot, 'Beyle and Balzac', 393.
16 Eliot, *The Waste Land: A Facsimile*, 13.
17 John Webster, *The White Devil*, in *The Complete Works of John Webster*, 4 vols (London: Chatto & Windus, 1927), **1**, 5.6.203.
18 Webster, 5.6.203–5.
19 Revelation, 3.20.
20 T.S. Eliot, 'Ode: on Independence Day, July 4th 1918', in James E. Miller, Jr. *T.S. Eliot's Personal Waste Land: Exorcism of the Demons* (University Park, Pen: Pennsylvania State University Press, 1977), 48–9 (first publ. in *Ara Vos Prec* (London: Ovid, 1920)).

21 Cleanth Brooks, 'The Waste Land: Critique of the Myth', in The Waste Land: A Collection of Critical Essays, ed. by Jay Martin (Englewood Cliffs, NJ: Prentice-Hall, 1968), 59–86 (67–9) (first publ. in Modern Poetry and the Tradition (Chapel Hill, NC: University of North Carolina Press, 1939), 136–72).
22 Eliot, Letter to P.E. More.
23 Smith, 96.
24 Webster, 5.6.155–9
25 Bedient, 198.
26 Jewel Spears Brooker, 'F.H. Bradley's doctrine of experience in T.S. Eliot's The Waste Land and Four Quartets', Modern Philology, 77 (1979), 146–57 (150–1).
27 William Shakespeare, Coriolanus, in William Shakespeare: The Complete Works (Baltimore: Penguin, 1969), 5.3.24–5.
28 Eliot, The Waste Land: A Facsimile, 105.
29 Eliot, The Waste Land: A Facsimile, 107.
30 Eliot, 'Beyle and Balzac', 393.
31 Eliot, The Waste Land: A Facsimile, 79.
32 Gordon, Eliot's New Life, 169–71.

6 A Broken Coriolanus

1 T.S. Eliot, 'Literature and the modern world', American Prefaces, 1.2 (Nov 1935), 19–22 (20).
2 T.S. Eliot, Letter to William Force Stead (9 Aug 1930), in Ronald Schuchard, 'Eliot and the horrific moment', The Southern Review, 21 (1985), 1045–56 (1046).
3 Schuchard, 1050.
4 T.S. Eliot, Letter to Mary Hutchinson (6 Aug 1919), The Letters of T.S. Eliot, 1, 326.
5 Schuchard, 1049–50.
6 T.S. Eliot, 'Mr Middleton Murry's Synthesis', Criterion, 6 (1927), 340–7 (343).
7 T.S. Eliot, 'Why Mr Russell is a Christian', Criterion, 6 (1927), 177–9 (179, 178).
8 T.S. Eliot, 'London Letter', Dial, 73 (1922), 329–31 (331).
9 T.S. Eliot, Letter to Henry Eliot (31 Dec 1922), The Letters of T.S. Eliot, 1, 617.
10 T.S. Eliot, Letter to Sydney Schiff (25 July 1919), The Letters of T.S. Eliot, 1, 324.
11 Eliot, 'London Letter', Dial, 73 (1922), 331.
12 D.H. Lawrence, Aaron's Rod, ed. Mara Kalnins (Cambridge: Cambridge University Press, 1988), 296–9.
13 Eliot, After Strange Gods, 39; T.S. Eliot, 'Contemporary English

Prose: A Discussion of the Development of English Prose from Hobbes and Sir Thomas Browne to Joyce and D.H. Lawrence', *Vanity Fair*, **20.11** (July 1923), 51, 98 (51).

14   T.S. Eliot, Review of *Son of Woman*, by John Middleton Murry, *Criterion*, **10** (1931), 768–74 (771–2).

15   Eliot, Review of *Son of Woman*, 772.

16   Eliot, 'London Letter', *Dial*, 73 (1922), 331.

17   Eliot, Review of *Son of Woman*, 770, 769, 770, 770, 770, 770–1.

18   Eliot, Review of *Son of Woman*, 769, 769, 771.

19   Eliot, Review of *Son of Woman*, 769.

20   T.S. Eliot, 'The Poetic Drama', *Athenaeum*, **4698** (1920), 635–6 (635).

21   Eliot, 'The Poetic Drama', 636.

22   Eliot, Review of *Son of Woman*, 774.

23   Eliot, Review of *Son of Woman*, 770.

24   Ibid.

25   1.1.33–6, hereafter cited parenthetically in the text.

26   Ackroyd, 190–1.

27   Eliot, Review of *Son of Woman*, 770.

28   D.H. Lawrence, *Sons and Lovers*, ed. by Keith Sagar (Harmondsworth: Penguin, 1981), 492.

29   T.S. Eliot, Letter to John Middleton Murry (29 Oct 1931), in Ackroyd, 190.

30   Eliot, 'Ode'.

31   Eliot's epigraph is neither Shakespeare nor Sir Thomas North's Plutarch, but rather a conflation of both. In *Coriolanus*, one finds not Eliot's Volscians, but Volsces: 'To thee particularly and to all the Volsces / Great hurt and mischief' (4.5.67–8). The Volscians belong to North: 'to thy self particularly, and to all the Volscians generally, great hurt and mischief' (*Plutarch's Lives: Englished by Sir Thomas North*, 10 vols (London: Dent, 1898), **1**, 35–6). Eliot seems also to have introduced to Shakespeare's line North's comma. Ironically, his letter to the editor of the *TLS* ten years after his use of *Coriolanus*'s speech to Aufidius (letter to the editor, *TLS*, **1391** (1928), 687) draws attention to the very matter of the punctuation of this passage in order to emphasize the importance of the distinction between punctuation in prose and punctuation in poetry:

> your reviewer . . . quotes the well-known passage from North's Plutarch (Coriolanus's speech to Aufidius), and follows it with the equally famous version of Shakespeare, which he prints as prose. He observes that the version of Shakespeare is 'a far better piece of prose than the original'.
>
> I make precisely the opposite observation. . . . What I think

your reviewer has overlooked is this: that verse, whatever else it may or may not be, is itself a system of *punctuation*; the usual marks of punctuation themselves are differently employed.

32 Gordon, *Eliot's Early Years*, 75–6.

33 Ackroyd, 66.

34 Stephen Spender, *Eliot* (London: Fontana, 1975), 56.

35 Smith, 38.

36 Ackroyd, 88.

37 Ezra Pound, Letter to Henry Ware Eliot (28 June 1915), *The Letters of T.S. Eliot*, **1**, 99.

38 Bertrand Russell, Letter to J.H. Woods (4 March 1916), *The Letters of T.S. Eliot*, **1**, 133.

39 T.S. Eliot, Letter to John Quinn (4 March 1918), *The Letters of T.S. Eliot*, **1**, 222.

40 Ibid.

41 T.S. Eliot, Letter to John Quinn (6 Jan 1919), *The Letters of T.S. Eliot*, **1**, 266.

42 T.S. Eliot, Letter to John Quinn (26 Jan 1919), *The Letters of T.S. Eliot*, **1**, 269.

43 Ackroyd, 71.

44 Vivien Eliot, Letter to Richard Aldington (15? July 1922), *The Letters of T.S. Eliot*, **1**, 544.

45 On 23 June 1918, while living at Marlow, Eliot wrote as follows to his mother: 'I . . . read this week most of Catullus' (*The Letters of T.S. Eliot*, **1**, 235). See also Walt Whitman, 'O Hymen, O Hymenee', in *Complete Poetry and Collected Prose* (New York: Library of America, 1982), 265. The last two lines of the poem also accord with Eliot's theme of the danger in human sexuality: 'Why can you not continue? O why do you now cease? / Is it because if you continued beyond the swift moment you would soon certainly kill me?'

46 Smith, 38.

47 Ovid, *The Metamorphoses of Ovid*, trans. Mary M. Innes (Harmondsworth: Penguin, 1955), 113.

48 Ovid, 112.

49 Ovid, 113.

50 Ackroyd, 84.

51 Ibid.

52 T.S. Eliot, Letter to Henry Eliot (15 Feb 1920), *The Letters of T.S. Eliot*, **1**, 363.

53 Ibid.

54 Eliot, Review of *Son of Woman*, 770.

55 Davidson, 94.

56 See William Wordsworth, *The Prose Works of William Wordsworth*, ed. W.J.B. Owen and Jane Worthington Smyser, 3 vols (Oxford: Clarendon Press, 1974), **3**, 69: 'Shakespeare expresses his own feelings in his own person.'

57 Eliot, 'Beyle and Balzac', 393.

7 *The Confidential Clark Lectures*

1 Eliot, 'Beyle and Balzac', 393.

2 John Middleton Murry, 'Eliot and the "Classical" Revival', in *T.S. Eliot: The Critical Heritage*, ed. by Micheal Grant, 2 vols (London: Routledge & Kegan Paul, 1982), **1**, 222–9 (227–8) (first publ. in *Adelphi*, **3** (1926), 585–95).

3 Murry, 'Eliot and the "Classical" Revival', 228.

4 Ibid.

5 F.A. Lea, *The Life of John Middleton Murry* (London: Methuen, 1959), 130.

6 Eliot indirectly makes this point in his definition of metaphysical poetry, ironically transferring to his discussion of poetry's metaphysics his dissertation's discussion of philosophy's metaphysics: 'We have first therefore to consider how much community of intension may be found between the term [metaphysical] as thus used [by Dryden and Johnson] and the term as we can use it' (*Varieties*, 46). (In the Houghton Library copy of The Clark Lectures, there is a stroke through the 's' in 'intension', and 't?' appears in the margin – as though Eliot (if indeed the marginal comment is his) were recalling that on the many occasions that he used the word in just this way in the dissertation he spelled it with a 't'.)

7 Michaels, 196.

8 Michaels, 179.

9 That Eliot regards Yeats's occultism as a form of romantic mysticism is clear from phrases that he regularly uses to characterize the effect of Yeats's interest in trance, occultism, theosophy and so on. By 'self-induced trance states, calculated symbolism, mediums, theosophy, crystal-gazing, folklore and hobgoblins . . . the author was trying to get as poet something like the exaltation to be obtained, I believe, from hashish or nitrous oxide' (*The Use of Poetry and the Use of Criticism*, 140). Eliot associates Yeats's verse – 'stimulated by folklore, occultism, mythology and symbolism, crystal-gazing and hermetic writings' – with Swinburne's, which 'has the effect of repeated doses of gin and water' (*After Strange Gods*, 48). Similarly, Yeats's 'supernatural world' is 'a highly sophisticated lower mythology summoned, like a physician, to supply the fading pulse of poetry with some transient stimulant so that the dying patient

may utter his last words' (*After Strange Gods*, 50). Eliot sees Yeats's spiritualism and theosophy as displaying the same 'spiritual hashish' and 'drugging of the emotions' that he finds in romantic mysticism (*Varieties*, 106).

10 Eliot, 'Leibniz's Monads', in KE, 202.
11 Michaels, 190.
12 Aristotle, *Metaphysics*, trans. Hugh Tredennick (Cambridge, Mass: Harvard University Press, 1935).
13 Aristotle, *The Nichomachean Ethics of Aristotle*, trans. Sir David Ross (London: Oxford University Press, 1954), 1177a.
14 Aristotle, *The Nichomachean Ethics of Aristotle*, 1177b–1178b.
15 Eliot, Review of *Son of Woman*, 773.
16 Dante Alighieri, *Vita Nuova*, in Smith, 7.
17 Smith, 7.
18 Manganiello, 95.
19 Eliot, Review of *Son of Woman*, 773.
20 See Michel Foucault, *The History of Sexuality, Volume I: An Introduction*, trans. Robert Hurley (New York: Vintage, 1980).
21 Henry Ware Eliot, Sr, Letter to Thomas Lamb Eliot (7 March 1914), in Gordon, *Eliot's Early Years*, 27.
22 T.S. Eliot, Letter to Henry Eliot (15 Feb 1920), *The Letters of T.S. Eliot*, **1**, 363.
23 T.S. Eliot, Letter to John Quinn (4 March 1918), in *The Letters of T.S. Eliot*, **1**, 223–4.
24 T.S. Eliot, in William Turner Levy and Victor Scherle, *Affectionately, T.S. Eliot* (New York: Lippincott, 1968), 121.
25 Eliot, 'Beyle and Balzac', 393.
26 Eliot, Letter to P.E. More.
27 Eliot, Review of *Son of Woman*, 772.
28 Ibid.
29 Eliot, Review of *Son of Woman*, 770.
30 Eliot, Review of *Son of Woman*, 770, 774.
31 Eliot, Review of *Son of Woman*, 771–3.
32 Eliot, Review of *Son of Woman*, 772. See also John Middleton Murry, *Son of Woman: The Story of D.H. Lawrence* (London: Cape, 1954), 363.
33 Murry, 363; Eliot, Review of *Son of Woman*, 772–3.
34 Eliot, Review of *Son of Woman*, 772.
35 T.S. Eliot, Letter to Bertrand Russell (21 Apr 1925), in Bertrand Russell, *The Autobiography of Bertrand Russell* (London: Allen & Unwin, 1975), 410.
36 T.S. Eliot, Letter to Bertrand Russell (15 Oct 1923), in *The Autobiography of Bertrand Russell*, 409.

37 Bertrand Russell, *The Autobiography of Bertrand Russell*, 242–6.
38 Bertrand Russell, Letter to Ottoline Morrell (July 1915), in *The Autobiography of Bertrand Russell*, 278.
39 Bertrand Russell, Letter to Ottoline Morrell (May 1914), in *Ottoline: The Early Memoirs of Lady Ottoline Morrell*, ed. Robert Gathorne-Hardy (London: Faber, 1963), 257.
40 Bertrand Russell, Letter to Ottoline Morrell (Sep 1916), in *The Autobiography of Bertrand Russell*, 301–2.
41 Ackroyd, 66.
42 T.S. Eliot, Letter to Conrad Aiken (31 Dec 1914), *The Letters of T.S. Eliot*, **1**, 75.
43 T.S. Eliot, Letter to Bertrand Russell (7 May 1925), in *The Autobiography of Bertrand Russell*, 410.
44 T.S. Eliot, Letter to William Force Stead (2 Dec 1930), in Gordon, *Eliot's New Life*, 67.
45 Eliot, Review of *Son of Woman*, 773.
46 Eliot, Review of *Son of Woman*, 772.
47 Murry, *Son of Woman*, 379.
48 Eliot, Review of *Son of Woman*, 773, 772.

8 Risking Enchantment *in* Four Quartets

1 Anon., *TLS*, **1084** (1922), 690, in *T.S. Eliot, the Critical Heritage*, **1**, 134–5; Gilbert Seldes, Review of *The Waste Land*, *Nation*, **115** (1922), 614–16, in *T.S. Eliot, the Critical Heritage*, **1**, 144–51 (150); Conrad Aiken, 'An anatomy of melancholy', *New Republic*, **33** (1923), 294–5, in *T.S. Eliot, the Critical Heritage*, **1**, 156–61 (160–1).
2 T.S. Eliot, *The Waste Land: A Facsimile*, 1.
3 T.S. Eliot, '*Paris Review* interview', 105.
4 David Perkins, *A History of Modern Poetry: Modernism and After* (Cambridge, Mass: Belknap Press, 1987), 126.
5 T.S. Eliot, 'The idea of a literary review', *Criterion*, **4** (1926), 1–6 (5–6).
6 T.S. Eliot, 'Commentary', *Criterion*, **4** (1926), 417–20 (420).
7 Ezra Pound, 'A few don'ts by an imagist', *Poetry* **1.6** (1913) (repr. in 'A retrospect', in *The Literary Essays of Ezra Pound*, ed. T.S. Eliot (New York: New Directions, 1954), 3–14 (4–5)).
8 Françoise de Castro, 'Interview with T.S. Eliot' (1948), Hayward Bequest, King's College Library, Cambridge, 3 (my translation).
9 Gardner, *The Art of T.S. Eliot*, 168, 181, 184, 2.
10 Sharp, 275.
11 Paul Murray, *T.S. Eliot and Mysticism: The Secret History of 'Four Quartets'* (New York: St Martin's Press, 1991), 256–7.
12 Sri, 4, 124.

13 Kearns, 245.
14 Kearns, 130.
15 James, *The Varieties of Religious Experience*, 422–3.
16 James, *The Varieties of Religious Experience*, 423.
17 Ibid.
18 James, *The Varieties of Religious Experience*, 424.
19 Gordon, *Eliot's New Life*, 48, 46, 46, 96, 96.
20 Christopher J.R. Armstrong, *Evelyn Underhill (1875–1941): An Introduction to her Life and Writings* (London and Oxford: Mowbrays, 1975), 254–8.
21 Margaret Cropper, *Evelyn Underhill* (London: Longman, Green, 1958), 184, 189.
22 T.S. Eliot, in Helen Gardner, *The Composition of Four Quartets* (London: Faber & Faber, 1978), 69–70, 70, 70.
23 Samuel Mather, *The Self-Justiciary Convicted and Condemned* (Boston: Green, 1707), 13.
24 Luke 4.8.
25 John 1.1–9.
26 Eliot, *After Strange Gods*, 64.
27 Ibid.
28 See William Wordsworth, 'Lines Composed a Few Miles Above Tintern Abbey', l. 106.
29 Eliot, 'A prediction in regard to three English authors', 29.
30 Bertrand Russell, *The Autobiography of Bertrand Russell*, 343.
31 Bergson's impact upon *Four Quartets* has long been acknowledged. See particularly Smidt, Smith and Bergsten.
32 Douglass, 104–5, 95, 93.
33 Douglass, 99, 102, 103, 104.
34 Murry, 258.
35 James, *Pragmatism*, 97, 28, 106–7.
36 Richard Rorty, *The Consequences of Pragmatism* (Minneapolis: University of Minnesota Press, 1982), xiv, xv, xlii, xlii–xliii.
37 Rorty, xxxvii.
38 Eliot, letter to B. Dobrée.
39 Michaels, 200.
40 See Davidson, 75–96.
41 Shusterman, 119.
42 Hans-Georg Gadamer, *Truth and Method* (New York: Seabury, 1975), 271.
43 See Shusterman, Chapter 7.
44 Michaels, 174.
45 Michaels, 174, 196.
46 Bradley, 406–7.

47 T.S. Eliot, 'The interpretation of primitive ritual' (1913), Hayward Bequest, King's College Library, Cambridge, 9.

48 T.S. Eliot, 'Description and explanation' (1914), Hayward Bequest, King's College Library, Cambridge, 6.

49 T.S. Eliot, 'Introduction', in Charlotte Eliot, *Savonarola: A Dramatic Poem* (London: Cobden-Sanderson, 1926), viii.

50 T.S. Eliot, *Notes Towards the Definition of Culture*, (New York: Harcourt, Brace, 1948), 30.

51 Eliot, *Notes Towards the Definition of Culture*, 126.

52 Michaels, 199.

53 James, *Pragmatism*, 97.

54 T.S. Eliot, 'The validity of artificial distinction', Case I of Philosophy Notes, Eliot Collection, Houghton Library, Harvard University, in Hay, 77.

Appendix: Dating 'The Love Song of Saint Sebastian'

1 *The Letters of T.S. Eliot*, **1**, 43–7, hereafter cited parenthetically.

2 Gordon, *Eliot's Early Years*, 61–2.

Index